W9-DJL-586

A   I have a diver down; keep well clear at slow speed.

B   I am taking in, or discharging, or carrying dangerous goods.

C   Yes, affirmative or 'The significance of the previous group should be read in the affirmative.'

D   Keep clear of me — I am maneuvering with difficulty.

E   I am altering my course to starboard.

F   I am disabled. Communicate with me.

G   I require a pilot. When made by fishing vessels operating in close proximity on the fishing grounds it means : 'I am hauling nets.'

H   I have a pilot on board.

I   I am altering my course to port.

J   I am on fire and have dangerous cargo on board : keep well clear of me.

K   I wish to communicate with you.

L   You should stop your vessel instantly.

M   My vessel is stopped and making no way through the water.

N   No, negative or 'The significance of the previous group should be read in the negative.' This signal may be given only visually or by sound. For voice or radio transmission the signal should be 'No.'

O   Man overboard.

P   In harbor [Blue Peter] hoisted at the foremast head. 'All persons should report on board as the vessel is about to proceed to sea.'
    At sea. It may be used by fishing vessels to mean 'My nets have come fast upon an obstruction.'

Q   My vessel is healthy and I request free pratique.

R   see page 82

S   I am operating stern propulsion.

T   Keep clear of me ; I am engaged in pair trawling.

U   You are running into danger.

V   I require assistance.

W   I require medical assistance.

X   Stop carrying out your intentions and watch for my signals.

Y   I am dragging my anchor.

Z   I require a tug. When made by fishing vessels operating in close proximity on the fishing grounds it means : 'I am shooting nets.'

THE YACHTSMAN'S POCKET ALMANAC

1981

EDITED BY NICHOLAS DENT

Technical consultant:
CAPTAIN J. L. STRANGE, BSc, MNI, MRIN

US Editor:
GARY JOBSON

SIMON AND SCHUSTER
NEW YORK

Preface

This book is designed to provide the yachtsman with a handy
source of reference on all aspects of cruising under sail or
power. In accommodating so many topics within a pocket-
sized book, priority has been given to information that is
likely to be needed quickly at sea or in harbor. Further
information can be obtained in a more leisurely way from
official and other publications. Every yachtsman should take
the trouble to acquaint himself with these publications, some
of which are listed on page 152, before putting to sea. This
book is primarily intended as a reminder of the important
details of what has been previously ascertained in this way.

The material has been organized in such a way as to yield
all the information in the most efficient manner possible.
After a short period of familiarization it should be possible to
find any subject with the minimum of delay. To further
simplify this task there is a comprehensive index.

This symbol has been used in certain parts of the book
to indicate paragraph[s] that are primarily concerned
with sailing yachts or other sailing vessels.

This symbol has been used in certain parts of the book
to indicate paragraph[s] that are primarily concerned
with motor yachts or other power-driven vessels, including
sailing vessels under power.

Editorial: Christopher Parker and Lloyd Lindo
Design: Martin Bronkhorst, Sue Lee, Jeremy Bratt and Lisa Tai

The Yachtsman's Pocket Almanac was edited and
designed by Mitchell Beazley Publishers
87–89 Shaftesbury Avenue, London W1V 7AD
© Mitchell Beazley Publishers 1979, 1980
All rights reserved
Library of Congress Cataloging in Publication Data
Dent, Nick
The Yachtsman's Pocket Almanac
1 Yachts and yachting 2 Sailing
I Jobson, Gary II Title
GV813.D37 1980 797.1 79-25571
ISBN 0 671 25512 6

A Fireside Book
Published by Simon and Schuster
A Division of Gulf & Western
Corporation
Simon and Schuster Building
Rockefeller Center
1230 Avenue of the Americas
New York, New York 10020

Typeset by Tradespools Limited and Photoprint Plates Limited
Printed and bound in Great Britain

Contents

Inside front cover: **Distress signals**
Single-letter code signals

Acknowledgements

The U.S. editor gratefully ackowledges the following for their assistance and permission to reproduce previously published material:

    U.S. Department of Commerce, National Oceanic and Atmospheric Administration, National Ocean Survey
    National Weather Service, U.S. Department of Commerce
    Davis Instruments Corporation
    Defense Mapping Agency Hydrographic/Topographic Center
    United States Coast Guard
    Sail and Power by Richard Henderson
    Waterway Guide
    United States Yacht Racing Union
    Bermuda Department of Tourism
    Department National Revenue, Canada
    Offshore Racing Council
    Coast Navigation

The permission of the Controller of Her Majesty's Stationery Office has been obtained for the reproduction of information from the following sources:

    The Nautical Almanac 1981
    Safety on Small Craft

The editor would also like to thank the staff of the following British establishments for their kind and helpful assistance in the preparation of this book:

    Her Majesty's Nautical Almanac Office
    The Hydrographic Department
    The Corporation of Trinity House
    The Post Office
    The British Broadcasting Corporation
    The Meteorological Office
    Captain O. M. Watts Ltd
    J. D. Potter Ltd
    Her Majesty's Stationery Office Bookshop
    Westminster Central Reference Library

1 NAUTICAL ALMANAC
Introduction
HOW TO USE THE TABLES

Monthly tables [pages 6–29] These tables give the Greenwich hour angle [GHA] and declination [DEC] of the sun at two-hourly intervals throughout the year. The times are Greenwich Mean Time [GMT] and expressed in whole hours [i.e. 08 is 0800]. Declination is either north or south of latitude 0° according to whether the degree is preceded by the letter 'N' or 'S'.

Meridian passage [right-hand pages 7–29] These tables give the time of the sun's meridian passage on longitude 0° [i.e. the time of local noon on the Greenwich meridian] on each day of the month. The times are GMT.

Sun GHA correction table [page 30] Since the sun's GHA changes rapidly throughout the day and it is listed only for one time in every two hours in the monthly table, it is necessary to *add* a correction for each minute and second that has elapsed since the previous listed time. If you are in the first hour of the two-hour period use the column headed 'Minutes' and find the correction for the number of whole minutes past the hour. Then use the column headed 'Seconds' and find the correction for the number of seconds past the last whole minute. If you are in the second hour of the two-hour period use the column headed '1 hour + minutes' instead of the 'Minutes' column.

For example, if the time is 1419 and 43 seconds the total correction is $4°45'.0 + 10'.8 = 4°55'.8$. If the time is 1519 and 43 seconds the total correction is $19°45'.0 + 10'.8 = 19°55'.8$. Both would be added to the GHA for 1400.

Sun altitude correction table [page 31] This correction is *added* to your sextant altitude. It includes an allowance for refraction and for the sun's semi-diameter. Use whichever side of the table is appropriate for the current month. The sextant altitude will fall between two of the figures listed in the column headed 'Altitude'. The correction is read off in the column opposite at this point.

Dip of sea horizon [page 31] This correction is *subtracted* from the sextant altitude in order to allow for your height above sea level. Your height of eye [in feet or meters] will fall between two of the figures listed in the column headed 'Eye Height'. The correction is read off in the column opposite at this point.

Distance of sea horizon [page 32] This table gives the distance of the horizon for various heights above sea level.

Times of sunrise and sunset [page 32] This table gives the times [GMT] of sunrise and sunset on latitude 38° north at three-day intervals throughout the year.

Vertical sextant angles [pages 33–36] For an explanation of the use of this table *see* page 58.

Tidal prediction For an explanation of the use of tidal prediction and tidal difference tables *see* pages 37–47.

January

SUN GHA, DECLINATION, MERIDIAN PASSAGE

1 THURSDAY

GMT	GHA	DEC
00	179° 08.9	S23° 01.5
02	209 08.3	01.1
04	239 07.7	00.7
06	269 07.1	S23 00.3
08	299 06.5	22 59.9
10	329 05.9	59.5
12	359 05.3	S22 59.1
14	29 04.7	58.6
16	59 04.1	58.2
18	89 03.5	S22 57.8
20	119 02.9	57.3
22	149 02.4	56.9

2 FRIDAY

GMT	GHA	DEC
00	179° 01.8	S22° 56.5
02	209 01.2	56.0
04	239 00.6	55.6
06	269 00.0	S22 55.1
08	298 59.4	54.7
10	328 58.8	54.2
12	358 58.3	S22 53.8
14	28 57.7	53.3
16	58 57.1	52.9
18	88 56.5	S22 52.4
20	118 55.9	51.9
22	148 55.4	51.5

3 SATURDAY

GMT	GHA	DEC
00	178° 54.8	S22° 51.0
02	208 54.2	50.5
04	238 53.6	50.0
06	268 53.0	S22 49.5
08	298 52.5	49.0
10	328 51.9	48.6
12	358 51.3	S22 48.1
14	28 50.7	47.6
16	58 50.2	47.1
18	88 49.6	S22 46.6
20	118 49.0	46.0
22	148 48.4	45.5

4 SUNDAY

GMT	GHA	DEC
00	178° 47.9	S22° 45.0
02	208 47.3	44.5
04	238 46.7	44.0
06	268 46.2	S22 43.5
08	298 45.6	42.9
10	328 45.0	42.4
12	358 44.4	S22 41.9
14	28 43.9	41.3
16	58 43.3	40.8
18	88 42.7	S22 40.3
20	118 42.2	39.7
22	148 41.6	39.2

5 MONDAY

GMT	GHA	DEC
00	178° 41.1	S22° 38.6
02	208 40.5	38.1
04	238 39.9	37.5
06	268 39.4	S22 37.0
08	298 38.8	36.4
10	328 38.2	35.8
12	358 37.7	S22 35.3
14	28 37.1	34.7
16	58 36.6	34.1
18	88 36.0	S22 33.5
20	118 35.5	32.9
22	148 34.9	32.4

6 TUESDAY

GMT	GHA	DEC
00	178° 34.4	S22° 31.8
02	208 33.8	31.2
04	238 33.2	30.6
06	268 32.7	S22 30.0
08	298 32.1	29.4
10	328 31.6	28.8
12	358 31.0	S22 28.2
14	28 30.5	27.6
16	58 29.9	27.0
18	88 29.4	S22 26.3
20	118 28.9	25.7
22	148 28.3	25.1

7 WEDNESDAY

GMT	GHA	DEC
00	178° 27.8	S22° 24.5
02	208 27.2	23.8
04	238 26.7	23.2
06	268 26.1	S22 22.6
08	298 25.6	21.9
10	328 25.1	21.3
12	358 24.5	S22 20.7
14	28 24.0	20.0
16	58 23.4	19.4
18	88 22.9	S22 18.7
20	118 22.4	18.1
22	148 21.8	17.4

8 THURSDAY

GMT	GHA	DEC
00	178° 21.3	S22° 16.7
02	208 20.8	16.1
04	238 20.2	15.4
06	268 19.7	S22 14.7
08	298 19.2	14.1
10	328 18.6	13.4
12	358 18.1	S22 12.7
14	28 17.6	12.0
16	58 17.1	11.3
18	88 16.5	S22 10.6
20	118 16.0	10.0
22	148 15.5	09.3

9 FRIDAY

GMT	GHA	DEC
00	178° 15.0	S22° 08.6
02	208 14.4	07.9
04	238 13.9	07.2
06	268 13.4	S22 06.4
08	298 12.9	05.7
10	328 12.4	05.0
12	358 11.9	S22 04.3
14	28 11.3	03.6
16	58 10.8	02.9
18	88 10.3	S22 02.1
20	118 09.8	01.4
22	148 09.3	00.7

10 SATURDAY

GMT	GHA	DEC
00	178° 08.8	S21° 59.9
02	208 08.3	59.2
04	238 07.8	58.5
06	268 07.2	S21 57.7
08	298 06.7	57.0
10	328 06.2	56.2
12	358 05.7	S21 55.5
14	28 05.2	54.7
16	58 04.7	54.0
18	88 04.2	S21 53.2
20	118 03.7	52.4
22	148 03.2	51.7

11 SUNDAY

GMT	GHA	DEC
00	178° 02.7	S21° 50.9
02	208 02.2	50.1
04	238 01.7	49.4
06	268 01.2	S21 48.6
08	298 00.7	47.8
10	328 00.2	47.0
12	357 59.8	S21 46.2
14	27 59.3	45.4
16	57 58.8	44.6
18	87 58.3	S21 43.9
20	117 57.8	43.1
22	147 57.3	42.3

12 MONDAY

GMT	GHA	DEC
00	177° 56.8	S21° 41.4
02	207 56.3	40.6
04	237 55.9	39.8
06	267 55.4	S21 39.0
08	297 54.9	38.2
10	327 54.4	37.4
12	357 53.9	S21 36.6
14	27 53.5	35.7
16	57 53.0	34.9
18	87 52.5	S21 34.1
20	117 52.0	33.2
22	147 51.6	32.4

13 TUESDAY

GMT	GHA	DEC
00	177° 51.1	S21° 31.6
02	207 50.6	30.7
04	237 50.1	29.9
06	267 49.7	S21 29.0
08	297 49.2	28.2
10	327 48.7	27.3
12	357 48.3	S21 26.5
14	27 47.8	25.6
16	57 47.3	24.7
18	87 46.9	S21 23.9
20	117 46.4	23.0
22	147 46.0	22.1

14 WEDNESDAY

GMT	GHA	DEC
00	177° 45.5	S21° 21.3
02	207 45.0	20.4
04	237 44.6	19.5
06	267 44.1	S21 18.6
08	297 43.7	17.7
10	327 43.2	16.8
12	357 42.8	S21 16.0
14	27 42.3	15.1
16	57 41.9	14.2
18	87 41.4	S21 13.3
20	117 41.0	12.4
22	147 40.5	11.5

15 THURSDAY

GMT	GHA	DEC
00	177° 40.1	S21° 10.5
02	207 39.6	09.6
04	237 39.2	08.7
06	267 38.8	S21 07.8
08	297 38.3	06.9
10	327 37.9	06.0
12	357 37.4	S21 05.0
14	27 37.0	04.1
16	57 36.6	03.2
18	87 36.1	S21 02.2
20	117 35.7	01.3
22	147 35.3	21 00.4

16 FRIDAY

GMT	GHA	DEC
00	177° 34.8	S20° 59.4
02	207 34.4	58.5
04	237 34.0	57.5
06	267 33.6	S20 56.6
08	297 33.1	55.6
10	327 32.7	54.7
12	357 32.3	S20 53.7
14	27 31.9	52.8
16	57 31.4	51.8
18	87 31.0	S20 50.8
20	117 30.6	49.9
22	147 30.2	48.9

17 SATURDAY

GMT	GHA	DEC
00	177° 29.8	S20° 47.9
02	207 29.4	46.9
04	237 28.9	46.0
06	267 28.5	S20 45.0
08	297 28.1	44.0
10	327 27.7	43.0
12	357 27.3	S20 42.0
14	27 26.9	41.0
16	57 26.5	40.0
18	87 26.1	S20 39.0
20	117 25.7	38.0
22	147 25.3	37.0

18 SUNDAY

GMT	GHA	DEC
00	177° 24.9	S20° 36.0
02	207 24.5	35.0
04	237 24.1	34.0
06	267 23.7	S20 33.0
08	297 23.3	31.9
10	327 22.9	30.9
12	357 22.5	S20 29.9
14	27 22.1	28.9
16	57 21.7	27.8
18	87 21.3	S20 26.8
20	117 20.9	25.8
22	147 20.6	24.7

19 MONDAY

GMT	GHA	DEC
00	177° 20.2	S20° 23.7
02	207 19.8	22.7
04	237 19.4	21.6
06	267 19.0	S20 20.6
08	297 18.6	19.5
10	327 18.3	18.5
12	357 17.9	S20 17.4
14	27 17.5	16.3
16	57 17.1	15.3
18	87 16.8	S20 14.2
20	117 16.4	13.1
22	147 16.0	12.1

20 TUESDAY

GMT	GHA	DEC
00	177° 15.6	S20° 11.0
02	207 15.3	09.9
04	237 14.9	08.9
06	267 14.5	S20 07.8
08	297 14.2	06.7
10	327 13.8	05.6
12	357 13.5	S20 04.5
14	27 13.1	03.4
16	57 12.7	02.3
18	87 12.4	S20 01.2
20	117 12.0	20 00.1
22	147 11.7	59.0

21 WEDNESDAY

GMT	GHA	DEC
00	177° 11.3	S19° 57.9
02	207 11.0	56.8
04	237 10.6	55.7
06	267 10.3	S19 54.6
08	297 09.9	53.5
10	327 09.6	52.4
12	357 09.2	S19 51.3
14	27 08.9	50.1
16	57 08.5	49.0
18	87 08.2	S19 47.9
20	117 07.8	46.8
22	147 07.5	45.6

22 THURSDAY

GMT	GHA	DEC
00	177° 07.2	S19° 44.5
02	207 06.8	43.4
04	237 06.5	42.2
06	267 06.2	S19 41.1
08	297 05.8	39.9
10	327 05.5	38.8
12	357 05.2	S19 37.6
14	27 04.8	36.5
16	57 04.5	35.3
18	87 04.2	S19 34.2
20	117 03.8	33.0
22	147 03.5	31.9

23 FRIDAY

GMT	GHA	DEC
00	177° 03.2	S19° 30.7
02	207 02.9	29.5
04	237 02.6	28.3
06	267 02.2	S19 27.2
08	297 01.9	26.0
10	327 01.6	24.8
12	357 01.3	S19 23.6
14	27 01.0	22.5
16	57 00.7	21.3
18	87 00.4	S19 20.1
20	117 00.1	18.9
22	146 59.7	17.7

24 SATURDAY

GMT	GHA	DEC
00	176° 59.4	S19° 16.5
02	206 59.1	15.3
04	236 58.8	14.1
06	266 58.5	S19 12.9
08	296 58.2	11.7
10	326 57.9	10.5
12	356 57.6	S19 09.3
14	26 57.3	08.1
16	56 57.0	06.9
18	86 56.7	S19 05.7
20	116 56.4	04.4
22	146 56.2	03.2

25 SUNDAY

GMT	GHA	DEC
00	176° 55.9	S19° 02.0
02	206 55.6	00.8
04	236 55.3	18 59.5
06	266 55.0	S18 58.3
08	296 54.7	57.1
10	326 54.4	55.8
12	356 54.2	S18 54.6
14	26 53.9	53.4
16	56 53.6	52.1
18	86 53.3	S18 50.9
20	116 53.0	49.6
22	146 52.8	48.4

26 MONDAY

GMT	GHA	DEC
00	176° 52.5	S18° 47.1
02	206 52.2	45.9
04	236 51.9	44.6
06	266 51.7	S18 43.3
08	296 51.4	42.1
10	326 51.1	40.8
12	356 50.9	S18 39.6
14	26 50.6	38.3
16	56 50.3	37.0
18	86 50.1	S18 35.7
20	116 49.8	34.5
22	146 49.6	33.2

27 TUESDAY

GMT	GHA	DEC
00	176° 49.3	S18° 31.9
02	206 49.0	30.6
04	236 48.8	29.3
06	266 48.5	S18 28.0
08	296 48.3	26.7
10	326 48.0	25.5
12	356 47.8	S18 24.2
14	26 47.5	22.9
16	56 47.3	21.6
18	86 47.0	S18 20.3
20	116 46.8	19.0
22	146 46.6	17.7

28 WEDNESDAY

GMT	GHA	DEC
00	176° 46.3	S18° 16.4
02	206 46.1	15.0
04	236 45.8	13.7
06	266 45.6	S18 12.4
08	296 45.4	11.1
10	326 45.1	09.8
12	356 44.9	S18 08.5
14	26 44.7	07.1
16	56 44.4	05.8
18	86 44.2	S18 04.5
20	116 44.0	03.1
22	146 43.8	01.8

29 THURSDAY

GMT	GHA	DEC
00	176° 43.5	S18° 00.5
02	206 43.3	59.1
04	236 43.1	57.8
06	266 42.9	S17 56.4
08	296 42.7	55.1
10	326 42.4	53.8
12	356 42.2	S17 52.4
14	26 42.0	51.1
16	56 41.8	49.7
18	86 41.6	S17 48.3
20	116 41.4	47.0
22	146 41.2	45.6

30 FRIDAY

GMT	GHA	DEC
00	176° 40.9	S17° 44.3
02	206 40.7	42.9
04	236 40.5	41.5
06	266 40.3	S17 40.2
08	296 40.1	38.8
10	326 39.9	37.4
12	356 39.7	S17 36.0
14	26 39.5	34.7
16	56 39.3	33.3
18	86 39.1	S17 31.9
20	116 38.9	30.5
22	146 38.8	29.1

31 SATURDAY

GMT	GHA	DEC
00	176° 38.6	S17° 27.7
02	206 38.4	26.4
04	236 38.2	25.0
06	266 38.0	S17 23.6
08	296 37.8	22.2
10	326 37.6	20.8
12	356 37.4	S17 19.4
14	26 37.3	18.0
16	56 37.1	16.6
18	86 36.9	S17 15.2
20	116 36.7	13.7
22	146 36.6	12.3

MERIDIAN PASSAGE

Day	hr min	Day	hr min
1	12 04	17	12 10
2	12 04	18	12 10
3	12 05	19	12 11
4	12 05	20	12 11
5	12 05	21	12 11
6	12 06	22	12 12
7	12 06	23	12 12
8	12 07	24	12 12
9	12 07	25	12 12
10	12 08	26	12 13
11	12 08	27	12 13
12	12 08	28	12 13
13	12 09	29	12 13
14	12 09	30	12 13
15	12 09	31	12 14
16	12 10		

February

SUN GHA, DECLINATION, MERIDIAN PASSAGE

1 SUNDAY

GMT	GHA	DEC
00	176° 36'.4	S17° 10'.9
02	206 36.2	09.5
04	236 36.0	08.1
06	266 35.9	S17 06.7
08	296 35.7	05.2
10	326 35.5	03.8
12	356 35.4	S17 02.4
14	26 35.2	01.0
16	56 35.0	16 59.5
18	86 34.9	S16 58.1
20	116 34.7	56.7
22	146 34.6	55.2

2 MONDAY

GMT	GHA	DEC
00	176° 34'.4	S16° 53'.8
02	206 34.2	52.3
04	236 34.1	50.9
06	266 33.9	S16 49.5
08	296 33.8	48.0
10	326 33.6	46.6
12	356 33.5	S16 45.1
14	26 33.3	43.7
16	56 33.2	42.2
18	86 33.0	S16 40.7
20	116 32.9	39.3
22	146 32.8	37.8

3 TUESDAY

GMT	GHA	DEC
00	176° 32'.6	S16° 36'.4
02	206 32.5	34.9
04	236 32.3	33.4
06	266 32.2	S16 32.0
08	296 32.1	30.5
10	326 31.9	29.0
12	356 31.8	S16 27.5
14	26 31.7	26.1
16	56 31.5	24.6
18	86 31.4	S16 23.1
20	116 31.3	21.6
22	146 31.2	20.1

4 WEDNESDAY

GMT	GHA	DEC
00	176° 31'.0	S16° 18'.6
02	206 30.9	17.2
04	236 30.8	15.7
06	266 30.7	S16 14.2
08	296 30.5	12.7
10	326 30.4	11.2
12	356 30.3	S16 09.7
14	26 30.2	08.2
16	56 30.1	06.7
18	86 30.0	S16 05.2
20	116 29.9	03.7
22	146 29.8	02.2

5 THURSDAY

GMT	GHA	DEC
00	176° 29'.7	S16° 00'.6
02	206 29.5	59.1
04	236 29.4	57.6
06	266 29.3	S15 56.1
08	296 29.2	54.6
10	326 29.1	53.1
12	356 29.0	S15 51.5
14	26 28.9	50.0
16	56 28.8	48.5
18	86 28.8	S15 47.0
20	116 28.7	45.4
22	146 28.6	43.9

6 FRIDAY

GMT	GHA	DEC
00	176° 28'.5	S15° 42'.4
02	206 28.4	40.8
04	236 28.3	39.3
06	266 28.2	S15 37.8
08	296 28.1	36.2
10	326 28.0	34.7
12	356 28.0	S15 33.1
14	26 27.9	31.6
16	56 27.8	30.0
18	86 27.7	S15 28.5
20	116 27.7	26.9
22	146 27.6	25.4

7 SATURDAY

GMT	GHA	DEC
00	176° 27'.5	S15° 23'.8
02	206 27.4	22.3
04	236 27.4	20.7
06	266 27.3	S15 19.1
08	296 27.2	17.6
10	326 27.2	16.0
12	356 27.1	S15 14.5
14	26 27.0	12.9
16	56 27.0	11.3
18	86 26.9	S15 09.7
20	116 26.8	08.2
22	146 26.8	06.6

8 SUNDAY

GMT	GHA	DEC
00	176° 26'.7	S15° 05'.0
02	206 26.6	03.4
04	236 26.6	01.9
06	266 26.6	S15 00.3
08	296 26.5	58.7
10	326 26.5	57.1
12	356 26.4	S14 55.5
14	26 26.4	53.9
16	56 26.3	52.3
18	86 26.3	S14 50.8
20	116 26.2	49.2
22	146 26.2	47.6

9 MONDAY

GMT	GHA	DEC
00	176° 26'.2	S14° 46'.0
02	206 26.1	44.4
04	236 26.1	42.8
06	266 26.1	S14 41.2
08	296 26.0	39.6
10	326 26.0	37.9
12	356 26.0	S14 36.3
14	26 25.9	34.7
16	56 25.9	33.1
18	86 25.9	S14 31.5
20	116 25.8	29.9
22	146 25.8	28.3

10 TUESDAY

GMT	GHA	DEC
00	176° 25'.8	S14° 26'.7
02	206 25.8	25.0
04	236 25.8	23.4
06	266 25.7	S14 21.8
08	296 25.7	20.2
10	326 25.7	18.5
12	356 25.7	S14 16.9
14	26 25.7	15.3
16	56 25.7	13.7
18	86 25.7	S14 12.0
20	116 25.6	10.4
22	146 25.6	08.7

11 WEDNESDAY

GMT	GHA	DEC
00	176° 25'.6	S14° 07'.1
02	206 25.6	05.5
04	236 25.6	03.8
06	266 25.6	S14 02.2
08	296 25.6	14 00.5
10	326 25.6	58.9
12	356 25.6	S13 57.2
14	26 25.6	55.6
16	56 25.6	53.9
18	86 25.6	S13 52.3
20	116 25.6	50.6
22	146 25.6	49.0

12 THURSDAY

GMT	GHA	DEC
00	176° 25'.7	S13° 47'.3
02	206 25.7	45.7
04	236 25.7	44.0
06	266 25.7	S13 42.3
08	296 25.7	40.7
10	326 25.7	39.0
12	356 25.8	S13 37.4
14	26 25.8	35.7
16	56 25.8	34.0
18	86 25.8	S13 32.3
20	116 25.8	30.7
22	146 25.8	29.0

13 FRIDAY

GMT	GHA	DEC
00	176° 25'.9	S13° 27'.3
02	206 25.9	25.6
04	236 25.9	24.0
06	266 26.0	S13 22.3
08	296 26.0	20.6
10	326 26.0	18.9
12	356 26.1	S13 17.2
14	26 26.1	15.5
16	56 26.1	13.9
18	86 26.2	S13 12.2
20	116 26.2	10.5
22	146 26.2	08.8

14 SATURDAY

GMT	GHA	DEC
00	176° 26'.3	S13° 07'.1
02	206 26.3	05.4
04	236 26.4	03.7
06	266 26.4	S13 02.0
08	296 26.5	13 00.3
10	326 26.5	58.6
12	356 26.6	S12 56.9
14	26 26.6	55.2
16	56 26.7	53.5
18	86 26.7	S12 51.8
20	116 26.8	50.1
22	146 26.8	48.4

15 SUNDAY

GMT	GHA	DEC
00	176° 26'.9	S12° 46'.7
02	206 26.9	44.9
04	236 27.0	43.2
06	266 27.1	S12 41.5
08	296 27.1	39.8
10	326 27.1	38.1
12	356 27.3	S12 36.4
14	26 27.3	34.6
16	56 27.4	32.9
18	86 27.5	S12 31.2
20	116 27.5	29.5
22	146 27.6	27.7

16 MONDAY

GMT	GHA	DEC
00	176° 27.7	S12° 26.0
02	206 27.8	24.3
04	236 27.8	22.5
06	266 27.9	S12 20.8
08	296 28.0	19.1
10	326 28.1	17.3
12	356 28.1	S12 15.6
14	26 28.2	13.9
16	56 28.3	12.1
18	86 28.4	S12 10.4
20	116 28.5	08.7
22	146 28.6	06.9

17 TUESDAY

GMT	GHA	DEC
00	176° 28.6	S12° 05.2
02	206 28.7	03.4
04	236 28.8	01.7
06	266 28.9	S11 59.9
08	296 29.0	58.2
10	326 29.1	56.4
12	356 29.2	S11 54.7
14	26 29.3	52.9
16	56 29.4	51.2
18	86 29.5	S11 49.4
20	116 29.6	47.6
22	146 29.7	45.9

18 WEDNESDAY

GMT	GHA	DEC
00	176° 29.8	S11° 44.1
02	206 29.9	42.4
04	236 30.0	40.6
06	266 30.1	S11 38.8
08	296 30.2	37.1
10	326 30.3	35.3
12	356 30.4	S11 33.5
14	26 30.5	31.8
16	56 30.7	30.0
18	86 30.8	S11 28.2
20	116 30.9	26.5
22	146 31.0	24.7

19 THURSDAY

GMT	GHA	DEC
00	176° 31.1	S11° 22.9
02	206 31.2	21.1
04	236 31.4	19.4
06	266 31.5	S11 17.6
08	296 31.6	15.8
10	326 31.7	14.0
12	356 31.8	S11 12.2
14	26 32.0	10.4
16	56 32.1	08.7
18	86 32.2	S11 06.9
20	116 32.4	05.1
22	146 32.5	03.3

20 FRIDAY

GMT	GHA	DEC
00	176° 32.6	S11° 01.5
02	206 32.7	10 59.7
04	236 32.9	57.9
06	266 33.0	S10 56.1
08	296 33.1	54.3
10	326 33.3	52.5
12	356 33.4	S10 50.7
14	26 33.6	48.9
16	56 33.7	47.1
18	86 33.8	S10 45.3
20	116 34.0	43.5
22	146 34.1	41.7

21 SATURDAY

GMT	GHA	DEC
00	176° 34.3	S10° 39.9
02	206 34.4	38.1
04	236 34.6	36.3
06	266 34.7	S10 34.5
08	296 34.9	32.7
10	326 35.0	30.9
12	356 35.2	S10 29.1
14	26 35.3	27.3
16	56 35.5	25.5
18	86 35.6	S10 23.6
20	116 35.8	21.8
22	146 35.9	20.0

22 SUNDAY

GMT	GHA	DEC
00	176° 36.1	S10° 18.2
02	206 36.2	16.4
04	236 36.4	14.6
06	266 36.6	S10 12.7
08	296 36.7	10.9
10	326 36.9	09.1
12	356 37.1	S10 07.3
14	26 37.2	05.4
16	56 37.4	03.6
18	86 37.6	S10 01.8
20	116 37.7	10 00.0
22	146 37.9	58.1

23 MONDAY

GMT	GHA	DEC
00	176° 38.1	S 9° 56.3
02	206 38.2	54.5
04	236 38.4	52.6
06	266 38.6	S 9 50.8
08	296 38.8	49.0
10	326 38.9	47.1
12	356 39.1	S 9 45.3
14	26 39.3	43.5
16	56 39.5	41.6
18	86 39.6	S 9 39.8
20	116 39.8	37.9
22	146 40.0	36.1

24 TUESDAY

GMT	GHA	DEC
00	176° 40.2	S 9° 34.3
02	206 40.4	32.4
04	236 40.6	30.6
06	266 40.7	S 9 28.7
08	296 40.9	26.9
10	326 41.1	25.0
12	356 41.3	S 9 23.2
14	26 41.5	21.3
16	56 41.7	19.5
18	86 41.9	S 9 17.6
20	116 42.1	15.8
22	146 42.3	13.9

25 WEDNESDAY

GMT	GHA	DEC
00	176° 42.5	S 9° 12.1
02	206 42.7	10.2
04	236 42.8	08.4
06	266 43.0	S 9 06.5
08	296 43.2	04.6
10	326 43.4	02.8
12	356 43.6	S 9 00.9
14	26 43.8	8 59.1
16	56 44.0	57.2
18	86 44.3	S 8 55.3
20	116 44.5	53.5
22	146 44.7	51.6

26 THURSDAY

GMT	GHA	DEC
00	176° 44.9	S 8° 49.7
02	206 45.1	47.9
04	236 45.3	46.0
06	266 45.5	S 8 44.1
08	296 45.7	42.3
10	326 45.9	40.4
12	356 46.1	S 8 38.5
14	26 46.3	36.6
16	56 46.5	34.8
18	86 46.8	S 8 32.9
20	116 47.0	31.0
22	146 47.2	29.1

27 FRIDAY

GMT	GHA	DEC
00	176° 47.4	S 8° 27.3
02	206 47.6	25.4
04	236 47.9	23.5
06	266 48.1	S 8 21.6
08	296 48.3	19.8
10	326 48.5	17.9
12	356 48.7	S 8 16.0
14	26 49.0	14.1
16	56 49.2	12.2
18	86 49.4	S 8 10.3
20	116 49.6	08.5
22	146 49.9	06.6

28 SATURDAY

GMT	GHA	DEC
00	176° 50.1	S 8° 04.7
02	206 50.3	02.8
04	236 50.6	00.9
06	266 50.8	S 7 59.0
08	296 51.0	57.1
10	326 51.2	55.2
12	356 51.5	S 7 53.3
14	26 51.7	51.5
16	56 51.9	49.6
18	86 52.2	S 7 47.7
20	116 52.4	45.8
22	146 52.7	43.9

MERIDIAN PASSAGE

Day	hr min	Day	hr min
1	12 14	17	12 14
2	12 14	18	12 14
3	12 14	19	12 14
4	12 14	20	12 14
5	12 14	21	12 14
6	12 14	22	12 13
7	12 14	23	12 13
8	12 14	24	12 13
9	12 14	25	12 13
10	12 14	26	12 13
11	12 14	27	12 13
12	12 14	28	12 13
13	12 14		
14	12 14		
15	12 14		
16	12 14		

March

SUN GHA, DECLINATION, MERIDIAN PASSAGE

1 SUNDAY

GMT	GHA	DEC
00	176° 52.9	S 7° 42.0
02	206 53.1	40.1
04	236 53.4	38.2
06	266 53.6	S 7 36.3
08	296 53.9	34.4
10	326 54.1	32.5
12	356 54.3	S 7 30.6
14	26 54.6	28.7
16	56 54.8	26.8
18	86 55.1	S 7 24.9
20	116 55.3	23.0
22	146 55.6	21.1

2 MONDAY

GMT	GHA	DEC
00	176 55.8	S 7° 19.2
02	206 56.1	17.3
04	236 56.3	15.4
06	266 56.6	S 7 13.4
08	296 56.8	11.5
10	326 57.1	09.6
12	356 57.3	S 7 07.7
14	26 57.6	05.8
16	56 57.8	03.9
18	86 58.1	S 7 02.0
20	116 58.4	7 00.1
22	146 58.6	58.2

3 TUESDAY

GMT	GHA	DEC
00	176 58.9	S 6° 56.2
02	206 59.1	54.3
04	236 59.4	52.4
06	266 59.7	S 6 50.5
08	296 59.9	48.6
10	327 00.2	46.7
12	357 00.4	S 6 44.7
14	27 00.7	42.8
16	57 01.0	40.9
18	87 01.2	S 6 39.0
20	117 01.5	37.1
22	147 01.8	35.1

4 WEDNESDAY

GMT	GHA	DEC
00	177° 02.0	S 6° 33.2
02	207 02.3	31.3
04	237 02.6	29.4
06	267 02.9	S 6 27.5
08	297 03.1	25.5
10	327 03.4	23.6
12	357 03.7	S 6 21.7
14	27 03.9	19.8
16	57 04.2	17.8
18	87 04.5	S 6 15.9
20	117 04.8	14.0
22	147 05.0	12.0

5 THURSDAY

GMT	GHA	DEC
00	177 05.3	S 6° 10.1
02	207 05.6	08.2
04	237 05.9	06.3
06	267 06.2	S 6 04.3
08	297 06.4	02.4
10	327 06.7	6 00.5
12	357 07.0	S 5 58.5
14	27 07.3	56.6
16	57 07.6	54.7
18	87 07.9	S 5 52.7
20	117 08.1	50.8
22	147 08.4	48.8

6 FRIDAY

GMT	GHA	DEC
00	177° 08.7	S 5° 46.9
02	207 09.0	45.0
04	237 09.3	43.0
06	267 09.6	S 5 41.1
08	297 09.9	39.2
10	327 10.2	37.2
12	357 10.4	S 5 35.3
14	27 10.7	33.3
16	57 11.0	31.4
18	87 11.3	S 5 29.5
20	117 11.6	27.5
22	147 11.9	25.6

7 SATURDAY

GMT	GHA	DEC
00	177° 12.2	S 5° 23.6
02	207 12.5	21.7
04	237 12.8	19.7
06	267 13.1	S 5 17.8
08	297 13.4	15.9
10	327 13.7	13.9
12	357 14.0	S 5 12.0
14	27 14.3	10.0
16	57 14.6	08.1
18	87 14.9	S 5 06.1
20	117 15.2	04.2
22	147 15.5	02.2

8 SUNDAY

GMT	GHA	DEC
00	177° 15.8	S 5° 00.3
02	207 16.1	58.3
04	237 16.4	56.4
06	267 16.7	S 4 54.4
08	297 17.0	52.5
10	327 17.2	50.5
12	357 17.5	S 4 48.6
14	27 17.9	46.6
16	57 18.2	44.7
18	87 18.6	S 4 42.7
20	117 18.9	40.8
22	147 19.2	38.8

9 MONDAY

GMT	GHA	DEC
00	177° 19.5	S 4° 36.9
02	207 19.8	34.9
04	237 20.1	33.0
06	267 20.4	S 4 31.0
08	297 20.7	29.1
10	327 21.1	27.1
12	357 21.4	S 4 25.1
14	27 21.7	23.2
16	57 22.0	21.2
18	87 22.3	S 4 19.3
20	117 22.6	17.3
22	147 23.0	15.4

10 TUESDAY

GMT	GHA	DEC
00	177° 23.3	S 4° 13.4
02	207 23.6	11.4
04	237 23.9	09.5
06	267 24.2	S 4 07.5
08	297 24.6	05.6
10	327 24.9	03.6
12	357 25.2	S 4 01.6
14	27 25.5	59.7
16	57 25.8	57.7
18	87 26.2	S 3 55.8
20	117 26.5	53.8
22	147 26.8	51.8

11 WEDNESDAY

GMT	GHA	DEC
00	177° 27.1	S 3° 49.9
02	207 27.5	47.9
04	237 27.8	45.9
06	267 28.1	S 3 44.0
08	297 28.5	42.0
10	327 28.8	40.0
12	357 29.1	S 3 38.1
14	27 29.4	36.1
16	57 29.8	34.2
18	87 30.1	S 3 32.2
20	117 30.4	30.2
22	147 30.8	28.3

12 THURSDAY

GMT	GHA	DEC
00	177° 31.1	S 3° 26.3
02	207 31.4	24.3
04	237 31.8	22.4
06	267 32.1	S 3 20.4
08	297 32.4	18.4
10	327 32.8	16.5
12	357 33.1	S 3 14.5
14	27 33.4	12.5
16	57 33.8	10.6
18	87 34.1	S 3 08.6
20	117 34.5	06.6
22	147 34.8	04.6

13 FRIDAY

GMT	GHA	DEC
00	177° 35.1	S 3° 02.7
02	207 35.5	3 00.7
04	237 35.8	58.7
06	267 36.2	S 2 56.8
08	297 36.5	54.8
10	327 36.8	52.8
12	357 37.2	S 2 50.9
14	27 37.5	48.9
16	57 37.9	46.9
18	87 38.2	S 2 44.9
20	117 38.6	43.0
22	147 38.9	41.0

14 SATURDAY

GMT	GHA	DEC
00	177° 39.2	S 2° 39.0
02	207 39.6	37.1
04	237 39.9	35.1
06	267 40.3	S 2 33.1
08	297 40.6	31.1
10	327 41.0	29.2
12	357 41.3	S 2 27.2
14	27 41.7	25.2
16	57 42.0	23.3
18	87 42.4	S 2 21.3
20	117 42.7	19.3
22	147 43.1	17.3

15 SUNDAY

GMT	GHA	DEC
00	177° 43.4	S 2° 15.4
02	207 43.8	13.4
04	237 44.1	11.4
06	267 44.5	S 2 09.4
08	297 44.8	07.5
10	327 45.2	05.5
12	357 45.5	S 2 03.5
14	27 45.9	01.5
16	57 46.3	1 59.6
18	87 46.6	S 1 57.6
20	117 47.0	55.6
22	147 47.3	53.6

	16 MONDAY				**22 SUNDAY**				**28 SATURDAY**	
GMT	GHA	DEC		GMT	GHA	DEC		GMT	GHA	DEC
00	177° 47.7	S 1° 51.7		00	178° 14.2	N 0° 30.6		00	178° 41.5	N 2° 52.0
02	207 48.0	49.7		02	208 14.5	32.5		02	208 41.9	54.0
04	237 48.4	47.7		04	238 14.9	34.5		04	238 42.3	55.9
06	267 48.7	S 1 45.7		06	268 15.3	N 0 36.5		06	268 42.7	N 2 57.9
08	297 49.1	43.8		08	298 15.7	38.4		08	298 43.0	2 59.8
10	327 49.5	41.8		10	328 16.1	40.4		10	328 43.4	01.8
12	357 49.8	S 1 39.8		12	358 16.4	N 0 42.4		12	358 43.8	N 3 03.7
14	27 50.2	37.8		14	28 16.8	44.4		14	28 44.2	05.7
16	57 50.5	35.9		16	58 17.2	46.3		16	58 44.5	07.6
18	87 50.9	S 1 33.9		18	88 17.6	N 0 48.3		18	88 44.9	N 3 09.6
20	117 51.3	31.9		20	118 17.9	50.3		20	118 45.3	11.5
22	147 51.6	29.9		22	148 18.3	52.2		22	148 45.7	13.5

	17 TUESDAY				**23 MONDAY**				**29 SUNDAY**	
00	177° 52.0	S 1° 28.0		00	178° 18.7	N 0° 54.2		00	178° 46.1	N 3° 15.4
02	207 52.3	26.0		02	208 19.1	56.2		02	208 46.4	17.4
04	237 52.7	24.0		04	238 19.5	58.2		04	238 46.8	19.3
06	267 53.1	S 1 22.0		06	268 19.8	N 1 00.1		06	268 47.2	N 3 21.3
08	297 53.4	20.1		08	298 20.2	02.1		08	298 47.6	23.2
10	327 53.8	18.1		10	328 20.6	04.1		10	328 48.0	25.2
12	357 54.2	S 1 16.1		12	358 21.0	N 1 06.0		12	358 48.3	N 3 27.1
14	27 54.5	14.1		14	28 21.4	08.0		14	28 48.7	29.1
16	57 54.9	12.2		16	58 21.7	10.0		16	58 49.1	31.0
18	87 55.2	S 1 10.2		18	88 22.1	N 1 11.9		18	88 49.5	N 3 33.0
20	117 55.6	08.2		20	118 22.5	13.9		20	118 49.8	34.9
22	147 56.0	06.2		22	148 22.9	15.9		22	148 50.2	36.9

	18 WEDNESDAY				**24 TUESDAY**				**30 MONDAY**	
00	177° 56.3	S 1° 04.2		00	178° 23.3	N 1° 17.8		00	178° 50.6	N 3° 38.8
02	207 56.7	02.3		02	208 23.6	19.8		02	208 51.0	40.7
04	237 57.1	1 00.3		04	238 24.0	21.8		04	238 51.3	42.7
06	267 57.4	S 0 58.3		06	268 24.4	N 1 23.8		06	268 51.7	N 3 44.6
08	297 57.8	56.3		08	298 24.8	25.7		08	298 52.1	46.6
10	327 58.2	54.4		10	328 25.2	27.7		10	328 52.5	48.5
12	357 58.5	S 0 52.4		12	358 25.5	N 1 29.7		12	358 52.9	N 3 50.5
14	27 58.9	50.4		14	28 25.9	31.6		14	28 53.2	52.4
16	57 59.3	48.4		16	58 26.3	33.6		16	58 53.6	54.3
18	87 59.6	S 0 46.5		18	88 26.7	N 1 35.6		18	88 54.0	N 3 56.3
20	118 00.0	44.5		20	118 27.1	37.5		20	118 54.4	58.2
22	148 00.4	42.5		22	148 27.4	39.5		22	148 54.7	4 00.2

	19 THURSDAY				**25 WEDNESDAY**				**31 TUESDAY**	
00	178° 00.7	S 0° 40.5		00	178° 27.8	N 1° 41.5		00	178° 55.1	N 4° 02.1
02	208 01.1	38.6		02	208 28.2	43.4		02	208 55.5	04.0
04	238 01.5	36.6		04	238 28.6	45.4		04	238 55.9	06.0
06	268 01.8	S 0 34.6		06	268 29.0	N 1 47.3		06	268 56.2	N 4 07.9
08	298 02.2	32.6		08	298 29.3	49.3		08	298 56.6	09.8
10	328 02.6	30.7		10	328 29.7	51.3		10	328 57.0	11.8
12	358 03.0	S 0 28.7		12	358 30.1	N 1 53.2		12	358 57.4	N 4 13.7
14	28 03.3	26.7		14	28 30.5	55.2		14	28 57.7	15.7
16	58 03.7	24.7		16	58 30.9	57.2		16	58 58.1	17.6
18	88 04.1	S 0 22.8		18	88 31.2	N 1 59.1		18	88 58.5	N 4 19.5
20	118 04.4	20.8		20	118 31.6	01.1		20	118 58.8	21.5
22	148 04.8	18.8		22	148 32.0	03.1		22	148 59.2	23.4

	20 FRIDAY				**26 THURSDAY**						
00	178° 05.2	S 0° 16.8		00	178° 32.4	N 2° 05.0				
02	208 05.6	14.8		02	208 32.8	07.0				
04	238 05.9	12.9		04	238 33.1	08.9				
06	268 06.3	S 0 10.9		06	268 33.5	N 2 10.9				
08	298 06.7	08.9		08	298 33.9	12.9				
10	328 07.0	06.9		10	328 34.3	14.8				
12	358 07.4	S 0 05.0		12	358 34.7	N 2 16.8				
14	28 07.8	03.0		14	28 35.0	18.7				
16	58 08.2	S 0 01.0		16	58 35.4	20.7				
18	88 08.5	N 0 00.9		18	88 35.8	N 2 22.7				
20	118 08.9	02.9		20	118 36.2	24.6				
22	148 09.3	04.9		22	148 36.6	26.6				

	21 SATURDAY				**27 FRIDAY**		
00	178° 09.7	N 0° 06.9		00	178° 37.0	N 2° 28.5
02	208 10.0	08.8		02	208 37.3	30.5
04	238 10.4	10.8		04	238 37.7	32.5
06	268 10.8	N 0 12.8		06	268 38.1	N 2 34.4
08	298 11.2	14.8		08	298 38.5	36.4
10	328 11.5	16.7		10	328 38.9	38.3
12	358 11.9	N 0 18.7		12	358 39.2	N 2 40.3
14	28 12.3	20.7		14	28 39.6	42.2
16	58 12.7	22.7		16	58 40.0	44.2
18	88 13.0	N 0 24.6		18	88 40.4	N 2 46.2
20	118 13.4	26.6		20	118 40.8	48.1
22	148 13.8	28.6		22	148 41.1	50.1

MERIDIAN PASSAGE

Day	hr min	Day	hr min
1	12 12	17	12 08
2	12 12	18	12 08
3	12 12	19	12 08
4	12 12	20	12 08
5	12 12	21	12 07
6	12 11	22	12 07
7	12 11	23	12 07
8	12 11	24	12 06
9	12 11	25	12 06
10	12 10	26	12 06
11	12 10	27	12 05
12	12 10	28	12 05
13	12 10	29	12 05
14	12 09	30	12 04
15	12 09	31	12 04
16	12 09		

April

SUN GHA, DECLINATION, MERIDIAN PASSAGE

1 WEDNESDAY

GMT	GHA	DEC
00	178° 59.6	N 4° 25.3
02	209 00.0	27.3
04	239 00.3	29.2
06	269 00.7	N 4 31.1
08	299 01.1	33.0
10	329 01.4	35.0
12	359 01.8	N 4 36.9
14	29 02.2	38.8
16	59 02.6	40.8
18	89 02.9	N 4 42.7
20	119 03.3	44.6
22	149 03.7	46.5

2 THURSDAY

GMT	GHA	DEC
00	179° 04.0	N 4° 48.5
02	209 04.4	50.4
04	239 04.8	52.3
06	269 05.2	N 4 54.2
08	299 05.5	56.2
10	329 05.9	58.1
12	359 06.3	N 5 00.0
14	29 06.6	01.9
16	59 07.0	03.8
18	89 07.4	N 5 05.8
20	119 07.7	07.7
22	149 08.1	09.6

3 FRIDAY

GMT	GHA	DEC
00	179° 08.5	N 5° 11.5
02	209 08.8	13.4
04	239 09.2	15.3
06	269 09.6	N 5 17.3
08	299 09.9	19.2
10	329 10.3	21.1
12	359 10.7	N 5 23.0
14	29 11.0	24.9
16	59 11.4	26.8
18	89 11.8	N 5 28.7
20	119 12.1	30.7
22	149 12.5	32.6

4 SATURDAY

GMT	GHA	DEC
00	179° 12.9	N 5° 34.5
02	209 13.2	36.4
04	239 13.6	38.3
06	269 13.9	N 5 40.2
08	299 14.3	42.1
10	329 14.7	44.0
12	359 15.0	N 5 45.9
14	29 15.4	47.8
16	59 15.8	49.7
18	89 16.1	N 5 51.6
20	119 16.5	53.5
22	149 16.8	55.4

5 SUNDAY

GMT	GHA	DEC
00	179° 17.2	N 5° 57.3
02	209 17.6	5 59.2
04	239 17.9	01.1
06	269 18.3	N 6 03.0
08	299 18.6	04.9
10	329 19.0	06.8
12	359 19.4	N 6 08.7
14	29 19.7	10.6
16	59 20.1	12.5
18	89 20.4	N 6 14.4
20	119 20.8	16.3
22	149 21.2	18.2

6 MONDAY

GMT	GHA	DEC
00	179° 21.5	N 6° 20.1
02	209 21.9	22.0
04	239 22.2	23.9
06	269 22.6	N 6 25.8
08	299 22.9	27.7
10	329 23.3	29.6
12	359 23.6	N 6 31.4
14	29 24.0	33.3
16	59 24.4	35.2
18	89 24.7	N 6 37.1
20	119 25.1	39.0
22	149 25.4	40.9

7 TUESDAY

GMT	GHA	DEC
00	179° 25.8	N 6° 42.8
02	209 26.1	44.6
04	239 26.5	46.5
06	269 26.8	N 6 48.4
08	299 27.2	50.3
10	329 27.5	52.2
12	359 27.9	N 6 54.0
14	29 28.2	55.9
16	59 28.6	57.8
18	89 28.9	N 6 59.7
20	119 29.3	01.5
22	149 29.6	03.4

8 WEDNESDAY

GMT	GHA	DEC
00	179° 30.0	N 7° 05.3
02	209 30.3	07.2
04	239 30.7	09.0
06	269 31.0	N 7 10.9
08	299 31.4	12.8
10	329 31.7	14.7
12	359 32.1	N 7 16.5
14	29 32.4	18.4
16	59 32.8	20.3
18	89 33.1	N 7 22.1
20	119 33.4	24.0
22	149 33.8	25.8

9 THURSDAY

GMT	GHA	DEC
00	179° 34.1	N 7° 27.7
02	209 34.5	29.6
04	239 34.8	31.4
06	269 35.2	N 7 33.3
08	299 35.5	35.2
10	329 35.8	37.0
12	359 36.2	N 7 38.9
14	29 36.5	40.7
16	59 36.9	42.6
18	89 37.2	N 7 44.4
20	119 37.5	46.3
22	149 37.9	48.1

10 FRIDAY

GMT	GHA	DEC
00	179° 38.2	N 7° 50.0
02	209 38.6	51.9
04	239 38.9	53.7
06	269 39.2	N 7 55.6
08	299 39.6	57.4
10	329 39.9	7 59.2
12	359 40.3	N 8 01.1
14	29 40.6	02.9
16	59 40.9	04.8
18	89 41.3	N 8 06.6
20	119 41.6	08.5
22	149 41.9	10.3

11 SATURDAY

GMT	GHA	DEC
00	179° 42.3	N 8° 12.2
02	209 42.6	14.0
04	239 42.9	15.8
06	269 43.3	N 8 17.7
08	299 43.6	19.5
10	329 43.9	21.3
12	359 44.3	N 8 23.2
14	29 44.6	25.0
16	59 44.9	26.8
18	89 45.2	N 8 28.7
20	119 45.6	30.5
22	149 45.9	32.3

12 SUNDAY

GMT	GHA	DEC
00	179° 46.2	N 8° 34.2
02	209 46.6	36.0
04	239 46.9	37.8
06	269 47.2	N 8 39.7
08	299 47.5	41.5
10	329 47.9	43.3
12	359 48.2	N 8 45.1
14	29 48.5	46.9
16	59 48.8	48.8
18	89 49.2	N 8 50.6
20	119 49.5	52.4
22	149 49.8	54.2

13 MONDAY

GMT	GHA	DEC
00	179° 50.1	N 8° 56.0
02	209 50.4	57.9
04	239 50.8	8 59.7
06	269 51.1	N 9 01.5
08	299 51.4	03.3
10	329 51.7	05.1
12	359 52.0	N 9 06.9
14	29 52.4	08.7
16	59 52.7	10.5
18	89 53.0	N 9 12.4
20	119 53.3	14.2
22	149 53.6	16.0

14 TUESDAY

GMT	GHA	DEC
00	179° 53.9	N 9° 17.8
02	209 54.3	19.6
04	239 54.6	21.4
06	269 54.9	N 9 23.2
08	299 55.2	25.0
10	329 55.5	26.8
12	359 55.8	N 9 28.6
14	29 56.1	30.4
16	59 56.4	32.2
18	89 56.8	N 9 34.0
20	119 57.1	35.8
22	149 57.4	37.5

15 WEDNESDAY

GMT	GHA	DEC
00	179° 57.7	N 9° 39.3
02	209 58.0	41.1
04	239 58.3	42.9
06	269 58.6	N 9 44.7
08	299 58.9	46.5
10	329 59.2	48.3
12	359 59.5	N 9 50.1
14	29 59.8	51.8
16	60 00.1	53.6
18	90 00.4	N 9 55.4
20	120 00.7	57.2
22	150 01.0	59.0

16 THURSDAY

GMT	GHA	DEC
00	180° 01.3	N10° 00.7
02	210 01.6	02.5
04	240 01.9	04.3
06	270 02.2	N10 06.1
08	300 02.5	07.8
10	330 02.8	09.6
12	0 03.1	N10 11.4
14	30 03.4	13.2
16	60 03.7	14.9
18	90 04.0	N10 16.7
20	120 04.3	18.5
22	150 04.6	20.2

17 FRIDAY

GMT	GHA	DEC
00	180° 04.9	N10° 22.0
02	210 05.2	23.7
04	240 05.5	25.5
06	270 05.8	N10 27.3
08	300 06.1	29.0
10	330 06.4	30.8
12	0 06.7	N10 32.5
14	30 07.0	34.3
16	60 07.2	36.0
18	90 07.5	N10 37.8
20	120 07.8	39.6
22	150 08.1	41.3

18 SATURDAY

GMT	GHA	DEC
00	180° 08.4	N10° 43.1
02	210 08.7	44.8
04	240 09.0	46.5
06	270 09.2	N10 48.3
08	300 09.5	50.0
10	330 09.8	51.8
12	0 10.1	N10 53.5
14	30 10.4	55.3
16	60 10.7	57.0
18	90 10.9	N10 58.7
20	120 11.2	11 00.5
22	150 11.5	02.2

19 SUNDAY

GMT	GHA	DEC
00	180° 11.8	N11° 03.9
02	210 12.0	05.7
04	240 12.3	07.4
06	270 12.6	N11 09.1
08	300 12.9	10.9
10	330 13.2	12.6
12	0 13.4	N11 14.3
14	30 13.7	16.0
16	60 14.0	17.8
18	90 14.2	N11 19.5
20	120 14.5	21.2
22	150 14.8	22.9

20 MONDAY

GMT	GHA	DEC
00	180° 15.0	N11° 24.7
02	210 15.3	26.4
04	240 15.6	28.1
06	270 15.9	N11 29.8
08	300 16.1	31.5
10	330 16.4	33.2
12	0 16.6	N11 34.9
14	30 16.9	36.7
16	60 17.2	38.4
18	90 17.4	N11 40.1
20	120 17.7	41.8
22	150 18.0	43.5

21 TUESDAY

GMT	GHA	DEC
00	180° 18.2	N11° 45.2
02	210 18.5	46.9
04	240 18.7	48.6
06	270 19.0	N11 50.3
08	300 19.3	52.0
10	330 19.5	53.7
12	0 19.8	N11 55.4
14	30 20.0	57.1
16	60 20.3	58.8
18	90 20.5	N12 00.4
20	120 20.8	02.1
22	150 21.0	03.8

22 WEDNESDAY

GMT	GHA	DEC
00	180° 21.3	N12° 05.5
02	210 21.5	07.2
04	240 21.8	08.9
06	270 22.0	N12 10.6
08	300 22.3	12.2
10	330 22.5	13.9
12	0 22.8	N12 15.6
14	30 23.0	17.3
16	60 23.3	19.0
18	90 23.5	N12 20.6
20	120 23.7	22.3
22	150 24.0	24.0

23 THURSDAY

GMT	GHA	DEC
00	180° 24.2	N12° 25.6
02	210 24.5	27.3
04	240 24.7	29.0
06	270 24.9	N12 30.6
08	300 25.2	32.3
10	330 25.4	34.0
12	0 25.7	N12 35.6
14	30 25.9	37.3
16	60 26.1	38.9
18	90 26.4	N12 40.6
20	120 26.6	42.3
22	150 26.8	43.9

24 FRIDAY

GMT	GHA	DEC
00	180° 27.1	N12° 45.6
02	210 27.3	47.2
04	240 27.5	48.9
06	270 27.7	N12 50.5
08	300 28.0	52.2
10	330 28.2	53.8
12	0 28.4	N12 55.5
14	30 28.7	57.1
16	60 28.9	58.7
18	90 29.1	N13 00.4
20	120 29.3	02.0
22	150 29.5	03.7

25 SATURDAY

GMT	GHA	DEC
00	180° 29.8	N13° 05.3
02	210 30.0	06.9
04	240 30.2	08.6
06	270 30.4	N13 10.2
08	300 30.6	11.8
10	330 30.9	13.4
12	0 31.1	N13 15.1
14	30 31.3	16.7
16	60 31.5	18.3
18	90 31.7	N13 19.9
20	120 31.9	21.6
22	150 32.1	23.2

26 SUNDAY

GMT	GHA	DEC
00	180° 32.4	N13° 24.8
02	210 32.6	26.4
04	240 32.8	28.0
06	270 33.0	N13 29.6
08	300 33.3	31.2
10	330 33.4	32.9
12	0 33.6	N13 34.5
14	30 33.8	36.1
16	60 34.0	37.7
18	90 34.2	N13 39.3
20	120 34.4	40.9
22	150 34.6	42.5

27 MONDAY

GMT	GHA	DEC
00	180° 34.8	N13° 44.1
02	210 35.0	45.7
04	240 35.2	47.3
06	270 35.4	N13 48.9
08	300 35.6	50.5
10	330 35.8	52.0
12	0 36.0	N13 53.6
14	30 36.2	55.2
16	60 36.4	56.8
18	90 36.6	N13 58.4
20	120 36.8	14 00.0
22	150 36.9	01.6

28 TUESDAY

GMT	GHA	DEC
00	180° 37.1	N14° 03.1
02	210 37.3	04.7
04	240 37.5	06.3
06	270 37.7	N14 07.9
08	300 37.9	09.4
10	330 38.1	11.0
12	0 38.3	N14 12.6
14	30 38.4	14.1
16	60 38.6	15.7
18	90 38.8	N14 17.3
20	120 39.0	18.8
22	150 39.2	20.4

29 WEDNESDAY

GMT	GHA	DEC
00	180° 39.3	N14° 22.0
02	210 39.5	23.5
04	240 39.7	25.1
06	270 39.9	N14 26.6
08	300 40.0	28.2
10	330 40.2	29.7
12	0 40.4	N14 31.3
14	30 40.6	32.8
16	60 40.7	34.4
18	90 40.9	N14 35.9
20	120 41.1	37.5
22	150 41.2	39.0

30 THURSDAY

GMT	GHA	DEC
00	180° 41.4	N14° 40.6
02	210 41.6	42.1
04	240 41.7	43.6
06	270 41.9	N14 45.2
08	300 42.1	46.7
10	330 42.2	48.2
12	0 42.4	N14 49.8
14	30 42.5	51.3
16	60 42.7	52.8
18	90 42.9	N14 54.3
20	120 43.0	55.9
22	150 43.2	57.4

MERIDIAN PASSAGE

Day	hr min	Day	hr min
1	12 04	17	12 00
2	12 04	18	11 59
3	12 03	19	11 59
4	12 03	20	11 59
5	12 03	21	11 59
6	12 02	22	11 58
7	12 02	23	11 58
8	12 02	24	11 58
9	12 02	25	11 58
10	12 01	26	11 58
11	12 01	27	11 58
12	12 01	28	11 57
13	12 01	29	11 57
14	12 00	30	11 57
15	12 00		
16	12 00		

May

SUN GHA, DECLINATION, MERIDIAN PASSAGE

1 FRIDAY		
GMT	GHA	DEC
00	180° 43.3	N14° 58.9
02	210 43.5	15 00.4
04	240 43.6	01.9
06	270 43.8	N15 03.5
08	300 43.9	05.0
10	330 44.1	06.5
12	0 44.2	N15 08.0
14	30 44.4	09.5
16	60 44.5	11.0
18	90 44.7	N15 12.5
20	120 44.8	14.0
22	150 45.0	15.5

2 SATURDAY		
00	180° 45.1	N15° 17.0
02	210 45.3	18.5
04	240 45.4	20.0
06	270 45.6	N15 21.5
08	300 45.7	23.0
10	330 45.8	24.5
12	0 46.0	N15 26.0
14	30 46.1	27.5
16	60 46.2	28.9
18	90 46.4	N15 30.4
20	120 46.5	31.9
22	150 46.6	33.4

3 SUNDAY		
00	180° 46.8	N15° 34.9
02	210 46.9	36.3
04	240 47.0	37.8
06	270 47.2	N15 39.3
08	300 47.3	40.8
10	330 47.4	42.2
12	0 47.6	N15 43.7
14	30 47.7	45.2
16	60 47.8	46.6
18	90 47.9	N15 48.1
20	120 48.1	49.5
22	150 48.2	51.0

4 MONDAY		
00	180° 48.3	N15° 52.5
02	210 48.4	53.9
04	240 48.5	55.4
06	270 48.7	N15 56.8
08	300 48.8	58.3
10	330 48.9	15 59.7
12	0 49.0	N16 01.2
14	30 49.1	02.6
16	60 49.2	04.0
18	90 49.3	N16 05.5
20	120 49.5	06.9
22	150 49.6	08.4

5 TUESDAY		
00	180° 49.7	N16° 09.8
02	210 49.8	11.2
04	240 49.9	12.7
06	270 50.0	N16 14.1
08	300 50.1	15.5
10	330 50.2	16.9
12	0 50.3	N16 18.4
14	30 50.4	19.8
16	60 50.5	21.2
18	90 50.6	N16 22.6
20	120 50.7	24.0
22	150 50.8	25.4

6 WEDNESDAY		
GMT	GHA	DEC
00	180° 50.9	N16° 26.9
02	210 51.0	28.3
04	240 51.1	29.7
06	270 51.2	N16 31.1
08	300 51.3	32.5
10	330 51.4	33.9
12	0 51.5	N16 35.3
14	30 51.6	36.7
16	60 51.7	38.1
18	90 51.8	N16 39.5
20	120 51.9	40.9
22	150 51.9	42.3

7 THURSDAY		
00	180° 52.0	N16° 43.6
02	210 52.1	45.0
04	240 52.2	46.4
06	270 52.3	N16 47.8
08	300 52.4	49.2
10	330 52.4	50.6
12	0 52.5	N16 51.9
14	30 52.6	53.3
16	60 52.7	54.7
18	90 52.8	N16 56.1
20	120 52.8	57.4
22	150 52.9	58.8

8 FRIDAY		
00	180° 53.0	N17° 00.2
02	210 53.1	01.5
04	240 53.1	02.9
06	270 53.2	N17 04.2
08	300 53.3	05.6
10	330 53.3	07.0
12	0 53.4	N17 08.3
14	30 53.5	09.7
16	60 53.6	11.0
18	90 53.6	N17 12.4
20	120 53.7	13.7
22	150 53.7	15.0

9 SATURDAY		
00	180° 53.8	N17° 16.4
02	210 53.9	17.7
04	240 53.9	19.1
06	270 54.0	N17 20.4
08	300 54.1	21.7
10	330 54.1	23.1
12	0 54.2	N17 24.4
14	30 54.2	25.7
16	60 54.3	27.0
18	90 54.3	N17 28.4
20	120 54.4	29.7
22	150 54.4	31.0

10 SUNDAY		
00	180° 54.5	N17° 32.3
02	210 54.5	33.6
04	240 54.6	35.0
06	270 54.6	N17 36.3
08	300 54.7	37.6
10	330 54.7	38.9
12	0 54.8	N17 40.2
14	30 54.8	41.5
16	60 54.9	42.8
18	90 54.9	N17 44.1
20	120 55.0	45.4
22	150 55.0	46.7

11 MONDAY		
GMT	GHA	DEC
00	180° 55.0	N17° 48.0
02	210 55.1	49.3
04	240 55.1	50.5
06	270 55.2	N17 51.8
08	300 55.2	53.1
10	330 55.2	54.4
12	0 55.3	N17 55.7
14	30 55.3	57.0
16	60 55.3	58.2
18	90 55.4	N17 59.5
20	120 55.4	00.8
22	150 55.4	02.1

12 TUESDAY		
00	180° 55.4	N18° 03.3
02	210 55.5	04.6
04	240 55.5	05.8
06	270 55.5	N18 07.1
08	300 55.5	08.4
10	330 55.6	09.6
12	0 55.6	N18 10.9
14	30 55.6	12.1
16	60 55.6	13.4
18	90 55.7	N18 14.6
20	120 55.7	15.9
22	150 55.7	17.1

13 WEDNESDAY		
00	180° 55.7	N18° 18.4
02	210 55.7	19.6
04	240 55.7	20.8
06	270 55.8	N18 22.1
08	300 55.8	23.3
10	330 55.8	24.5
12	0 55.8	N18 25.8
14	30 55.8	27.0
16	60 55.8	28.2
18	90 55.8	N18 29.4
20	120 55.8	30.7
22	150 55.8	31.9

14 THURSDAY		
00	180° 55.8	N18° 33.1
02	210 55.8	34.3
04	240 55.8	35.5
06	270 55.8	N18 36.7
08	300 55.8	37.9
10	330 55.8	39.1
12	0 55.8	N18 40.3
14	30 55.8	41.5
16	60 55.8	42.7
18	90 55.8	N18 43.9
20	120 55.8	45.1
22	150 55.8	46.3

15 FRIDAY		
00	180° 55.8	N18° 47.5
02	210 55.8	48.7
04	240 55.8	49.9
06	270 55.8	N18 51.1
08	300 55.8	52.3
10	330 55.8	53.4
12	0 55.8	N18 54.6
14	30 55.8	55.8
16	60 55.7	57.0
18	90 55.7	N18 58.1
20	120 55.7	59.3
22	150 55.7	19 00.5

16 SATURDAY

GMT	GHA	DEC
00	180° 55.7	N19° 01.6
02	210 55.7	02.8
04	240 55.6	03.9
06	270 55.6	N19 05.1
08	300 55.6	06.3
10	330 55.6	07.4
12	0 55.5	N19 08.6
14	30 55.5	09.7
16	60 55.5	10.8
18	90 55.5	N19 12.0
20	120 55.4	13.1
22	150 55.4	14.3

17 SUNDAY

GMT	GHA	DEC
00	180° 55.4	N19° 15.4
02	210 55.4	16.5
04	240 55.3	17.7
06	270 55.3	N19 18.8
08	300 55.3	19.9
10	330 55.2	21.1
12	0 55.2	N19 22.2
14	30 55.2	23.3
16	60 55.1	24.4
18	90 55.1	N19 25.5
20	120 55.0	26.6
22	150 55.0	27.8

18 MONDAY

GMT	GHA	DEC
00	180° 55.0	N19° 28.9
02	210 54.9	30.0
04	240 54.9	31.1
06	270 54.8	N19 32.2
08	300 54.8	33.3
10	330 54.7	34.4
12	0 54.7	N19 35.5
14	30 54.6	36.6
16	60 54.6	37.6
18	90 54.5	N19 38.7
20	120 54.5	39.8
22	150 54.4	40.9

19 TUESDAY

GMT	GHA	DEC
00	180° 54.4	N19° 42.0
02	210 54.3	43.1
04	240 54.3	44.1
06	270 54.2	N19 45.2
08	300 54.2	46.3
10	330 54.1	47.4
12	0 54.1	N19 48.4
14	30 54.0	49.5
16	60 53.9	50.5
18	90 53.9	N19 51.6
20	120 53.8	52.7
22	150 53.8	53.7

20 WEDNESDAY

GMT	GHA	DEC
00	180° 53.7	N19° 54.8
02	210 53.6	55.8
04	240 53.6	56.9
06	270 53.5	N19 57.9
08	300 53.4	59.0
10	330 53.4	20 00.0
12	0 53.3	N20 01.0
14	30 53.2	02.1
16	60 53.2	03.1
18	90 53.1	N20 04.1
20	120 53.0	05.2
22	150 52.9	06.2

21 THURSDAY

GMT	GHA	DEC
00	180° 52.9	N20° 07.2
02	210 52.8	08.2
04	240 52.7	09.3
06	270 52.6	N20 10.3
08	300 52.5	11.3
10	330 52.5	12.3
12	0 52.4	N20 13.3
14	30 52.3	14.3
16	60 52.2	15.3
18	90 52.1	N20 16.3
20	120 52.1	17.3
22	150 52.0	18.3

22 FRIDAY

GMT	GHA	DEC
00	180° 51.9	N20° 19.3
02	210 51.8	20.3
04	240 51.7	21.3
06	270 51.6	N20 22.3
08	300 51.5	23.3
10	330 51.4	24.3
12	0 51.3	N20 25.2
14	30 51.3	26.2
16	60 51.2	27.2
18	90 51.1	N20 28.2
20	120 51.0	29.1
22	150 50.9	30.1

23 SATURDAY

GMT	GHA	DEC
00	180° 50.8	N20° 31.1
02	210 50.7	32.0
04	240 50.6	33.0
06	270 50.5	N20 34.0
08	300 50.4	34.9
10	330 50.3	35.9
12	0 50.2	N20 36.8
14	30 50.1	37.8
16	60 50.0	38.7
18	90 49.9	N20 39.7
20	120 49.8	40.6
22	150 49.6	41.5

24 SUNDAY

GMT	GHA	DEC
00	180° 49.5	N20° 42.5
02	210 49.4	43.4
04	240 49.3	44.3
06	270 49.2	N20 45.3
08	300 49.1	46.2
10	330 49.0	47.1
12	0 48.9	N20 48.1
14	30 48.8	49.0
16	60 48.6	49.9
18	90 48.5	N20 50.8
20	120 48.4	51.7
22	150 48.3	52.6

25 MONDAY

GMT	GHA	DEC
00	180° 48.2	N20° 53.5
02	210 48.1	54.4
04	240 47.9	55.3
06	270 47.8	N20 56.2
08	300 47.7	57.1
10	330 47.6	58.0
12	0 47.4	N20 58.9
14	30 47.3	20 59.8
16	60 47.2	00.7
18	90 47.1	N21 01.6
20	120 46.9	02.5
22	150 46.8	03.3

26 TUESDAY

GMT	GHA	DEC
00	180° 46.7	N21° 04.2
02	210 46.5	05.1
04	240 46.4	06.0
06	270 46.3	N21 06.8
08	300 46.1	07.7
10	330 46.0	08.6
12	0 45.9	N21 09.4
14	30 45.7	10.3
16	60 45.6	11.1
18	90 45.5	N21 12.0
20	120 45.3	12.9
22	150 45.2	13.7

27 WEDNESDAY

GMT	GHA	DEC
00	180° 45.1	N21° 14.5
02	210 44.9	15.4
04	240 44.8	16.2
06	270 44.6	N21 17.1
08	300 44.5	17.9
10	330 44.3	18.7
12	0 44.2	N21 19.6
14	30 44.0	20.4
16	60 43.9	21.2
18	90 43.8	N21 22.1
20	120 43.6	22.9
22	150 43.5	23.7

28 THURSDAY

GMT	GHA	DEC
00	180° 43.3	N21° 24.5
02	210 43.2	25.3
04	240 43.0	26.1
06	270 42.8	N21 26.9
08	300 42.7	27.7
10	330 42.5	28.5
12	0 42.4	N21 29.3
14	30 42.2	30.1
16	60 42.1	30.9
18	90 41.9	N21 31.7
20	120 41.8	32.5
22	150 41.6	33.3

29 FRIDAY

GMT	GHA	DEC
00	180° 41.4	N21° 34.1
02	210 41.3	34.9
04	240 41.1	35.7
06	270 40.9	N21 36.4
08	300 40.8	37.2
10	330 40.6	38.0
12	0 40.5	N21 38.8
14	30 40.3	39.5
16	60 40.1	40.3
18	90 40.0	N21 41.0
20	120 39.8	41.8
22	150 39.6	42.6

30 SATURDAY

GMT	GHA	DEC
00	180° 39.4	N21° 43.3
02	210 39.3	44.1
04	240 39.1	44.8
06	270 38.9	N21 45.6
08	300 38.8	46.3
10	330 38.6	47.0
12	0 38.4	N21 47.8
14	30 38.2	48.5
16	60 38.1	49.2
18	90 37.9	N21 50.0
20	120 37.7	50.7
22	150 37.5	51.4

31 MONDAY

GMT	GHA	DEC
00	180° 37.4	N21° 52.2
02	210 37.2	52.9
04	240 37.0	53.6
06	270 36.8	N21 54.3
08	300 36.6	55.0
10	330 36.4	55.7
12	0 36.3	N21 56.4
14	30 36.1	57.1
16	60 35.9	57.8
18	90 35.7	N21 58.5
20	120 35.5	59.2
22	150 35.3	21 59.9

MERIDIAN PASSAGE

Day	hr min	Day	hr min
1	11 57	17	11 56
2	11 57	18	11 56
3	11 57	19	11 56
4	11 57	20	11 56
5	11 57	21	11 57
6	11 57	22	11 57
7	11 57	23	11 57
8	11 56	24	11 57
9	11 56	25	11 57
10	11 56	26	11 57
11	11 56	27	11 57
12	11 56	28	11 57
13	11 56	29	11 57
14	11 56	30	11 57
15	11 56	31	11 58
16	11 56		

June
SUN GHA, DECLINATION, MERIDIAN PASSAGE

1 MONDAY

GMT	GHA	DEC
00	180° 35.1	N22° 00.6
02	210 35.0	01.3
04	240 34.8	02.0
06	270 34.6	N22 02.7
08	300 34.4	03.3
10	330 34.2	04.0
12	0 34.0	N22 04.7
14	30 33.8	05.4
16	60 33.6	06.0
18	90 33.4	N22 06.7
20	120 33.2	07.4
22	150 33.0	08.0

2 TUESDAY

GMT	GHA	DEC
00	180° 32.8	N22° 08.7
02	210 32.6	09.3
04	240 32.4	10.0
06	270 32.2	N22 10.7
08	300 32.0	11.3
10	330 31.8	11.9
12	0 31.6	N22 12.6
14	30 31.4	13.2
16	60 31.2	13.9
18	90 31.0	N22 14.5
20	120 30.8	15.1
22	150 30.6	15.8

3 WEDNESDAY

GMT	GHA	DEC
00	180° 30.4	N22° 16.4
02	210 30.2	17.0
04	240 30.0	17.6
06	270 29.8	N22 18.2
08	300 29.6	18.9
10	330 29.4	19.5
12	0 29.2	N22 20.1
14	30 29.0	20.7
16	60 28.8	21.3
18	90 28.6	N22 21.9
20	120 28.3	22.5
22	150 28.1	23.1

4 THURSDAY

GMT	GHA	DEC
00	180° 27.9	N22° 23.7
02	210 27.7	24.3
04	240 27.5	24.9
06	270 27.3	N22 25.5
08	300 27.1	26.0
10	330 26.8	26.6
12	0 26.6	N22 27.2
14	30 26.4	27.8
16	60 26.2	28.3
18	90 26.0	N22 28.9
20	120 25.8	29.5
22	150 25.5	30.0

5 FRIDAY

GMT	GHA	DEC
00	180° 25.3	N22° 30.6
02	210 25.1	31.2
04	240 24.9	31.7
06	270 24.7	N22 32.3
08	300 24.4	32.8
10	330 24.2	33.4
12	0 24.0	N22 33.9
14	30 23.8	34.5
16	60 23.6	35.0
18	90 23.3	N22 35.5
20	120 23.1	36.1
22	150 22.9	36.6

6 SATURDAY

GMT	GHA	DEC
00	180° 22.7	N22° 37.1
02	210 22.4	37.7
04	240 22.2	38.2
06	270 22.0	N22 38.7
08	300 21.7	39.2
10	330 21.5	39.7
12	0 21.3	N22 40.2
14	30 21.1	40.7
16	60 20.8	41.3
18	90 20.6	N22 41.8
20	120 20.4	42.3
22	150 20.1	42.8

7 SUNDAY

GMT	GHA	DEC
00	180° 19.9	N22° 43.3
02	210 19.7	43.7
04	240 19.4	44.2
06	270 19.2	N22 44.7
08	300 19.0	45.2
10	330 18.7	45.7
12	0 18.5	N22 46.2
14	30 18.3	46.6
16	60 18.0	47.1
18	90 17.8	N22 47.6
20	120 17.6	48.1
22	150 17.3	48.5

8 MONDAY

GMT	GHA	DEC
00	180° 17.1	N22° 49.0
02	210 16.8	49.4
04	240 16.6	49.9
06	270 16.4	N22 50.3
08	300 16.1	50.8
10	330 15.9	51.2
12	0 15.7	N22 51.7
14	30 15.4	52.1
16	60 15.2	52.6
18	90 14.9	N22 53.0
20	120 14.7	53.4
22	150 14.4	53.9

9 TUESDAY

GMT	GHA	DEC
00	180° 14.2	N22° 54.3
02	210 14.0	54.7
04	240 13.7	55.2
06	270 13.5	N22 55.6
08	300 13.2	56.0
10	330 13.0	56.4
12	0 12.7	N22 56.8
14	30 12.5	57.2
16	60 12.3	57.6
18	90 12.0	N22 58.0
20	120 11.8	58.4
22	150 11.5	58.8

10 WEDNESDAY

GMT	GHA	DEC
00	180° 11.3	N22° 59.2
02	210 11.0	59.6
04	240 10.8	23 00.0
06	270 10.5	N23 00.4
08	300 10.3	00.8
10	330 10.0	01.2
12	0 09.8	N23 01.5
14	30 09.5	01.9
16	60 09.3	02.3
18	90 09.0	N23 02.7
20	120 08.8	03.0
22	150 08.5	03.4

11 THURSDAY

GMT	GHA	DEC
00	180° 08.3	N23° 03.7
02	210 08.0	04.1
04	240 07.8	04.5
06	270 07.5	N23 04.8
08	300 07.3	05.2
10	330 07.0	05.5
12	0 06.8	N23 05.9
14	30 06.5	06.2
16	60 06.3	06.5
18	90 06.0	N23 06.9
20	120 05.8	07.2
22	150 05.5	07.5

12 FRIDAY

GMT	GHA	DEC
00	180° 05.2	N23° 07.9
02	210 05.0	08.2
04	240 04.7	08.5
06	270 04.5	N23 08.8
08	300 04.2	09.1
10	330 04.0	09.5
12	0 03.7	N23 09.8
14	30 03.5	10.1
16	60 03.2	10.4
18	90 02.9	N23 10.7
20	120 02.7	11.0
22	150 02.4	11.3

13 SATURDAY

GMT	GHA	DEC
00	180° 02.2	N23° 11.6
02	210 01.9	11.9
04	240 01.7	12.1
06	270 01.4	N23 12.4
08	300 01.1	12.7
10	330 00.9	13.0
12	0 00.6	N23 13.3
14	30 00.1	13.5
16	60 00.1	13.8
18	89 59.8	N23 14.1
20	119 59.6	14.3
22	149 59.3	14.6

14 SUNDAY

GMT	GHA	DEC
00	179° 59.1	N23° 14.9
02	209 58.8	15.1
04	239 58.5	15.4
06	269 58.3	N23 15.6
08	299 58.0	15.9
10	329 57.8	16.1
12	359 57.5	N23 16.3
14	29 57.2	16.6
16	59 57.0	16.8
18	89 56.7	N23 17.1
20	119 56.4	17.3
22	149 56.2	17.5

15 MONDAY

GMT	GHA	DEC
00	179° 55.9	N23° 17.7
02	209 55.7	18.0
04	239 55.4	18.2
06	269 55.1	N23 18.4
08	299 54.9	18.6
10	329 54.6	18.8
12	359 54.3	N23 19.0
14	29 54.1	19.2
16	59 53.8	19.4
18	89 53.5	N23 19.6
20	119 53.3	19.8
22	149 53.0	20.0

16 TUESDAY

GMT	GHA	DEC
00	179° 52'8	N23° 20'2
02	209 52.5	20.4
04	239 52.2	20.6
06	269 52.0	N23 20.8
08	299 51.7	20.9
10	329 51.4	21.1
12	359 51.2	N23 21.3
14	29 50.9	21.5
16	59 50.6	21.6
18	89 50.4	N23 21.8
20	119 50.1	21.9
22	149 49.8	22.1

17 WEDNESDAY

GMT	GHA	DEC
00	179° 49'6	N23° 22'3
02	209 49.3	22.4
04	239 49.0	22.6
06	269 48.8	N23 22.7
08	299 48.5	22.9
10	329 48.2	23.0
12	359 48.0	N23 23.1
14	29 47.7	23.3
16	59 47.4	23.4
18	89 47.1	N23 23.5
20	119 46.9	23.7
22	149 46.6	23.8

18 THURSDAY

GMT	GHA	DEC
00	179° 46'3	N23° 23'9
02	209 46.1	24.0
04	239 45.8	24.1
06	269 45.5	N23 24.3
08	299 45.3	24.4
10	329 45.0	24.5
12	359 44.7	N23 24.6
14	29 44.5	24.7
16	59 44.2	24.8
18	89 43.9	N23 24.9
20	119 43.6	25.0
22	149 43.4	25.0

19 FRIDAY

GMT	GHA	DEC
00	179° 43'1	N23° 25'1
02	209 42.8	25.2
04	239 42.6	25.3
06	269 42.3	N23 25.4
08	299 42.0	25.5
10	329 41.8	25.5
12	359 41.5	N23 25.6
14	29 41.2	25.7
16	59 40.9	25.7
18	89 40.7	N23 25.8
20	119 40.4	25.8
22	149 40.1	25.9

20 SATURDAY

GMT	GHA	DEC
00	179° 39'9	N23° 25'9
02	209 39.6	26.0
04	239 39.3	26.0
06	269 39.1	N23 26.1
08	299 38.8	26.1
10	329 38.5	26.2
12	359 38.2	N23 26.2
14	29 38.0	26.2
16	59 37.7	26.3
18	89 37.4	N23 26.3
20	119 37.1	26.3
22	149 36.9	26.3

21 SUNDAY

GMT	GHA	DEC
00	179° 36'6	N23° 26'4
02	209 36.3	26.4
04	239 36.1	26.4
06	269 35.8	N23 26.4
08	299 35.5	26.4
10	329 35.3	26.4
12	359 35.0	N23 26.4
14	29 34.7	26.4
16	59 34.4	26.4
18	89 34.2	N23 26.4
20	119 33.9	26.4
22	149 33.6	26.4

22 MONDAY

GMT	GHA	DEC
00	179° 33'4	N23° 26'3
02	209 33.1	26.3
04	239 32.8	26.3
06	269 32.5	N23 26.3
08	299 32.3	26.2
10	329 32.0	26.2
12	359 31.7	N23 26.2
14	29 31.5	26.1
16	59 31.2	26.1
18	89 30.9	N23 26.1
20	119 30.7	26.0
22	149 30.4	26.0

23 TUESDAY

GMT	GHA	DEC
00	179° 30'1	N23° 25'9
02	209 29.8	25.9
04	239 29.6	25.8
06	269 29.3	N23 25.8
08	299 29.0	25.7
10	329 28.8	25.6
12	359 28.5	N23 25.6
14	29 28.2	25.5
16	59 28.0	25.4
18	89 27.7	N23 25.3
20	119 27.4	25.3
22	149 27.2	25.2

24 WEDNESDAY

GMT	GHA	DEC
00	179° 26'9	N23° 25'1
02	209 26.6	25.0
04	239 26.4	24.9
06	269 26.1	N23 24.8
08	299 25.8	24.7
10	329 25.6	24.6
12	359 25.3	N23 24.5
14	29 25.0	24.4
16	59 24.8	24.3
18	89 24.5	N23 24.2
20	119 24.2	24.1
22	149 24.0	24.0

25 THURSDAY

GMT	GHA	DEC
00	179° 23'7	N23° 23'9
02	209 23.5	23.7
04	239 23.2	23.6
06	269 22.9	N23 23.5
08	299 22.6	23.3
10	329 22.4	23.2
12	359 22.1	N23 23.1
14	29 21.8	22.9
16	59 21.6	22.8
18	89 21.3	N23 22.7
20	119 21.0	22.5
22	149 20.8	22.4

26 FRIDAY

GMT	GHA	DEC
00	179° 20'5	N23° 22'2
02	209 20.3	22.1
04	239 20.0	21.9
06	269 19.7	N23 21.7
08	299 19.5	21.6
10	329 19.2	21.4
12	359 18.9	N23 21.2
14	29 18.7	21.1
16	59 18.4	20.9
18	89 18.1	N23 20.7
20	119 17.9	20.5
22	149 17.6	20.3

27 SATURDAY

GMT	GHA	DEC
00	179° 17'4	N23° 20'1
02	209 17.1	20.1
04	239 16.8	19.8
06	269 16.6	N23 19.6
08	299 16.3	19.4
10	329 16.1	19.2
12	359 15.8	N23 19.0
14	29 15.5	18.8
16	59 15.3	18.5
18	89 15.0	N23 18.3
20	119 14.8	18.1
22	149 14.5	17.9

28 SUNDAY

GMT	GHA	DEC
00	179° 14'2	N23° 17'7
02	209 14.0	17.4
04	239 13.7	17.2
06	269 13.5	N23 17.0
08	299 13.2	16.8
10	329 13.0	16.5
12	359 12.7	N23 16.3
14	29 12.5	16.0
16	59 12.2	15.8
18	89 11.9	N23 15.5
20	119 11.7	15.3
22	149 11.4	15.0

29 MONDAY

GMT	GHA	DEC
00	179° 11'2	N23° 14'8
02	209 10.9	14.5
04	239 10.7	14.3
06	269 10.4	N23 14.0
08	299 10.2	13.7
10	329 09.9	13.5
12	359 09.7	N23 13.2
14	29 09.4	12.9
16	59 09.2	12.6
18	89 08.9	N23 12.3
20	119 08.7	12.1
22	149 08.4	11.8

30 TUESDAY

GMT	GHA	DEC
00	179° 08'2	N23° 11'5
02	209 07.9	11.2
04	239 07.7	10.9
06	269 07.4	N23 10.6
08	299 07.2	10.3
10	329 06.9	10.0
12	359 06.7	N23 09.7
14	29 06.4	09.4
16	59 06.2	09.1
18	89 05.9	N23 08.7
20	119 05.7	08.4
22	149 05.4	08.1

MERIDIAN PASSAGE

Day	hr min	Day	hr min
1	11 58	17	12 01
2	11 58	18	12 01
3	11 58	19	12 01
4	11 58	20	12 01
5	11 58	21	12 02
6	11 59	22	12 02
7	11 59	23	12 02
8	11 59	24	12 02
9	11 59	25	12 03
10	11 59	26	12 03
11	12 00	27	12 03
12	12 00	28	12 03
13	12 00	29	12 03
14	12 00	30	12 04
15	12 00		
16	12 01		

July
SUN GHA, DECLINATION, MERIDIAN PASSAGE

1 WEDNESDAY

GMT	GHA	DEC
00	179° 05.2	N23° 07.8
02	209 04.9	07.5
04	239 04.7	07.1
06	269 04.4	N23 06.8
08	299 04.2	06.5
10	329 04.0	06.1
12	359 03.7	N23 05.8
14	29 03.5	05.4
16	59 03.2	05.1
18	89 03.0	N23 04.7
20	119 02.7	04.4
22	149 02.5	04.0

2 THURSDAY

GMT	GHA	DEC
00	179° 02.3	N23° 03.7
02	209 02.0	03.3
04	239 01.8	03.0
06	269 01.5	N23 02.6
08	299 01.3	02.2
10	329 01.1	01.8
12	359 01.0	N23 01.5
14	29 00.6	01.1
16	59 00.4	00.7
18	89 00.1	N23 00.3
20	118 59.9	22 59.9
22	148 59.7	59.6

3 FRIDAY

GMT	GHA	DEC
00	178° 59.4	N22° 59.2
02	209 59.2	58.8
04	238 59.0	58.4
06	268 58.7	N22 58.0
08	298 58.5	57.6
10	328 58.3	57.2
12	358 58.0	56.8
14	28 57.8	56.4
16	58 57.6	55.9
18	88 57.3	N22 55.5
20	118 57.1	55.1
22	148 56.9	54.7

4 SATURDAY

GMT	GHA	DEC
00	178° 56.6	N22° 54.3
02	208 56.4	53.8
04	238 56.2	53.4
06	268 56.0	N22 53.0
08	298 55.7	52.5
10	328 55.5	52.1
12	358 55.3	N22 51.7
14	28 55.1	51.2
16	58 54.8	50.8
18	88 54.6	N22 50.3
20	118 54.4	49.9
22	148 54.2	49.4

5 SUNDAY

GMT	GHA	DEC
00	178° 53.9	N22° 49.0
02	208 53.7	48.5
04	238 53.5	48.0
06	268 53.3	N22 47.6
08	298 53.1	47.1
10	328 52.8	46.6
12	358 52.6	N22 46.2
14	28 52.4	45.7
16	58 52.2	45.2
18	88 52.0	N22 44.7
20	118 51.8	44.2
22	148 51.5	43.7

6 MONDAY

GMT	GHA	DEC
00	178° 51.3	N22° 43.3
02	208 51.1	42.8
04	238 50.9	42.3
06	268 50.7	N22 41.8
08	298 50.5	41.3
10	328 50.3	40.8
12	358 50.1	N22 40.3
14	28 49.9	39.7
16	58 49.6	39.2
18	88 49.4	N22 38.7
20	118 49.2	38.2
22	148 49.0	37.7

7 TUESDAY

GMT	GHA	DEC
00	178° 48.8	N22° 37.2
02	208 48.6	36.6
04	238 48.4	36.1
06	268 48.2	N22 35.6
08	298 48.0	35.0
10	328 47.8	34.5
12	358 47.6	N22 34.0
14	28 47.4	33.4
16	58 47.2	32.9
18	88 47.0	N22 32.3
20	118 46.8	31.8
22	148 46.6	31.2

8 WEDNESDAY

GMT	GHA	DEC
00	178° 46.4	N22° 30.7
02	208 46.2	30.1
04	238 46.0	29.6
06	268 45.8	N22 29.0
08	298 45.6	28.4
10	328 45.4	27.9
12	358 45.2	N22 27.3
14	28 45.0	26.7
16	58 44.8	26.1
18	88 44.7	N22 25.5
20	118 44.5	25.0
22	148 44.3	24.4

9 THURSDAY

GMT	GHA	DEC
00	178° 44.1	N22° 23.8
02	208 43.9	23.2
04	238 43.7	22.6
06	268 43.5	N22 22.0
08	298 43.3	21.4
10	328 43.2	20.8
12	358 43.0	N22 20.2
14	28 42.8	19.6
16	58 42.6	19.0
18	88 42.4	N22 18.4
20	118 42.2	17.8
22	148 42.0	17.2

10 FRIDAY

GMT	GHA	DEC
00	178° 41.9	N22° 16.5
02	208 41.7	15.9
04	238 41.5	15.3
06	268 41.4	N22 14.7
08	298 41.2	14.0
10	328 41.0	13.4
12	358 40.8	N22 12.8
14	28 40.6	12.1
16	58 40.5	11.5
18	88 40.3	N22 10.8
20	118 40.1	10.2
22	148 40.0	09.5

11 SATURDAY

GMT	GHA	DEC
00	178° 39.8	N22° 08.9
02	208 39.6	08.2
04	238 39.5	07.6
06	268 39.3	N22 06.9
08	298 39.1	06.3
10	328 39.0	05.6
12	358 38.8	N22 04.9
14	28 38.6	04.3
16	58 38.5	03.6
18	88 38.3	N22 02.9
20	118 38.1	02.2
22	148 38.0	01.5

12 SUNDAY

GMT	GHA	DEC
00	178° 37.8	N22° 00.9
02	208 37.7	22 00.2
04	238 37.5	59.5
06	268 37.3	N21 58.8
08	298 37.2	58.1
10	328 37.0	57.4
12	358 36.9	N21 56.7
14	28 36.7	56.0
16	58 36.6	55.3
18	88 36.4	N21 54.6
20	118 36.3	53.9
22	148 36.1	53.2

13 MONDAY

GMT	GHA	DEC
00	178° 36.0	N21° 52.5
02	208 35.8	51.7
04	238 35.7	51.0
06	268 35.5	N21 50.3
08	298 35.4	49.6
10	328 35.2	48.8
12	358 35.1	N21 48.1
14	28 34.9	47.4
16	58 34.8	46.6
18	88 34.6	N21 45.9
20	118 34.5	45.2
22	148 34.4	44.4

14 TUESDAY

GMT	GHA	DEC
00	178° 34.2	N21° 43.7
02	208 34.1	42.9
04	238 33.9	42.2
06	268 33.8	N21 41.4
08	298 33.7	40.7
10	328 33.5	39.9
12	358 33.4	N21 39.1
14	28 33.3	38.4
16	58 33.1	37.6
18	88 33.0	N21 36.9
20	118 32.9	36.1
22	148 32.7	35.3

15 WEDNESDAY

GMT	GHA	DEC
00	178° 32.6	N21° 34.5
02	208 32.5	33.7
04	238 32.4	33.0
06	268 32.3	N21 32.2
08	298 32.1	31.4
10	328 32.0	30.6
12	358 31.8	N21 29.8
14	28 31.7	29.0
16	58 31.6	28.2
18	88 31.5	N21 27.4
20	118 31.4	26.6
22	148 31.2	25.8

16 THURSDAY

GMT	GHA	DEC
00	178° 31'.1	N21° 25'.0
02	208 31.0	24.2
04	238 30.9	23.4
06	268 30.8	N21 22.6
08	298 30.7	21.8
10	328 30.5	20.9
12	358 30.4	N21 20.1
14	28 30.3	19.3
16	58 30.2	18.5
18	88 30.1	N21 17.6
20	118 30.0	16.8
22	148 29.9	16.0

17 FRIDAY

GMT	GHA	DEC
00	178° 29'.8	N21° 15'.1
02	208 29.7	14.3
04	238 29.5	13.4
06	268 29.4	N21 12.6
08	298 29.3	11.8
10	328 29.2	10.9
12	358 29.1	N21 10.0
14	28 29.0	09.2
16	58 28.9	08.3
18	88 28.8	N21 07.5
20	118 28.7	06.6
22	148 28.6	05.8

18 SATURDAY

GMT	GHA	DEC
00	178° 28'.5	N21° 04'.9
02	208 28.4	04.0
04	238 28.3	03.1
06	268 28.2	N21 02.3
08	298 28.1	01.4
10	328 28.1	00.5
12	358 28.0	N20 59.6
14	28 27.9	58.7
16	58 27.8	57.9
18	88 27.7	N20 57.0
20	118 27.6	56.1
22	148 27.5	55.2

19 SUNDAY

GMT	GHA	DEC
00	178° 27'.4	N20° 54'.3
02	208 27.3	53.4
04	238 27.3	52.5
06	268 27.2	N20 51.6
08	298 27.1	50.7
10	328 27.0	49.8
12	358 26.9	N20 48.8
14	28 26.8	47.9
16	58 26.8	47.0
18	88 26.7	N20 46.1
20	118 26.6	45.2
22	148 26.5	44.3

20 MONDAY

GMT	GHA	DEC
00	178° 26'.5	N20° 43'.3
02	208 26.4	42.4
04	238 26.3	41.5
06	268 26.2	N20 40.5
08	298 26.2	39.6
10	328 26.1	38.7
12	358 26.0	N20 37.7
14	28 26.0	36.8
16	58 25.9	35.8
18	88 25.8	N20 34.9
20	118 25.8	33.9
22	348 25.7	33.0

21 TUESDAY

GMT	GHA	DEC
00	178° 25'.6	N20° 32'.0
02	208 25.6	31.1
04	238 25.5	30.1
06	268 25.4	N20 29.2
08	298 25.4	28.2
10	328 25.3	27.2
12	358 25.3	N20 26.2
14	28 25.2	25.3
16	58 25.1	24.3
18	88 25.1	N20 23.3
20	118 25.0	22.3
22	148 25.0	21.4

22 WEDNESDAY

GMT	GHA	DEC
00	178° 24'.9	N20° 20'.4
02	208 24.9	19.4
04	238 24.8	18.4
06	268 24.8	N20 17.4
08	298 24.7	16.4
10	328 24.7	15.4
12	358 24.6	N20 14.4
14	28 24.6	13.4
16	58 24.5	12.4
18	88 24.5	N20 11.4
20	118 24.4	10.4
22	148 24.4	09.4

23 THURSDAY

GMT	GHA	DEC
00	178° 24'.4	N20° 08'.4
02	208 24.3	07.4
04	238 24.3	06.4
06	268 24.2	N20 05.3
08	298 24.2	04.3
10	328 24.2	03.3
12	358 24.1	N20 02.3
14	28 24.1	01.2
16	58 24.1	N20 00.2
18	88 24.0	N19 59.2
20	118 24.0	58.1
22	148 24.0	57.1

24 FRIDAY

GMT	GHA	DEC
00	178° 23'.9	N19° 56'.1
02	208 23.9	55.0
04	238 23.9	54.0
06	268 23.9	N19 52.9
08	298 23.8	51.9
10	328 23.8	50.8
12	358 23.8	N19 49.8
14	28 23.8	48.7
16	58 23.7	47.7
18	88 23.7	N19 46.6
20	118 23.7	45.5
22	148 23.7	44.5

25 SATURDAY

GMT	GHA	DEC
00	178° 23'.7	N19° 43'.4
02	208 23.6	42.3
04	238 23.6	41.3
06	268 23.6	N19 40.2
08	298 23.6	39.1
10	328 23.6	38.0
12	358 23.6	N19 36.9
14	28 23.6	35.9
16	58 23.6	34.8
18	88 23.5	N19 33.7
20	118 23.5	32.6
22	148 23.5	31.5

26 SUNDAY

GMT	GHA	DEC
00	178° 23'.5	N19° 30'.4
02	208 23.5	29.3
04	238 23.5	28.2
06	268 23.5	N19 27.1
08	298 23.5	26.0
10	328 23.5	24.9
12	358 23.5	N19 23.8
14	28 23.5	22.7
16	58 23.5	21.6
18	88 23.5	N19 20.5
20	118 23.5	19.3
22	148 23.5	18.2

27 MONDAY

GMT	GHA	DEC
00	178° 23'.5	N19° 17'.1
02	208 23.5	16.0
04	238 23.6	14.8
06	268 23.6	N19 13.7
08	298 23.6	12.6
10	328 23.6	11.5
12	358 23.6	N19 10.3
14	28 23.6	09.2
16	58 23.6	08.0
18	88 23.6	N19 06.9
20	118 23.7	05.8
22	148 23.7	04.6

28 TUESDAY

GMT	GHA	DEC
00	178° 23'.7	N19° 03'.5
02	208 23.7	02.3
04	238 23.7	01.2
06	268 23.8	N19 00.0
08	298 23.8	58.9
10	328 23.8	57.7
12	358 23.8	N18 56.5
14	28 23.9	55.4
16	58 23.9	54.2
18	88 23.9	N18 53.0
20	118 23.9	51.9
22	148 24.0	50.7

29 WEDNESDAY

GMT	GHA	DEC
00	178° 24'.0	N18° 49'.5
02	208 24.0	48.3
04	238 24.1	47.2
06	268 24.1	N18 46.0
08	298 24.1	44.8
10	328 24.2	43.6
12	358 24.2	N18 42.4
14	28 24.2	41.2
16	58 24.3	40.1
18	88 24.4	N18 38.9
20	118 24.4	37.7
22	148 24.4	36.5

30 THURSDAY

GMT	GHA	DEC
00	178° 24'.4	N18° 35'.3
02	208 24.5	34.1
04	238 24.5	32.9
06	268 24.6	N18 31.7
08	298 24.6	30.5
10	328 24.7	29.2
12	358 24.7	N18 28.0
14	28 24.8	26.8
16	58 24.8	25.6
18	88 24.9	N18 24.4
20	118 24.9	23.2
22	148 25.0	21.9

31 FRIDAY

GMT	GHA	DEC
00	178° 25'.1	N18° 20'.7
02	208 25.1	19.5
04	238 25.2	18.3
06	268 25.2	N18 17.0
08	298 25.3	15.8
10	328 25.3	14.6
12	358 25.4	N18 13.3
14	28 25.4	12.1
16	58 25.5	10.8
18	88 25.6	N18 09.6
20	118 25.7	08.4
22	148 25.7	07.1

MERIDIAN PASSAGE

Day	hr min	Day	hr min
1	12 04	17	12 06
2	12 04	18	12 06
3	12 04	19	12 06
4	12 04	20	12 06
5	12 04	21	12 06
6	12 05	22	12 06
7	12 05	23	12 06
8	12 05	24	12 06
9	12 05	25	12 06
10	12 05	26	12 06
11	12 05	27	12 06
12	12 06	28	12 06
13	12 06	29	12 06
14	12 06	30	12 06
15	12 06	31	12 06
16	12 06		

August

SUN GHA, DECLINATION, MERIDIAN PASSAGE

1 SATURDAY

GMT	GHA	DEC
00	178° 25.8	N18° 05.9
02	208 25.9	04.6
04	238 25.9	03.3
06	268 26.0	N18 02.1
08	298 26.1	00.8
10	328 26.2	17 59.6
12	358 26.2	N17 58.3
14	28 26.3	57.1
16	58 26.4	55.8
18	88 26.5	N17 54.5
20	118 26.6	53.2
22	148 26.6	52.0

2 SUNDAY

GMT	GHA	DEC
00	178° 26.7	N17° 50.7
02	208 26.8	49.4
04	238 26.9	48.1
06	268 27.0	N17 46.9
08	298 27.1	45.6
10	328 27.1	44.3
12	358 27.2	N17 43.0
14	28 27.3	41.7
16	58 27.4	40.4
18	88 27.5	N17 39.1
20	118 27.6	37.9
22	148 27.7	36.6

3 MONDAY

GMT	GHA	DEC
00	178° 27.8	N17° 35.3
02	208 27.9	34.0
04	238 28.0	32.7
06	268 28.1	N17 31.4
08	298 28.2	30.0
10	328 28.3	28.7
12	358 28.4	N17 27.4
14	28 28.5	26.1
16	58 28.6	24.8
18	88 28.7	N17 23.5
20	118 28.8	22.2
22	148 28.9	20.9

4 TUESDAY

GMT	GHA	DEC
00	178° 29.0	N17° 19.5
02	208 29.1	18.2
04	238 29.2	16.9
06	268 29.3	N17 15.6
08	298 29.4	14.2
10	328 29.6	12.9
12	358 29.7	N17 11.6
14	28 29.8	10.2
16	58 29.9	08.9
18	88 30.0	N17 07.5
20	118 30.1	06.2
22	148 30.2	04.9

5 WEDNESDAY

GMT	GHA	DEC
00	178° 30.4	N17° 03.5
02	208 30.5	02.2
04	238 30.6	00.8
06	268 30.7	N16 59.5
08	298 30.9	58.1
10	328 31.0	56.8
12	358 31.1	N16 55.4
14	28 31.2	54.1
16	58 31.4	52.7
18	88 31.5	N16 51.3
20	118 31.6	50.0
22	148 31.8	48.6

6 THURSDAY

GMT	GHA	DEC
00	178° 31.9	N16° 47.2
02	208 32.0	45.9
04	238 32.2	44.5
06	268 32.3	N16 43.1
08	298 32.4	41.7
10	328 32.6	40.4
12	358 32.7	N16 39.0
14	28 32.9	37.6
16	58 33.0	36.2
18	88 33.1	N16 34.8
20	118 33.3	33.5
22	148 33.4	32.1

7 FRIDAY

GMT	GHA	DEC
00	178° 33.6	N16° 30.7
02	208 33.7	29.3
04	238 33.9	27.9
06	268 34.0	N16 26.5
08	298 34.2	25.1
10	328 34.3	23.7
12	358 34.5	N16 22.3
14	28 34.6	20.9
16	58 34.8	19.5
18	88 34.9	N16 18.1
20	118 35.1	16.7
22	148 35.2	15.3

8 SATURDAY

GMT	GHA	DEC
00	178° 35.4	N16° 13.9
02	208 35.5	12.4
04	238 35.7	11.0
06	268 35.9	N16 09.6
08	298 36.0	08.2
10	328 36.2	06.8
12	358 36.4	N16 05.3
14	28 36.5	03.9
16	58 36.7	02.5
18	88 36.9	N16 01.1
20	118 37.0	15 59.6
22	148 37.2	58.2

9 SUNDAY

GMT	GHA	DEC
00	178° 37.4	N15° 56.8
02	208 37.6	55.3
04	238 37.7	53.9
06	268 37.9	N15 52.5
08	298 38.1	51.0
10	328 38.2	49.6
12	358 38.4	N15 48.1
14	28 38.6	46.7
16	58 38.8	45.2
18	88 39.0	N15 43.8
20	118 39.1	42.3
22	148 39.3	40.9

10 MONDAY

GMT	GHA	DEC
00	178° 39.4	N15° 39.4
02	208 39.7	38.0
04	238 39.9	36.5
06	268 40.1	N15 35.1
08	298 40.3	33.6
10	328 40.4	32.1
12	358 40.6	N15 30.7
14	28 40.8	29.2
16	58 41.0	27.7
18	88 41.2	N15 26.3
20	118 41.4	24.8
22	148 41.6	23.3

11 TUESDAY

GMT	GHA	DEC
00	178° 41.8	N15° 21.8
02	208 42.0	20.4
04	238 42.2	18.9
06	268 42.4	N15 17.4
08	298 42.6	15.9
10	328 42.8	14.4
12	358 43.0	N15 13.0
14	28 43.2	11.5
16	58 43.4	10.0
18	88 43.6	N15 08.5
20	118 43.8	07.0
22	148 44.0	05.5

12 WEDNESDAY

GMT	GHA	DEC
00	178° 44.2	N15° 04.0
02	208 44.4	02.5
04	238 44.6	01.0
06	268 44.8	N14 59.5
08	298 45.0	58.0
10	328 45.3	56.5
12	358 45.5	N14 55.0
14	28 45.7	53.5
16	58 45.9	52.0
18	88 46.1	N14 50.5
20	118 46.3	49.0
22	148 46.5	47.5

13 THURSDAY

GMT	GHA	DEC
00	178° 46.8	N14° 45.9
02	208 47.0	44.4
04	238 47.2	42.9
06	268 47.4	N14 41.4
08	298 47.7	39.9
10	328 47.9	38.3
12	358 48.1	N14 36.8
14	28 48.3	35.3
16	58 48.6	33.8
18	88 48.8	N14 32.2
20	118 49.0	30.7
22	148 49.2	29.2

14 FRIDAY

GMT	GHA	DEC
00	178° 49.5	N14° 27.6
02	208 49.7	26.1
04	238 49.9	24.6
06	268 50.2	N14 23.0
08	298 50.4	21.5
10	328 50.6	19.9
12	358 50.9	N14 18.4
14	28 51.1	16.8
16	58 51.3	15.3
18	88 51.6	N14 13.7
20	118 51.8	12.2
22	148 52.1	10.6

15 SATURDAY

GMT	GHA	DEC
00	178° 52.3	N14° 09.1
02	208 52.6	07.5
04	238 52.8	06.0
06	268 53.0	N14 04.4
08	298 53.3	02.9
10	328 53.5	01.3
12	358 53.8	N13 59.7
14	28 54.0	58.2
16	58 54.3	56.6
18	88 54.5	N13 55.0
20	118 54.8	53.5
22	148 55.0	51.9

16 SUNDAY

GMT	GHA	DEC
00	178° 55.3	N13° 50.3
02	208 55.5	48.8
04	238 55.8	47.2
06	268 56.0	N13 45.6
08	298 56.3	44.0
10	328 56.6	42.4
12	358 56.8	N13 40.9
14	28 57.1	39.3
16	58 57.3	37.7
18	88 57.6	N13 36.1
20	118 57.9	34.5
22	148 58.1	32.9

17 MONDAY

GMT	GHA	DEC
00	178° 58.4	N13° 31.3
02	208 58.6	29.7
04	238 58.9	28.2
06	268 59.2	N13 26.6
08	298 59.4	25.0
10	328 59.7	23.4
12	359 00.0	N13 21.8
14	29 00.3	20.2
16	59 00.5	18.6
18	89 00.8	N13 17.0
20	119 01.1	15.4
22	149 01.3	13.7

18 TUESDAY

GMT	GHA	DEC
00	179° 01.6	N13° 12.1
02	209 02.1	10.5
04	239 02.2	08.9
06	269 02.4	N13 07.3
08	299 02.7	05.7
10	329 03.0	04.1
12	359 03.3	N13 02.5
14	29 03.6	00.8
16	59 03.8	12 59.2
18	89 04.1	N12 57.6
20	119 04.4	56.0
22	149 04.7	54.4

19 WEDNESDAY

GMT	GHA	DEC
00	179° 05.0	N12° 52.7
02	209 05.3	51.1
04	239 05.5	49.5
06	269 05.8	N12 47.8
08	299 06.1	46.2
10	329 06.4	44.6
12	359 06.7	N12 42.9
14	29 07.0	41.3
16	59 07.3	39.7
18	89 07.6	N12 38.0
20	119 07.9	36.4
22	149 08.1	34.8

20 THURSDAY

GMT	GHA	DEC
00	179° 08.4	N12° 33.1
02	209 08.7	31.5
04	239 09.0	29.8
06	269 09.3	N12 28.2
08	299 09.6	26.5
10	329 09.9	24.9
12	359 10.2	N12 23.2
14	29 10.5	21.6
16	59 10.8	19.9
18	89 11.1	N12 18.3
20	119 11.4	16.6
22	149 11.7	15.0

21 FRIDAY

GMT	GHA	DEC
00	179° 12.0	N12° 13.3
02	209 12.3	11.6
04	239 12.6	10.0
06	269 12.9	N12 08.3
08	299 13.3	06.7
10	329 13.6	05.0
12	359 13.9	N12 03.3
14	29 14.2	01.7
16	59 14.5	12 00.0
18	89 14.8	N11 58.3
20	119 15.1	56.6
22	149 15.4	55.0

22 SATURDAY

GMT	GHA	DEC
00	179° 15.7	N11° 53.3
02	209 16.0	51.6
04	239 16.4	49.9
06	269 16.7	N11 48.3
08	299 17.0	46.6
10	329 17.3	44.9
12	359 17.6	N11 43.2
14	29 17.9	41.5
16	59 18.3	39.9
18	89 18.6	N11 38.2
20	119 18.9	36.5
22	149 19.2	34.8

23 SUNDAY

GMT	GHA	DEC
00	179° 19.5	N11° 33.1
02	209 19.9	31.4
04	239 20.2	29.7
06	269 20.5	N11 28.0
08	299 20.8	26.3
10	329 21.2	24.6
12	359 21.5	N11 22.9
14	29 21.8	21.2
16	59 22.1	19.5
18	89 22.5	N11 17.8
20	119 22.8	16.1
22	149 23.1	14.4

24 MONDAY

GMT	GHA	DEC
00	179° 23.5	N11° 12.7
02	209 23.8	11.0
04	239 24.1	09.3
06	269 24.5	N11 07.6
08	299 24.8	05.9
10	329 25.1	04.2
12	359 25.5	N11 02.5
14	29 25.8	11 00.8
16	59 26.1	59.0
18	89 26.5	N10 57.3
20	119 26.8	55.6
22	149 27.2	53.9

25 TUESDAY

GMT	GHA	DEC
00	179° 27.5	N10° 52.2
02	209 27.8	50.4
04	239 28.2	48.7
06	269 28.5	N10 47.0
08	299 28.8	45.3
10	329 29.2	43.5
12	359 29.5	N10 41.8
14	29 29.9	40.1
16	59 30.2	38.4
18	89 30.6	N10 36.6
20	119 30.9	34.9
22	149 31.3	33.2

26 WEDNESDAY

GMT	GHA	DEC
00	179° 31.6	N10° 31.4
02	209 32.0	29.7
04	239 32.3	28.0
06	269 32.7	N10 26.2
08	299 33.0	24.5
10	329 33.4	22.7
12	359 33.7	N10 21.0
14	29 34.1	19.3
16	59 34.4	17.5
18	89 34.8	N10 15.8
20	119 35.1	14.0
22	149 35.5	12.3

27 THURSDAY

GMT	GHA	DEC
00	179° 35.8	N10° 10.5
02	209 36.2	08.8
04	239 36.5	07.0
06	269 36.9	N10 05.3
08	299 37.3	03.5
10	329 37.6	01.8
12	359 38.0	N10 00.0
14	29 38.3	58.3
16	59 38.7	56.5
18	89 39.1	N 9 54.8
20	119 39.4	53.0
22	149 39.8	51.2

28 FRIDAY

GMT	GHA	DEC
00	179° 40.1	N 9° 49.5
02	209 40.5	47.7
04	239 40.9	46.0
06	269 41.2	N 9 44.2
08	299 41.6	42.4
10	329 42.0	40.7
12	359 42.3	N 9 38.9
14	29 42.7	37.1
16	59 43.1	35.3
18	89 43.4	N 9 33.6
20	119 43.8	31.8
22	149 44.2	30.0

29 SATURDAY

GMT	GHA	DEC
00	179° 44.5	N 9° 28.3
02	209 44.9	26.5
04	239 45.3	24.7
06	269 45.7	N 9 22.9
08	299 46.0	21.2
10	329 46.4	19.4
12	359 46.8	N 9 17.6
14	29 47.2	15.8
16	59 47.5	14.0
18	89 47.9	N 9 12.2
20	119 48.3	10.5
22	149 48.7	08.7

30 SUNDAY

GMT	GHA	DEC
00	179° 49.0	N 9° 06.9
02	209 49.4	05.1
04	239 49.8	03.3
06	269 50.2	N 9 01.5
08	299 50.5	8 59.7
10	329 50.9	57.9
12	359 51.3	N 8 56.2
14	29 51.7	54.4
16	59 52.1	52.6
18	89 52.5	N 8 50.8
20	119 52.8	49.0
22	149 53.2	47.2

31 MONDAY

GMT	GHA	DEC
00	179° 53.6	N 8° 45.4
02	209 54.0	43.6
04	239 54.4	41.8
06	269 54.8	N 8 40.0
08	299 55.1	38.2
10	329 55.5	36.4
12	359 55.9	N 8 34.6
14	29 56.3	32.8
16	59 56.7	31.0
18	89 57.1	N 8 29.2
20	119 57.5	27.3
22	149 57.9	25.5

MERIDIAN PASSAGE

Day	hr min	Day	hr min
1	12 06	17	12 04
2	12 06	18	12 04
3	12 06	19	12 04
4	12 06	20	12 03
5	12 06	21	12 03
6	12 06	22	12 03
7	12 06	23	12 02
8	12 06	24	12 02
9	12 05	25	12 02
10	12 05	26	12 02
11	12 05	27	12 01
12	12 05	28	12 01
13	12 05	29	12 01
14	12 05	30	12 01
15	12 04	31	12 00
16	12 04		

September
SUN GHA, DECLINATION, MERIDIAN PASSAGE

1 TUESDAY

GMT	GHA	DEC
00	179° 58'.3	N 8° 23'.7
02	209 58.6	21.9
04	239 59.0	20.1
06	269 59.4	N 8 18.3
08	299 59.8	16.5
10	330 00.2	14.7
12	0 00.6	N 8 12.9
14	30 01.0	11.0
16	60 01.4	09.2
18	90 01.8	N 8 07.4
20	120 02.2	05.6
22	150 02.6	03.8

2 WEDNESDAY

GMT	GHA	DEC
00	180° 03'.0	N 8° 01'.9
02	210 03.4	8 00.1
04	240 03.8	58.3
06	270 04.2	N 7 56.5
08	300 04.6	54.6
10	330 05.0	52.8
12	0 05.4	N 7 51.0
14	30 05.8	49.2
16	60 06.2	47.3
18	90 06.6	N 7 45.5
20	120 07.0	43.7
22	150 07.4	41.9

3 THURSDAY

GMT	GHA	DEC
00	180° 07'.8	N 7° 40'.0
02	210 08.2	38.2
04	240 08.6	36.4
06	270 09.0	N 7 34.5
08	300 09.4	32.7
10	330 09.8	30.9
12	0 10.2	N 7 29.0
14	30 10.6	27.2
16	60 11.0	25.3
18	90 11.4	N 7 23.5
20	120 11.8	21.7
22	150 12.3	19.8

4 FRIDAY

GMT	GHA	DEC
00	180° 12'.7	N 7° 18'.0
02	210 13.1	16.1
04	240 13.5	14.3
06	270 13.9	N 7 12.5
08	300 14.3	10.6
10	330 14.7	08.8
12	0 15.1	N 7 06.9
14	30 15.5	05.1
16	60 15.9	03.2
18	90 16.4	N 7 01.4
20	120 16.8	6 59.5
22	150 17.2	57.7

5 SATURDAY

GMT	GHA	DEC
00	180° 17'.6	N 6° 55'.8
02	210 18.0	54.0
04	240 18.4	52.1
06	270 18.8	N 6 50.3
08	300 19.3	48.4
10	330 19.7	46.6
12	0 20.1	N 6 44.7
14	30 20.5	42.8
16	60 20.9	41.0
18	90 21.3	N 6 39.1
20	120 21.8	37.3
22	150 22.2	35.4

6 SUNDAY

GMT	GHA	DEC
00	180° 22'.6	N 6° 33'.6
02	210 23.0	31.7
04	240 23.4	29.8
06	270 23.9	N 6 28.0
08	300 24.3	26.1
10	330 24.7	24.2
12	0 25.1	N 6 22.4
14	30 25.5	20.5
16	60 26.0	18.6
18	90 26.4	N 6 16.8
20	120 26.8	14.9
22	150 27.2	13.0

7 MONDAY

GMT	GHA	DEC
00	180° 27'.7	N 6° 11'.2
02	210 28.1	09.3
04	240 28.5	07.4
06	270 28.9	N 6 05.6
08	300 29.4	03.7
10	330 29.8	01.8
12	0 30.2	N 5 59.9
14	30 30.6	58.1
16	60 31.1	56.2
18	90 31.5	N 5 54.3
20	120 31.9	52.5
22	150 32.3	50.6

8 TUESDAY

GMT	GHA	DEC
00	180° 32'.8	N 5° 48'.7
02	210 33.2	46.8
04	240 33.6	44.9
06	270 34.1	N 5 43.1
08	300 34.5	41.2
10	330 34.9	39.3
12	0 35.3	N 5 37.4
14	30 35.8	35.5
16	60 36.2	33.7
18	90 36.6	N 5 31.8
20	120 37.1	29.9
22	150 37.5	28.0

9 WEDNESDAY

GMT	GHA	DEC
00	180° 37'.9	N 5° 26'.1
02	210 38.4	24.2
04	240 38.8	22.4
06	270 39.2	N 5 20.5
08	300 39.7	18.6
10	330 40.1	16.7
12	0 40.5	N 5 14.8
14	30 41.0	12.9
16	60 41.4	11.0
18	90 41.8	N 5 09.1
20	120 42.3	07.2
22	150 42.7	05.3

10 THURSDAY

GMT	GHA	DEC
00	180° 43'.1	N 5° 03'.5
02	210 43.6	01.6
04	240 44.0	4 59.7
06	270 44.4	N 4 57.8
08	300 44.9	55.9
10	330 45.3	54.0
12	0 45.8	N 4 52.1
14	30 46.2	50.2
16	60 46.6	48.3
18	90 47.1	N 4 46.4
20	120 47.5	44.5
22	150 47.9	42.6

11 FRIDAY

GMT	GHA	DEC
00	180° 48'.4	N 4° 40'.7
02	210 48.8	38.8
04	240 49.3	36.9
06	270 49.7	N 4 35.0
08	300 50.1	33.1
10	330 50.6	31.2
12	0 51.0	N 4 29.3
14	30 51.5	27.4
16	60 51.9	25.5
18	90 52.3	N 4 23.6
20	120 52.8	21.7
22	150 53.2	19.8

12 SATURDAY

GMT	GHA	DEC
00	180° 53'.7	N 4° 17'.9
02	210 54.1	16.0
04	240 54.5	14.1
06	270 55.0	N 4 12.2
08	300 55.4	10.2
10	330 55.9	08.3
12	0 56.3	N 4 06.4
14	30 56.8	04.5
16	60 57.2	02.6
18	90 57.6	N 4 00.7
20	120 58.1	58.8
22	150 58.5	56.9

13 SUNDAY

GMT	GHA	DEC
00	180° 59'.0	N 3° 55'.0
02	210 59.4	53.1
04	240 59.9	51.1
06	271 00.3	N 3 49.2
08	301 00.7	47.3
10	331 01.2	45.4
12	1 01.6	N 3 43.5
14	31 02.1	41.6
16	61 02.5	39.7
18	91 03.0	N 3 37.7
20	121 03.4	35.8
22	151 03.8	33.9

14 MONDAY

GMT	GHA	DEC
00	181° 04'.3	N 3° 32'.0
02	211 04.7	30.1
04	241 05.2	28.2
06	271 05.6	N 3 26.2
08	301 06.1	24.3
10	331 06.5	22.4
12	1 07.0	N 3 20.5
14	31 07.4	18.6
16	61 07.9	16.6
18	91 08.3	N 3 14.7
20	121 08.7	12.8
22	151 09.2	10.9

15 TUESDAY

GMT	GHA	DEC
00	181° 09'.6	N 3° 09'.0
02	211 10.1	07.0
04	241 10.5	05.1
06	271 11.0	N 3 03.2
08	301 11.4	01.3
10	331 11.9	2 59.3
12	1 12.3	N 2 57.4
14	31 12.8	55.5
16	61 13.2	53.6
18	91 13.7	N 2 51.6
20	121 14.1	49.7
22	151 14.5	47.8

16 WEDNESDAY

GMT	GHA	DEC
00	181° 15.0	N 2° 45.9
02	211 15.4	43.9
04	241 15.9	42.0
06	271 16.3	N 2 40.1
08	301 16.8	38.2
10	331 17.2	36.2
12	1 17.7	N 2 34.3
14	31 18.1	32.4
16	61 18.6	30.4
18	91 19.0	N 2 28.5
20	121 19.5	26.6
22	151 19.9	24.6

17 THURSDAY

GMT	GHA	DEC
00	181° 20.3	N 2° 22.7
02	211 20.8	20.8
04	241 21.2	18.9
06	271 21.7	N 2 16.9
08	301 22.1	15.0
10	331 22.6	13.1
12	1 23.0	N 2 11.1
14	31 23.5	09.2
16	61 23.9	07.3
18	91 24.4	N 2 05.3
20	121 24.8	03.4
22	151 25.3	01.5

18 FRIDAY

GMT	GHA	DEC
00	181° 25.7	N 1° 59.5
02	211 26.1	57.6
04	241 26.6	55.6
06	271 27.0	N 1 53.7
08	301 27.5	51.8
10	331 27.9	49.8
12	1 28.4	N 1 47.9
14	31 28.8	46.0
16	61 29.3	44.0
18	91 29.7	N 1 42.1
20	121 30.2	40.2
22	151 30.6	38.2

19 SATURDAY

GMT	GHA	DEC
00	181° 31.0	N 1° 36.3
02	211 31.5	34.3
04	241 31.9	32.4
06	271 32.4	N 1 30.5
08	301 32.8	28.5
10	331 33.3	26.6
12	1 33.7	N 1 24.6
14	31 34.2	22.7
16	61 34.6	20.8
18	91 35.0	N 1 18.8
20	121 35.5	16.9
22	151 35.9	14.9

20 SUNDAY

GMT	GHA	DEC
00	181° 36.4	N 1° 13.0
02	211 36.8	11.1
04	241 37.3	09.1
06	271 37.7	N 1 07.2
08	301 38.2	05.2
10	331 38.6	03.3
12	1 39.0	N 1 01.4
14	31 39.5	0 59.4
16	61 39.9	57.5
18	91 40.4	N 0 55.5
20	121 40.8	53.6
22	151 41.2	51.6

21 MONDAY

GMT	GHA	DEC
00	181° 41.7	N 0° 49.7
02	211 42.1	47.8
04	241 42.6	45.8
06	271 43.0	N 0 43.9
08	301 43.5	41.9
10	331 43.9	40.0
12	1 44.3	N 0 38.0
14	31 44.8	36.1
16	61 45.2	34.1
18	91 45.7	N 0 32.2
20	121 46.1	30.3
22	151 46.5	28.3

22 TUESDAY

GMT	GHA	DEC
00	181° 47.0	N 0° 26.4
02	211 47.4	24.4
04	241 47.9	22.5
06	271 48.3	N 0 20.5
08	301 48.7	18.6
10	331 49.2	16.6
12	1 49.6	N 0 14.7
14	31 50.0	12.7
16	61 50.5	10.8
18	91 50.9	N 0 08.8
20	121 51.4	06.9
22	151 51.8	05.0

23 WEDNESDAY

GMT	GHA	DEC
00	181° 52.2	N 0° 03.0
02	211 52.7	01.1
04	241 53.1	S 0 00.9
06	271 53.5	S 0 02.8
08	301 54.0	04.8
10	331 54.4	06.7
12	1 54.8	S 0 08.7
14	31 55.3	10.6
16	61 55.7	12.6
18	91 56.2	S 0 14.5
20	121 56.6	16.5
22	151 57.0	18.4

24 THURSDAY

GMT	GHA	DEC
00	181° 57.5	S 0° 20.4
02	211 57.9	22.3
04	241 58.3	24.3
06	271 58.8	S 0 26.2
08	301 59.2	28.2
10	331 59.6	30.1
12	2 00.1	S 0 32.1
14	32 00.5	34.0
16	62 00.9	36.0
18	92 01.3	S 0 37.9
20	122 01.8	39.8
22	152 02.2	41.8

25 FRIDAY

GMT	GHA	DEC
00	182° 02.6	S 0° 43.7
02	212 03.1	45.7
04	242 03.5	47.6
06	272 03.9	S 0 49.6
08	302 04.4	51.5
10	332 04.8	53.5
12	2 05.2	S 0 55.4
14	32 05.6	57.4
16	62 06.1	0 59.3
18	92 06.5	S 1 01.3
20	122 06.9	03.2
22	152 07.4	05.2

26 SATURDAY

GMT	GHA	DEC
00	182° 07.8	S 1° 07.1
02	212 08.2	09.1
04	242 08.6	11.0
06	272 09.1	S 1 13.0
08	302 09.5	14.9
10	332 09.9	16.9
12	2 10.3	S 1 18.8
14	32 10.8	20.8
16	62 11.2	22.7
18	92 11.6	S 1 24.7
20	122 12.0	26.6
22	152 12.5	28.6

27 SUNDAY

GMT	GHA	DEC
00	182° 12.9	S 1° 30.5
02	212 13.3	32.5
04	242 13.7	34.4
06	272 14.1	S 1 36.4
08	302 14.6	38.3
10	332 15.0	40.3
12	2 15.4	S 1 42.2
14	32 15.8	44.1
16	62 16.2	46.1
18	92 16.7	S 1 48.0
20	122 17.1	50.0
22	152 17.5	51.9

28 MONDAY

GMT	GHA	DEC
00	182° 17.9	S 1° 53.9
02	212 18.3	55.8
04	242 18.8	57.8
06	272 19.2	S 1 59.7
08	302 19.6	01.7
10	332 20.0	03.6
12	2 20.4	S 2 05.6
14	32 20.8	07.5
16	62 21.3	09.5
18	92 21.7	S 2 11.4
20	122 22.1	13.4
22	152 22.5	15.3

29 TUESDAY

GMT	GHA	DEC
00	182° 22.9	S 2° 17.3
02	212 23.3	19.2
04	242 23.7	21.1
06	272 24.2	S 2 23.1
08	302 24.6	25.0
10	332 25.0	27.0
12	2 25.4	S 2 28.9
14	32 25.8	30.9
16	62 26.2	32.8
18	92 26.6	S 2 34.8
20	122 27.0	36.7
22	152 27.4	38.6

30 WEDNESDAY

GMT	GHA	DEC
00	182° 27.9	S 2° 40.6
02	212 28.3	42.5
04	242 28.7	44.5
06	272 29.1	S 2 46.4
08	302 29.5	48.4
10	332 29.9	50.3
12	2 30.3	S 2 52.3
14	32 30.7	54.2
16	62 31.1	56.1
18	92 31.5	S 2 58.1
20	122 31.9	3 00.0
22	152 32.3	02.0

MERIDIAN PASSAGE

Day	hr min	Day	hr min
1	12 00	17	11 54
2	12 00	18	11 54
3	11 59	19	11 54
4	11 59	20	11 53
5	11 59	21	11 53
6	11 58	22	11 53
7	11 58	23	11 52
8	11 58	24	11 52
9	11 57	25	11 52
10	11 57	26	11 51
11	11 57	27	11 51
12	11 56	28	11 51
13	11 56	29	11 50
14	11 56	30	11 50
15	11 55		
16	11 55		

October

SUN GHA, DECLINATION, MERIDIAN PASSAGE

1 THURSDAY

GMT	GHA	DEC
00	182° 32'7	S 3° 03'9
02	212 33.1	05.8
04	242 33.5	07.8
06	272 33.9	S 3 09.7
08	302 34.3	11.7
10	332 34.7	13.6
12	2 35.1	S 3 15.6
14	32 35.5	17.5
16	62 35.9	19.4
18	92 36.3	S 3 21.4
20	122 36.7	23.3
22	152 37.1	25.2

2 FRIDAY

GMT	GHA	DEC
00	182° 37'5	S 3° 27'2
02	212 37.9	29.1
04	242 38.3	31.1
06	272 38.7	S 3 33.0
08	302 39.1	34.9
10	332 39.5	36.9
12	2 39.9	S 3 38.8
14	32 40.3	40.7
16	62 40.7	42.7
18	92 41.1	S 3 44.6
20	122 41.5	46.6
22	152 41.9	48.5

3 SATURDAY

GMT	GHA	DEC
00	182° 42'2	S 3° 50'4
02	212 42.6	52.3
04	242 43.0	54.3
06	272 43.4	S 3 56.2
08	302 43.8	58.2
10	332 44.2	4 00.1
12	2 44.6	S 4 02.0
14	32 45.0	04.0
16	62 45.4	.05.9
18	92 45.8	S 4 07.8
20	122 46.1	09.8
22	152 46.5	11.7

4 SUNDAY

GMT	GHA	DEC
00	182° 46'9	S 4° 13'6
02	212 47.3	15.6
04	242 47.7	17.5
06	272 48.1	S 4 19.4
08	302 48.5	21.4
10	332 48.8	23.3
12	2 49.2	S 4 25.2
14	32 49.6	27.1
16	62 50.0	29.1
18	92 50.4	S 4 31.0
20	122 50.7	32.9
22	152 51.1	34.9

5 MONDAY

GMT	GHA	DEC
00	182° 51'5	S 4° 36'8
02	212 51.9	38.7
04	242 52.2	40.6
06	272 52.6	S 4 42.6
08	302 53.0	44.5
10	332 53.4	46.4
12	2 53.7	S 4 48.3
14	32 54.1	50.3
16	62 54.5	52.2
18	92 54.9	S 4 54.1
20	122 55.2	56.0
22	152 55.6	57.9

6 TUESDAY

GMT	GHA	DEC
00	182° 56'0	S 4° 59'9
02	212 56.3	01.8
04	242 56.7	03.7
06	272 57.1	S 5 05.6
08	302 57.4	07.5
10	332 57.8	09.5
12	2 58.2	S 5 11.4
14	32 58.5	13.3
16	62 58.9	15.2
18	92 59.3	S 5 17.1
20	122 59.6	19.1
22	153 00.0	21.0

7 WEDNESDAY

GMT	GHA	DEC
00	183° 00'3	S 5° 22'9
02	213 00.7	24.8
04	243 01.1	26.7
06	273 01.4	S 5 28.6
08	303 01.8	30.5
10	333 02.1	32.5
12	3 02.5	S 5 34.4
14	33 02.8	36.3
16	63 03.2	38.2
18	93 03.6	S 5 40.1
20	123 03.9	42.0
22	153 04.3	43.9

8 THURSDAY

GMT	GHA	DEC
00	183° 04'6	S 5° 45'8
02	213 05.0	47.7
04	243 05.3	49.7
06	273 05.7	S 5 51.6
08	303 06.0	53.5
10	333 06.4	55.4
12	3 06.7	S 5 57.3
14	33 07.1	5 59.2
16	63 07.4	01.1
18	93 07.8	S 6 03.0
20	123 08.1	04.9
22	153 08.5	06.8

9 FRIDAY

GMT	GHA	DEC
00	183° 08'8	S 6° 08'7
02	213 09.1	10.6
04	243 09.5	12.5
06	273 09.8	S 6 14.4
08	303 10.2	16.3
10	333 10.5	18.2
12	3 10.9	S 6 20.1
14	33 11.2	22.0
16	63 11.5	23.9
18	93 11.9	S 6 25.8
20	123 12.2	27.7
22	153 12.6	29.6

10 SATURDAY

GMT	GHA	DEC
00	183° 12'9	S 6° 31'5
02	213 13.2	33.4
04	243 13.6	35.3
06	273 13.9	S 6 37.2
08	303 14.2	39.1
10	333 14.6	41.0
12	3 14.9	S 6 42.9
14	33 15.2	44.7
16	63 15.6	46.6
18	93 15.9	S 6 48.5
20	123 16.2	50.4
22	153 16.5	52.3

11 SUNDAY

GMT	GHA	DEC
00	183° 16'9	S 6° 54'2
02	213 17.2	56.1
04	243 17.5	58.0
06	273 17.8	S 6 59.9
08	303 18.2	01.7
10	333 18.5	03.6
12	3 18.8	S 7 05.5
14	33 19.1	07.4
16	63 19.5	09.3
18	93 19.8	S 7 11.2
20	123 20.1	13.0
22	153 20.4	14.9

12 MONDAY

GMT	GHA	DEC
00	183° 20'7	S 7° 16'8
02	213 21.0	18.7
04	243 21.4	20.6
06	273 21.7	S 7 22.4
08	303 22.0	24.3
10	333 22.3	26.2
12	3 22.6	S 7 28.1
14	33 22.9	29.9
16	63 23.2	31.8
18	93 23.5	S 7 33.7
20	123 23.8	35.6
22	153 24.2	37.4

13 TUESDAY

GMT	GHA	DEC
00	183° 24'5	S 7° 39'3
02	213 24.8	41.2
04	243 25.1	43.1
06	273 25.4	S 7 44.9
08	303 25.7	46.8
10	333 26.0	48.7
12	3 26.3	S 7 50.5
14	33 26.6	52.4
16	63 26.9	54.3
18	93 27.2	S 7 56.1
20	123 27.5	58.0
22	153 27.8	7 59.9

14 WEDNESDAY

GMT	GHA	DEC
00	183° 28'1	S 8° 01'7
02	213 28.4	03.6
04	243 28.7	05.4
06	273 29.0	S 8 07.3
08	303 29.2	09.2
10	333 29.5	11.0
12	3 29.8	S 8 12.9
14	33 30.1	14.7
16	63 30.4	16.6
18	93 30.7	S 8 18.5
20	123 31.0	20.3
22	153 31.3	22.2

15 THURSDAY

GMT	GHA	DEC
00	183° 31'5	S 8° 24'0
02	213 31.8	25.9
04	243 32.1	27.7
06	273 32.4	S 8 29.6
08	303 32.7	31.4
10	333 33.0	33.3
12	3 33.2	S 8 35.1
14	33 33.5	37.0
16	63 33.8	38.8
18	93 34.1	S 8 40.7
20	123 34.3	42.5
22	153 34.6	44.4

16 FRIDAY

GMT	GHA	DEC
00	183° 34'.9	S 8° 46'.2
02	213 35.2	48.0
04	243 35.4	49.9
06	273 35.7	S 8 51.7
08	303 36.0	53.6
10	333 36.2	55.4
12	3 36.5	S 8 57.2
14	33 36.8	8 59.1
16	63 37.0	00.9
18	93 37.3	S 9 02.8
20	123 37.5	04.6
22	153 37.8	06.4

17 SATURDAY

GMT	GHA	DEC
00	183° 38'.1	S 9° 08'.3
02	213 38.3	10.1
04	243 38.6	11.9
06	273 38.8	S 9 13.7
08	303 39.1	15.6
10	333 39.3	17.4
12	3 39.6	S 9 19.2
14	33 39.9	21.1
16	63 40.1	22.9
18	93 40.4	S 9 24.7
20	123 40.6	26.5
22	153 40.9	28.4

18 SUNDAY

GMT	GHA	DEC
00	183° 41'.1	S 9° 30'.2
02	213 41.3	32.0
04	243 41.6	33.8
06	273 41.8	S 9 35.6
08	303 42.1	37.5
10	333 42.3	39.3
12	3 42.6	S 9 41.1
14	33 42.8	42.9
16	63 43.0	44.7
18	93 43.3	S 9 46.5
20	123 43.5	48.4
22	153 43.7	50.2

19 MONDAY

GMT	GHA	DEC
00	183° 44'.0	S 9° 52'.0
02	213 44.2	53.8
04	243 44.4	55.6
06	273 44.7	S 9 57.4
08	303 44.9	9 59.2
10	333 45.1	01.0
12	3 45.4	S10 02.8
14	33 45.6	04.6
16	63 45.8	06.4
18	93 46.0	S10 08.2
20	123 46.2	10.0
22	153 46.5	11.8

20 TUESDAY

GMT	GHA	DEC
00	183° 46'.7	S10° 13'.6
02	213 46.9	15.4
04	243 47.1	17.2
06	273 47.3	S10 19.0
08	303 47.6	20.8
10	333 47.8	22.6
12	3 48.0	S10 24.4
14	33 48.2	26.2
16	63 48.4	28.0
18	93 48.6	S10 29.8
20	123 48.8	31.6
22	153 49.0	33.3

21 WEDNESDAY

GMT	GHA	DEC
00	183° 49'.2	S10° 35'.1
02	213 49.4	36.9
04	243 49.6	38.7
06	273 49.8	S10 40.5
08	303 50.0	42.3
10	333 50.2	44.0
12	3 50.4	S10 45.8
14	33 50.6	47.6
16	63 50.8	49.4
18	93 51.0	S10 51.1
20	123 51.2	52.9
22	153 51.4	54.7

22 THURSDAY

GMT	GHA	DEC
00	183° 51'.6	S10° 56'.5
02	213 51.8	58.2
04	243 52.0	11 00.0
06	273 52.2	S11 01.8
08	303 52.4	03.5
10	333 52.5	05.3
12	3 52.7	S11 07.1
14	33 52.9	08.8
16	63 53.1	10.6
18	93 53.3	S11 12.4
20	123 53.5	14.1
22	153 53.6	15.9

23 FRIDAY

GMT	GHA	DEC
00	183° 53'.8	S11° 17'.7
02	213 54.0	19.4
04	243 54.2	21.2
06	273 54.3	S11 22.9
08	303 54.5	24.7
10	333 54.7	26.4
12	3 54.9	S11 28.2
14	33 55.0	29.9
16	63 55.2	31.7
18	93 55.4	S11 33.4
20	123 55.5	35.2
22	153 55.7	36.9

24 SATURDAY

GMT	GHA	DEC
00	183° 55'.8	S11° 38'.7
02	213 56.0	40.4
04	243 56.2	42.1
06	273 56.3	S11 43.9
08	303 56.5	45.6
10	333 56.6	47.4
12	3 56.8	S11 49.1
14	33 56.9	50.8
16	63 57.1	52.6
18	93 57.3	S11 54.3
20	123 57.4	56.0
22	153 57.5	57.8

25 SUNDAY

GMT	GHA	DEC
00	183° 57'.7	S11° 59'.5
02	213 57.8	01.2
04	243 58.0	03.0
06	273 58.1	S12 04.6
08	303 58.3	06.4
10	333 58.4	08.1
12	3 58.6	S12 09.8
14	33 58.7	11.6
16	63 58.8	13.3
18	93 59.0	S12 15.0
20	123 59.1	16.7
22	153 59.2	18.4

26 MONDAY

GMT	GHA	DEC
00	183° 59'.4	S12° 20'.2
02	213 59.6	21.9
04	243 59.6	23.6
06	273 59.8	S12 25.3
08	303 59.9	27.0
10	334 00.0	28.7
12	4 00.1	S12 30.4
14	34 00.3	32.1
16	64 00.4	33.8
18	94 00.5	S12 35.5
20	124 00.6	37.2
22	154 00.7	38.9

27 TUESDAY

GMT	GHA	DEC
00	184° 00'.9	S12° 40'.6
02	214 01.0	42.3
04	244 01.1	44.0
06	274 01.2	S12 45.7
08	304 01.3	47.4
10	334 01.4	49.1
12	4 01.5	S12 50.8
14	34 01.6	52.5
16	64 01.8	54.1
18	94 01.9	S12 55.8
20	124 02.0	57.5
22	154 02.1	12 59.2

28 WEDNESDAY

GMT	GHA	DEC
00	184° 02'.2	S13° 00'.9
02	214 02.3	02.6
04	244 02.4	04.2
06	274 02.5	S13 05.9
08	304 02.6	07.6
10	334 02.7	09.3
12	4 02.8	S13 10.9
14	34 02.8	12.6
16	64 02.9	14.3
18	94 03.0	S13 15.9
20	124 03.1	17.6
22	154 03.2	19.3

29 THURSDAY

GMT	GHA	DEC
00	184° 03'.3	S13° 20'.9
02	214 03.4	22.6
04	244 03.5	24.3
06	274 03.5	S13 25.9
08	304 03.6	27.6
10	334 03.7	29.2
12	4 03.8	S13 30.9
14	34 03.9	32.6
16	64 03.9	34.2
18	94 04.0	S13 35.9
20	124 04.1	37.5
22	154 04.1	39.2

30 FRIDAY

GMT	GHA	DEC
00	184° 04'.2	S13° 40'.8
02	214 04.3	42.4
04	244 04.4	44.1
06	274 04.4	S13 45.7
08	304 04.5	47.4
10	334 04.6	49.0
12	4 04.6	S13 50.6
14	34 04.7	52.3
16	64 04.7	53.9
18	94 04.8	S13 55.5
20	124 04.9	57.2
22	154 04.9	58.8

31 SATURDAY

GMT	GHA	DEC
00	184° 05'.0	S14° 00'.4
02	214 05.0	02.1
04	244 05.1	03.7
06	274 05.1	S14 05.3
08	304 05.2	06.9
10	334 05.2	08.5
12	4 05.3	S14 10.2
14	34 05.3	11.8
16	64 05.3	13.4
18	94 05.4	S14 15.0
20	124 05.5	16.6
22	154 05.5	18.2

MERIDIAN PASSAGE

Day	hr min	Day	hr min
1	11 50	17	11 45
2	11 49	18	11 45
3	11 49	19	11 45
4	11 49	20	11 45
5	11 48	21	11 45
6	11 48	22	11 44
7	11 48	23	11 44
8	11 48	24	11 44
9	11 47	25	11 44
10	11 47	26	11 44
11	11 47	27	11 44
12	11 47	28	11 44
13	11 46	29	11 44
14	11 46	30	11 44
15	11 46	31	11 44
16	11 46		

November

SUN GHA, DECLINATION, MERIDIAN PASSAGE

1 SUNDAY

GMT	GHA	DEC
00	184° 05.5	S14° 19.8
02	214 05.5	21.5
04	244 05.6	23.1
06	274 05.6	S14 24.7
08	304 05.7	26.3
10	334 05.7	27.9
12	4 05.7	S14 29.5
14	34 05.7	31.1
16	64 05.8	32.7
18	94 05.8	S14 34.3
20	124 05.8	35.8
22	154 05.8	37.4

2 MONDAY

GMT	GHA	DEC
00	184° 05.9	S14° 39.0
02	214 05.9	40.6
04	244 05.9	42.2
06	274 05.9	S14 43.8
08	304 05.9	45.4
10	334 06.0	46.9
12	4 06.0	S14 48.5
14	34 06.0	50.1
16	64 06.0	51.7
18	94 06.0	S14 53.3
20	124 06.0	54.8
22	154 06.0	56.4

3 TUESDAY

GMT	GHA	DEC
00	184° 06.0	S14° 58.0
02	214 06.0	14 59.5
04	244 06.0	01.1
06	274 06.0	S15 02.7
08	304 06.0	04.2
10	334 06.0	05.8
12	4 06.0	S15 07.3
14	34 06.0	08.9
16	64 06.0	10.5
18	94 06.0	S15 12.0
20	124 06.0	13.6
22	154 06.0	15.1

4 WEDNESDAY

GMT	GHA	DEC
00	184° 06.0	S15° 16.7
02	214 06.0	18.2
04	244 06.0	19.8
06	274 05.9	S15 21.3
08	304 05.9	22.8
10	334 05.9	24.4
12	4 05.9	S15 25.9
14	34 05.9	27.5
16	64 05.8	29.0
18	94 05.8	S15 30.5
20	124 05.8	32.1
22	154 05.8	33.6

5 THURSDAY

GMT	GHA	DEC
00	184° 05.7	S15° 35.1
02	214 05.7	36.6
04	244 05.7	38.2
06	274 05.6	S15 39.7
08	304 05.6	41.2
10	334 05.6	42.7
12	4 05.5	S15 44.2
14	34 05.5	45.8
16	64 05.5	47.3
18	94 05.4	S15 48.8
20	124 05.4	50.3
22	154 05.3	51.8

6 FRIDAY

GMT	GHA	DEC
00	184° 05.3	S15° 53.3
02	214 05.2	54.8
04	244 05.2	56.3
06	274 05.2	S15 57.8
08	304 05.1	15 59.3
10	334 05.1	00.8
12	4 05.0	S16 02.3
14	34 04.9	03.8
16	64 04.9	05.3
18	94 04.8	S16 06.8
20	124 04.8	08.3
22	154 04.7	09.7

7 SATURDAY

GMT	GHA	DEC
00	184° 04.6	S16° 11.2
02	214 04.6	12.7
04	244 04.5	14.2
06	274 04.5	S16 15.7
08	304 04.4	17.1
10	334 04.3	18.6
12	4 04.2	S16 20.1
14	34 04.2	21.6
16	64 04.1	23.0
18	94 04.0	S16 24.5
20	124 03.9	26.0
22	154 03.9	27.4

8 SUNDAY

GMT	GHA	DEC
00	184° 03.8	S16° 28.9
02	214 03.7	30.3
04	244 03.6	31.8
06	274 03.5	S16 33.3
08	304 03.5	34.7
10	334 03.4	36.2
12	4 03.3	S16 37.6
14	34 03.2	39.1
16	64 03.1	40.5
18	94 03.0	S16 41.9
20	124 02.9	43.4
22	154 02.8	44.8

9 MONDAY

GMT	GHA	DEC
00	184° 02.7	S16° 46.3
02	214 02.6	47.7
04	244 02.5	49.1
06	274 02.4	S16 50.6
08	304 02.3	52.0
10	334 02.2	53.4
12	4 02.1	S16 54.8
14	34 02.0	56.3
16	64 01.9	57.7
18	94 01.8	S16 59.1
20	124 01.7	17 00.5
22	154 01.6	01.9

10 TUESDAY

GMT	GHA	DEC
00	184° 01.4	S17° 03.4
02	214 01.3	04.8
04	244 01.2	06.2
06	274 01.1	S17 07.6
08	304 01.0	09.0
10	334 00.9	10.4
12	4 00.7	S17 11.8
14	34 00.6	13.2*
16	64 00.5	14.6
18	94 00.4	S17 16.0
20	124 00.2	17.4
22	154 00.1	18.8

11 WEDNESDAY

GMT	GHA	DEC
00	184° 00.0	S17° 20.2
02	213 59.8	21.5
04	243 59.7	22.9
06	273 59.6	S17 24.3
08	303 59.4	25.7
10	333 59.3	27.1
12	3 59.1	S17 28.5
14	33 59.0	29.8
16	63 58.8	31.2
18	93 58.7	S17 32.6
20	123 58.6	33.9
22	153 58.4	35.3

12 THURSDAY

GMT	GHA	DEC
00	183° 58.3	S17° 36.7
02	213 58.1	38.0
04	243 58.0	39.4
06	273 57.8	S17 40.7
08	303 57.6	42.1
10	333 57.5	43.5
12	3 57.3	S17 44.8
14	33 57.2	46.2
16	63 57.0	47.5
18	93 56.8	S17 48.8
20	123 56.7	50.2
22	153 56.5	51.5

13 FRIDAY

GMT	GHA	DEC
00	183° 56.3	S17° 52.9
02	213 56.2	54.2
04	243 56.0	55.5
06	273 55.8	S17 56.9
08	303 55.7	58.2
10	333 55.5	17 59.5
12	3 55.3	S18 00.9
14	33 55.1	02.2
16	63 54.9	03.5
18	93 54.8	S18 04.8
20	123 54.6	06.1
22	153 54.4	07.4

14 SATURDAY

GMT	GHA	DEC
00	183° 54.2	S18° 08.8
02	213 54.0	10.1
04	243 53.8	11.4
06	273 53.7	S18 12.7
08	303 53.5	14.0
10	333 53.3	15.3
12	3 53.1	S18 16.6
14	33 52.9	17.9
16	63 52.7	19.2
18	93 52.5	S18 20.5
20	123 52.3	21.8
22	153 52.1	23.0

15 SUNDAY

GMT	GHA	DEC
00	183° 51.9	S18° 24.3
02	213 51.7	25.6
04	243 51.5	26.9
06	273 51.3	S18 28.2
08	303 51.0	29.4
10	333 50.8	30.7
12	3 50.6	S18 32.0
14	33 50.4	33.3
16	63 50.2	34.5
18	93 50.0	S18 35.8
20	123 49.8	37.1
22	153 49.5	38.3

16 MONDAY

GMT	GHA	DEC
00	183° 49'3	S18° 39'5
02	213 49.1	40.8
04	243 48.9	42.1
06	273 48.6	S18 43.3
08	303 48.4	44.6
10	333 48.2	45.8
12	3 48.0	S18 47.1
14	33 47.7	48.3
16	63 47.5	49.6
18	93 47.3	S18 50.8
20	123 47.0	52.0
22	153 46.8	53.3

17 TUESDAY

GMT	GHA	DEC
00	183° 46'5	S18° 54'5
02	213 46.3	55.7
04	243 46.1	57.0
06	273 45.8	S18 58.2
08	303 45.6	18 59.4
10	333 45.3	00.6
12	3 45.1	S19 01.8
14	33 44.8	03.0
16	63 44.6	04.3
18	93 44.3	S19 05.5
20	123 44.1	06.7
22	153 43.8	07.9

18 WEDNESDAY

GMT	GHA	DEC
00	183° 43'6	S19° 09'1
02	213 43.3	10.3
04	243 43.0	11.5
06	273 42.8	S19 12.7
08	303 42.5	13.9
10	333 42.3	15.1
12	3 42.0	S19 16.2
14	33 41.7	17.4
16	63 41.5	18.6
18	93 41.2	S19 19.8
20	123 40.9	21.0
22	153 40.6	22.1

19 THURSDAY

GMT	GHA	DEC
00	183° 40'4	S19° 23'3
02	213 40.1	24.5
04	243 39.8	25.7
06	273 39.5	S19 26.8
08	303 39.3	28.0
10	333 39.0	29.2
12	3 38.7	S19 30.3
14	33 38.4	31.5
16	63 38.1	32.6
18	93 37.8	S19 33.8
20	123 37.5	34.9
22	153 37.3	36.1

20 FRIDAY

GMT	GHA	DEC
00	183° 37'0	S19° 37'2
02	213 36.7	38.4
04	243 36.4	39.5
06	273 36.1	S19 40.6
08	303 35.8	41.8
10	333 35.5	42.9
12	3 35.2	S19 44.0
14	33 34.9	45.2
16	63 34.6	46.3
18	93 34.3	S19 47.4
20	123 34.0	48.5
22	153 33.7	49.6

21 SATURDAY

GMT	GHA	DEC
00	183° 33'4	S19° 50'7
02	213 33.0	51.9
04	243 32.7	53.0
06	273 32.4	S19 54.1
08	303 32.1	55.2
10	333 31.8	56.3
12	3 31.5	S19 57.4
14	33 31.2	58.5
16	63 30.8	19 59.6
18	93 30.5	S20 00.7
20	123 30.2	01.8
22	153 29.9	02.8

22 SUNDAY

GMT	GHA	DEC
00	183° 29'5	S20° 03'9
02	213 29.2	05.0
04	243 28.9	06.1
06	273 28.6	S20 07.2
08	303 28.2	08.2
10	333 27.9	09.3
12	3 27.6	S20 10.4
14	33 27.2	11.4
16	63 26.9	12.5
18	93 26.5	S20 13.6
20	123 26.2	14.6
22	153 25.9	15.7

23 MONDAY

GMT	GHA	DEC
00	183° 25'5	S20° 16'7
02	213 25.2	17.8
04	243 24.8	18.8
06	273 24.5	S20 19.9
08	303 24.1	20.9
10	333 23.8	22.0
12	3 23.4	S20 23.0
14	33 23.1	24.0
16	63 22.7	25.1
18	93 22.4	S20 26.1
20	123 22.0	27.1
22	153 21.7	28.1

24 TUESDAY

GMT	GHA	DEC
00	183° 21'3	S20° 29'2
02	213 21.0	30.2
04	243 20.6	31.2
06	273 20.2	S20 32.2
08	303 19.9	33.2
10	333 19.5	34.2
12	3 19.1	S20 35.2
14	33 18.8	36.2
16	63 18.4	37.2
18	93 18.0	S20 38.2
20	123 17.7	39.2
22	153 17.3	40.2

25 WEDNESDAY

GMT	GHA	DEC
00	183° 16'9	S20° 41'2
02	213 16.5	42.2
04	243 16.1	43.2
06	273 15.8	S20 44.2
08	303 15.4	45.2
10	333 15.0	46.1
12	3 14.6	S20 47.1
14	33 14.2	48.1
16	63 13.9	49.0
18	93 13.5	S20 50.0
20	123 13.1	51.0
22	153 12.7	51.9

26 THURSDAY

GMT	GHA	DEC
00	183° 12'3	S20° 52'9
02	213 11.9	53.9
04	243 11.5	54.8
06	273 11.1	S20 55.8
08	303 10.7	56.7
10	333 10.3	57.6
12	3 09.9	S20 58.6
14	33 09.5	20 59.5
16	63 09.1	00.5
18	93 08.7	S21 01.4
20	123 08.3	02.3
22	153 07.9	03.3

27 FRIDAY

GMT	GHA	DEC
00	183° 07'5	S21° 04'2
02	213 07.1	05.1
04	243 06.7	06.0
06	273 06.3	S21 06.9
08	303 05.9	07.9
10	333 05.5	08.8
12	3 05.1	S21 09.7
14	33 04.6	10.6
16	63 04.2	11.5
18	93 03.8	S21 12.4
20	123 03.4	13.3
22	153 03.0	14.2

28 SATURDAY

GMT	GHA	DEC
00	183° 02'6	S21° 15'1
02	213 02.1	16.0
04	243 01.7	16.8
06	273 01.3	S21 17.7
08	303 00.9	18.6
10	333 00.4	19.5
12	3 00.0	S21 20.4
14	32 59.6	21.2
16	62 59.1	22.1
18	92 58.7	S21 23.0
20	122 58.3	23.8
22	152 57.8	24.7

29 SUNDAY

GMT	GHA	DEC
00	182° 57'4	S21° 25'5
02	212 57.0	26.4
04	242 56.5	27.3
06	272 56.1	S21 28.1
08	302 55.7	29.0
10	332 55.2	29.8
12	2 54.8	S21 30.6
14	32 54.3	31.5
16	62 53.9	32.3
18	92 53.4	S21 33.1
20	122 53.0	34.0
22	152 52.5	34.8

30 MONDAY

GMT	GHA	DEC
00	182° 52'1	S21° 35'6
02	212 51.6	36.5
04	242 51.2	37.3
06	272 50.7	S21 38.1
08	302 50.3	38.9
10	332 49.8	39.7
12	2 49.4	S21 40.5
14	32 48.9	41.3
16	62 48.5	42.1
18	92 48.0	S21 42.9
20	122 47.5	43.7
22	152 47.1	44.5

MERIDIAN PASSAGE

Day	hr min	Day	hr min
1	11 44	17	11 45
2	11 44	18	11 45
3	11 44	19	11 45
4	11 44	20	11 46
5	11 44	21	11 46
6	11 44	22	11 46
7	11 44	23	11 46
8	11 44	24	11 47
9	11 44	25	11 47
10	11 44	26	11 47
11	11 44	27	11 48
12	11 44	28	11 48
13	11 44	29	11 48
14	11 44	30	11 49
15	11 45		
16	11 45		

December

SUN GHA, DECLINATION, MERIDIAN PASSAGE

1 TUESDAY		
GMT	GHA	DEC
00	182° 46'6	S21° 45'3
02	212 46.1	46.1
04	242 45.7	46.9
06	272 45.2	S21 47.6
08	302 44.8	48.4
10	332 44.3	49.2
12	2 43.8	S21 50.0
14	32 43.3	50.7
16	62 42.9	51.5
18	92 42.4	S21 52.3
20	122 41.9	53.0
22	152 41.4	53.8

2 WEDNESDAY		
00	182° 41'0	S21° 54'5
02	212 40.5	55.3
04	242 40.0	56.1
06	272 39.5	S21 56.8
08	302 39.1	57.5
10	332 38.6	58.3
12	2 38.1	S21 59.0
14	32 37.6	21 59.8
16	62 37.1	00.5
18	92 36.6	S22 01.2
20	122 36.2	01.9
22	152 35.7	02.7

3 THURSDAY		
00	182° 35'2	S22° 03'4
02	212 34.7	04.1
04	242 34.2	04.8
06	272 33.7	S22 05.5
08	302 33.2	06.2
10	332 32.7	06.9
12	2 32.2	S22 07.6
14	32 31.7	08.3
16	62 31.2	09.0
18	92 30.7	S22 09.7
20	122 30.2	10.4
22	152 29.7	11.1

4 FRIDAY		
00	182° 29'2	S22° 11'8
02	212 28.7	12.5
04	242 28.2	13.1
06	272 27.7	S22 13.8
08	302 27.2	14.5
10	332 26.7	15.2
12	2 26.2	S22 15.9
14	32 25.7	16.5
16	62 25.2	17.2
18	92 24.7	S22 17.8
20	122 24.2	18.5
22	152 23.7	19.1

5 SATURDAY		
00	182° 23'2	S22° 19'8
02	212 22.6	20.4
04	242 22.1	21.1
06	272 21.6	S22 21.7
08	302 21.1	22.3
10	332 20.6	23.0
12	2 20.1	S22 23.6
14	32 19.5	24.2
16	62 19.0	24.8
18	92 18.5	S22 25.4
20	122 18.0	26.1
22	152 17.5	26.7

6 SUNDAY		
00	182° 16'9	S22° 27'3
02	212 16.4	27.9
04	242 15.9	28.5
06	272 15.4	S22 29.1
08	302 14.8	29.7
10	332 14.3	30.3
12	2 13.8	S22 30.9
14	32 13.2	31.5
16	62 12.7	32.1
18	92 12.2	S22 32.7
20	122 11.6	33.3
22	152 11.1	33.8

7 MONDAY		
00	182° 10'6	S22° 34'4
02	212 10.0	35.0
04	242 09.5	35.6
06	272 09.0	S22 36.1
08	302 08.4	36.7
10	332 07.9	37.2
12	2 07.4	S22 37.8
14	32 06.8	38.4
16	62 06.3	38.9
18	92 05.7	S22 39.5
20	122 05.2	40.0
22	152 04.7	40.5

8 TUESDAY		
00	182° 04'1	S22° 41'1
02	212 03.6	41.6
04	242 03.0	42.1
06	272 02.5	S22 42.7
08	302 01.9	43.2
10	332 01.4	43.7
12	2 00.8	S22 44.2
14	32 00.3	44.8
16	61 59.7	45.3
18	91 59.2	S22 45.8
20	121 58.6	46.3
22	151 58.1	46.8

9 WEDNESDAY		
00	182° 57'5	S22° 47'3
02	211 57.0	47.8
04	241 56.4	48.3
06	271 55.8	S22 48.8
08	301 55.3	49.3
10	331 54.7	49.8
12	1 54.2	S22 50.2
14	31 53.6	50.7
16	61 53.1	51.2
18	91 52.5	S22 51.7
20	121 51.9	52.1
22	151 51.4	52.6

10 THURSDAY		
00	181° 50'8	S22° 53'1
02	211 50.3	53.5
04	241 49.7	54.0
06	271 49.1	S22 54.4
08	301 48.6	54.9
10	331 48.0	55.3
12	1 47.4	S22 55.8
14	31 46.9	56.2
16	61 46.3	56.7
18	91 45.7	S22 57.1
20	121 45.1	57.5
22	151 44.6	58.0

11 FRIDAY		
00	181° 44'0	S22° 58'4
02	211 43.4	58.8
04	241 42.9	59.2
06	271 42.3	S22 59.6
08	301 41.7	23 00.1
10	331 41.1	00.5
12	1 40.6	S23 00.9
14	31 40.0	01.3
16	61 39.4	01.7
18	91 38.8	S23 02.1
20	121 38.3	02.5
22	151 37.7	02.9

12 SATURDAY		
00	181° 37'1	S23° 03'3
02	211 36.5	03.6
04	241 35.9	04.0
06	271 35.4	S23 04.4
08	301 34.8	04.8
10	331 34.2	05.1
12	1 33.6	S23 05.5
14	31 33.0	05.9
16	61 32.5	06.2
18	91 31.9	S23 06.6
20	121 31.3	07.0
22	151 30.7	07.3

13 SUNDAY		
00	181° 30'1	S23° 07'7
02	211 29.5	08.0
04	241 28.9	08.3
06	271 28.4	S23 08.7
08	301 27.8	09.0
10	331 27.2	09.4
12	1 26.6	S23 09.7
14	31 26.0	10.0
16	61 25.4	10.3
18	91 24.8	S23 10.7
20	121 24.2	11.0
22	151 23.6	11.3

14 MONDAY		
00	181° 23'0	S23° 11'6
02	211 22.4	11.9
04	241 21.9	12.2
06	271 21.3	S23 12.5
08	301 20.7	12.8
10	331 20.1	13.1
12	1 19.5	S23 13.4
14	31 18.9	13.7
16	61 18.3	14.0
18	91 17.7	S23 14.3
20	121 17.1	14.5
22	151 16.5	14.8

15 TUESDAY		
00	181° 15'9	S23° 15'1
02	211 15.3	15.4
04	241 14.7	15.6
06	271 14.1	S23 15.9
08	301 13.5	16.2
10	331 12.9	16.4
12	1 12.3	S23 16.7
14	31 11.7	16.9
16	61 11.1	17.2
18	91 10.5	S23 17.4
20	121 09.9	17.6
22	151 09.3	17.9

16 WEDNESDAY

GMT	GHA	DEC
00	181° 08.7	S23° 18.1
02	211 08.1	18.3
04	241 07.5	18.6
06	271 06.9	S23 18.8
08	301 06.3	19.0
10	331 05.6	19.2
12	1 05.0	S23 19.4
14	31 04.4	19.7
16	61 03.8	19.9
18	91 03.2	S23 20.1
20	121 02.6	20.3
22	151 02.0	20.5

17 THURSDAY

GMT	GHA	DEC
00	181° 01.4	S23° 20.7
02	211 00.8	20.9
04	241 00.2	21.1
06	270 59.6	S23 21.2
08	300 58.9	21.4
10	330 58.3	21.6
12	0 57.7	S23 21.8
14	30 57.1	21.9
16	60 56.5	22.1
18	90 55.9	S23 22.3
20	120 55.3	22.4
22	150 54.7	22.6

18 FRIDAY

GMT	GHA	DEC
00	180° 54.1	S23° 22.8
02	210 53.4	22.9
04	240 52.8	23.1
06	270 52.2	S23 23.2
08	300 51.6	23.4
10	330 51.0	23.5
12	0 50.4	S23 23.6
14	30 49.7	23.8
16	60 49.1	23.9
18	90 48.5	S23 24.1
20	120 47.9	24.1
22	150 47.3	24.3

19 SATURDAY

GMT	GHA	DEC
00	180° 46.7	S23° 24.4
02	210 46.1	24.5
04	240 45.4	24.6
06	270 44.8	S23 24.7
08	300 44.2	24.8
10	330 43.6	24.9
12	0 43.0	S23 25.0
14	30 42.3	25.1
16	60 41.7	25.2
18	90 41.1	S23 25.3
20	120 40.5	25.4
22	150 39.9	25.5

20 SUNDAY

GMT	GHA	DEC
00	180° 39.2	S23° 25.5
02	210 38.6	25.6
04	240 38.0	25.7
06	270 37.4	S23 25.7
08	300 36.8	25.8
10	330 36.1	25.9
12	0 35.5	S23 25.9
14	30 34.9	26.0
16	60 34.3	26.0
18	90 33.7	S23 26.1
20	120 33.0	26.1
22	150 32.4	26.2

21 MONDAY

GMT	GHA	DEC
00	180° 31.8	S23° 26.2
02	210 31.2	26.2
04	240 30.6	26.3
06	270 29.9	S23 26.3
08	300 29.3	26.3
10	330 28.7	26.4
12	0 28.1	S23 26.4
14	30 27.4	26.4
16	60 26.8	26.4
18	90 26.2	S23 26.4
20	120 25.6	26.4
22	150 25.0	26.4

22 TUESDAY

GMT	GHA	DEC
00	180° 24.3	S23° 26.4
02	210 23.7	26.4
04	240 23.1	26.4
06	270 22.5	S23 26.4
08	300 21.8	26.4
10	330 21.2	26.4
12	0 20.6	S23 26.4
14	30 20.0	26.3
16	60 19.3	26.3
18	90 18.7	S23 26.3
20	120 18.1	26.2
22	150 17.5	26.2

23 WEDNESDAY

GMT	GHA	DEC
00	180° 16.8	S23° 26.2
02	210 16.2	26.1
04	240 15.6	26.1
06	270 15.0	S23 26.0
08	300 14.3	26.0
10	330 13.7	25.9
12	0 13.1	S23 25.9
14	30 12.5	25.8
16	60 11.9	25.7
18	90 11.2	S23 25.7
20	120 10.6	25.6
22	150 10.0	25.5

24 THURSDAY

GMT	GHA	DEC
00	180° 09.4	S23° 25.4
02	210 08.7	25.4
04	240 08.1	25.3
06	270 07.5	S23 25.2
08	300 06.9	25.1
10	330 06.2	25.0
12	0 05.6	S23 24.9
14	30 05.0	24.8
16	60 04.4	24.7
18	90 03.7	S23 24.6
20	120 03.1	24.5
22	150 02.5	24.4

25 FRIDAY

GMT	GHA	DEC
00	180° 01.9	S23° 24.2
02	210 01.3	24.1
04	240 00.6	24.0
06	270 00.0	S23 23.9
08	299 59.4	23.7
10	329 58.8	23.6
12	359 58.1	S23 23.5
14	29 57.5	23.3
16	59 56.9	23.2
18	89 56.3	S23 23.0
20	119 55.7	22.9
22	149 55.0	22.7

26 SATURDAY

GMT	GHA	DEC
00	179° 54.4	S23° 22.6
02	209 53.8	22.4
04	239 53.2	22.2
06	269 52.5	S23 22.1
08	299 51.9	21.9
10	329 51.3	21.7
12	359 50.7	S23 21.6
14	29 50.1	21.4
16	59 49.4	21.2
18	89 48.8	S23 21.0
20	119 48.2	20.8
22	149 47.6	20.6

27 SUNDAY

GMT	GHA	DEC
00	179° 47.0	S23° 20.4
02	209 46.3	20.2
04	239 45.7	20.0
06	269 45.1	S23 19.8
08	299 44.5	19.6
10	329 43.9	19.4
12	359 43.3	S23 19.2
14	29 42.6	19.0
16	59 42.0	18.7
18	89 41.4	S23 18.5
20	119 40.8	18.3
22	149 40.2	18.0

28 MONDAY

GMT	GHA	DEC
00	179° 39.6	S23° 17.8
02	209 38.9	17.6
04	239 38.3	17.3
06	269 37.7	S23 17.1
08	299 37.1	16.8
10	329 36.5	16.6
12	359 35.9	S23 16.3
14	29 35.3	16.1
16	59 34.6	15.8
18	89 34.0	S23 15.5
20	119 33.4	15.3
22	149 32.8	15.0

29 TUESDAY

GMT	GHA	DEC
00	179° 32.2	S23° 14.7
02	209 31.6	14.5
04	239 31.0	14.2
06	269 30.4	S23 13.9
08	299 29.8	13.6
10	329 29.1	13.3
12	359 28.5	S23 13.0
14	29 27.9	12.7
16	59 27.3	12.4
18	89 26.7	S23 12.1
20	119 26.1	11.8
22	149 25.5	11.5

30 WEDNESDAY

GMT	GHA	DEC
00	179° 24.9	S23° 11.2
02	209 24.3	10.9
04	239 23.7	10.6
06	269 23.1	S23 10.2
08	299 22.5	09.9
10	329 21.9	09.6
12	359 21.3	S23 09.3
14	29 20.6	08.9
16	59 20.0	08.6
18	89 19.4	S23 08.2
20	119 18.8	07.9
22	149 18.2	07.5

31 THURSDAY

GMT	GHA	DEC
00	179° 17.6	S23° 07.2
02	209 17.0	06.8
04	239 16.4	06.5
06	269 15.8	S23 06.1
08	299 15.2	05.8
10	329 14.6	05.4
12	359 14.0	S23 05.0
14	29 13.4	04.6
16	59 12.8	04.3
18	89 12.2	S23 03.9
20	119 11.7	03.5
22	149 11.1	03.1

MERIDIAN PASSAGE

Day	hr min	Day	hr min
1	11 49	17	11 56
2	11 49	18	11 57
3	11 50	19	11 57
4	11 50	20	11 58
5	11 51	21	11 58
6	11 51	22	11 59
7	11 51	23	11 59
8	11 52	24	12 00
9	11 52	25	12 00
10	11 53	26	12 01
11	11 53	27	12 01
12	11 54	28	12 02
13	11 54	29	12 02
14	11 55	30	12 03
15	11 55	31	12 03
16	11 56		

Sun GHA correction

FOR PAGE 6–29

Min.	Correct.		1 Hour+min.	Correct.		Secs.	Correct.	
1	0°	15′0	1 hr+1 min.	15°	15′0	1	0°	00′3
2	0	30.0	1 hr+2	15	30.0	2	0	00.5
3	0	45.0	1 hr+3	15	45.0	3	0	00.8
4	1	00.0	1 hr+4	16	00.0	4	0	01.0
5	1	15.0	1 hr+5	16	15.0	5	0	01.3
6	1	30.0	1 hr+6	16	30.0	6	0	01.5
7	1	45.0	1 hr+7	16	45.0	7	0	01.8
8	2	00.0	1 hr+8	17	00.0	8	0	02.0
9	2	15.0	1 hr+9	17	15.0	9	0	02.3
10	2	30.0	1 hr+10	17	30.0	10	0	02.5
11	2	45.0	1 hr+11	17	45.0	11	0	02.8
12	3	00.0	1 hr+12	18	00.0	12	0	03.0
13	3	15.0	1 hr+13	18	15.0	13	0	03.3
14	3	30.0	1 hr+14	18	30.0	14	0	03.5
15	3	45.0	1 hr+15	18	45.0	15	0	03.8
16	4	00.0	1 hr+16	19	00.0	16	0	04.0
17	4	15.0	1 hr+17	19	15.0	17	0	04.3
18	4	30.0	1 hr+18	19	30.0	18	0	04.5
19	4	45.0	1 hr+19	19	45.0	19	0	04.8
20	5	00.0	1 hr+20	20	00.0	20	0	05.0
21	5	15.0	1 hr+21	20	15.0	21	0	05.3
22	5	30.0	1 hr+22	20	30.0	22	0	05.5
23	5	45.0	1 hr+23	20	45.0	23	0	05.8
24	6	00.0	1 hr+24	21	00.0	24	0	06.0
25	6	15.0	1 hr+25	21	15.0	25	0	06.3
26	6	30.0	1 hr+26	21	30.0	26	0	06.5
27	6	45.0	1 hr+27	21	45.0	27	0	06.8
28	7	00.0	1 hr+28	22	00.0	28	0	07.0
29	7	15.0	1 hr+29	22	15.0	29	0	07.3
30	7	30.0	1 hr+30	22	30.0	30	0	07.5
31	7	45.0	1 hr+31	22	45.0	31	0	07.8
32	8	00.0	1 hr+32	23	00.0	32	0	08.0
33	8	15.0	1 hr+33	23	15.0	33	0	08.3
34	8	30.0	1 hr+34	23	30.0	34	0	08.5
35	8	45.0	1 hr+35	23	45.0	35	0	08.8
36	9	00.0	1 hr+36	24	00.0	36	0	09.0
37	9	15.0	1 hr+37	24	15.0	37	0	09.3
38	9	30.0	1 hr+38	24	30.0	38	0	09.5
39	9	45.0	1 hr+39	24	45.0	39	0	09.8
40	10	00.0	1 hr+40	25	00.0	40	0	10.0
41	10	15.0	1 hr+41	25	15.0	41	0	10.3
42	10	30.0	1 hr+42	25	30.0	42	0	10.5
43	10	45.0	1 hr+43	25	45.0	43	0	10.8
44	11	00.0	1 hr+44	26	00.0	44	0	11.0
45	11	15.0	1 hr+45	26	15.0	45	0	11.3
46	11	30.0	1 hr+46	26	30.0	46	0	11.5
47	11	45.0	1 hr+47	26	45.0	47	0	11.8
48	12	00.0	1 hr+48	27	00.0	48	0	12.0
49	12	15.0	1 hr+49	27	15.0	49	0	12.3
50	12	30.0	1 hr+50	27	30.0	50	0	12.5
51	12	45.0	1 hr+51	27	45.0	51	0	12.8
52	13	00.0	1 hr+52	28	00.0	52	0	13.0
53	13	15.0	1 hr+53	28	15.0	53	0	13.3
54	13	30.0	1 hr+54	28	30.0	54	0	13.5
55	13	45.0	1 hr+55	28	45.0	55	0	13.8
56	14	00.0	1 hr+56	29	00.0	56	0	14.0
57	14	15.0	1 hr+57	29	15.0	57	0	14.3
58	14	30.0	1 hr+58	29	30.0	58	0	14.5
59	14	45.0	1 hr+59	29	45.0	59	0	14.8
60	15	00.0	1 hr+60	30	00.0	60	0	15.0

Sun altitude correction

AND DIP OF SEA HORIZON

For an explanation of how to use these tables see page 5.

ALTITUDE CORRECTION TABLE				DIP OF SEA HORIZON			
APRIL-SEPT.		**OCT.-MARCH**		**FEET**		**METERS**	
Apparent Altitude	Add	Apparent Altitude	Add	Eye Height	Subtract	Eye Height	Subtract
10°03′	10.8	9°34′	10.8	1.9	1.4	0.6	1.4
10 15	10.9	9 45	10.9	2.2	1.5	0.7	1.5
10 27	11.0	9 56	11.0	2.6	1.6	0.8	1.6
10 40	11.1	10 08	11.1	2.9	1.7	0.9	1.7
10 54	11.2	10 21	11.2	3.3	1.8	1.0	1.8
11 08	11.3	10 34	11.3	3.6	1.9	1.1	1.9
11 23	11.4	10 47	11.4	4.0	2.0	1.2	2.0
11 38	11.5	11 01	11.5	4.5	2.1	1.3	2.1
11 54	11.6	11 15	11.6	4.9	2.2	1.5	2.2
12 10	11.7	11 30	11.7	5.4	2.3	1.6	2.3
12 28	11.8	11 46	11.8	5.9	2.4	1.8	2.4
12 46	11.9	12 02	11.9	6.4	2.5	1.9	2.5
13 05	12.0	12 19	12.0	6.9	2.6	2.1	2.6
13 24	12.1	12 37	12.1	7.5	2.7	2.3	2.7
13 45	12.2	12 55	12.2	8.0	2.8	2.4	2.8
14 07	12.3	13 14	12.3	8.6	2.9	2.6	2.9
14 30	12.4	13 35	12.4	9.2	3.0	2.8	3.0
14 54	12.5	13 56	12.5	9.8	3.1	3.0	3.1
15 19	12.6	14 18	12.6	10.5	3.2	3.2	3.2
15 46	12.7	14 42	12.7	11.2	3.3	3.4	3.3
16 14	12.8	15 06	12.8	11.9	3.4	3.6	3.4
16 44	12.9	15 32	12.9	12.6	3.5	3.8	3.5
17 15	13.0	15 59	13.0	13.3	3.6	4.0	3.6
17 48	13.1	16 28	13.1	14.1	3.7	4.3	3.7
18 24	13.2	16 59	13.2	14.9	3.8	4.5	3.8
19 01	13.3	17 32	13.3	15.7	3.9	4.7	3.9
19 42	13.4	18 06	13.4	16.5	4.0	5.0	4.0
20 25	13.5	18 42	13.5	17.4		5.2	
21 11	13.6	19 21	13.6				
22 00	13.7	20 03	13.7				
22 54	13.8	20 48	13.8				
23 51	13.9	21 35	13.9				
24 53	14.0	22 26	14.0				
26 00	14.1	23 22	14.1				
27 13	14.2	24 21	14.2				
28 33	14.3	25 26	14.3				
30 00	14.4	26 36	14.4				
31 35	14.5	27 52	14.5				
33 20	14.6	29 15	14.6				
35 17	14.7	30 46	14.7				
37 26	14.8	32 26	14.8				
39 50	14.9	34 17	14.9				
42 31	15.0	36 20	15.0				
45 31	15.1	38 36	15.1				
48 55	15.2	41 08	15.2				
52 44	15.3	43 59	15.3				
57 02	15.4	47 10	15.4				
61 51	15.5	50 46	15.5				
67 17	15.6	54 49	15.6				
73 16	15.7	59 23	15.7				
79 43	15.8	64 30	15.8				
86 32	15.9	70 12	15.9				
90 00		76 26	16.0				
		83 05	16.1				
		90 00					

Distance of sea horizon

AND TIMES OF SUNRISE AND SUNSET

DISTANCE OF SEA HORIZON

Height of eye	Distance		Height of eye	Distance		Height of eye	Distance	
1ft	1.1Nm	1.3mi	21ft	5.2Nm	6.0mi	41ft	7.3Nm	8.4mi
2	1.6	1.9	22	5.4	6.2	42	7.4	8.5
3	2.0	2.3	23	5.5	6.3	43	7.5	8.6
4	2.3	2.6	24	5.6	6.5	44	7.6	8.7
5	2.6	2.9	25	5.7	6.6	45	7.7	8.8
6	2.8	3.2	26	5.8	6.7	46	7.8	8.9
7	3.0	3.5	27	5.9	6.8	47	7.8	9.0
8	3.2	3.7	28	6.1	7.0	48	7.9	9.1
9	3.4	4.0	29	6.2	7.1	49	8.0	9.2
10	3.6	4.2	30	6.3	7.2	50	8.1	9.3
11	3.8	4.4	31	6.4	7.3	55	8.5	9.8
12	4.0	4.6	32	6.5	7.5	60	8.9	10.2
13	4.1	4.7	33	6.6	7.6	65	9.2	10.6
14	4.3	4.9	34	6.7	7.7	70	9.6	11.0
15	4.4	5.1	35	6.8	7.8	75	9.9	11.4
16	4.6	5.3	36	6.9	7.9	80	10.2	11.8
17	4.7	5.4	37	7.0	8.0	85	10.5	12.1
18	4.9	5.6	38	7.1	8.1	90	10.9	12.5
19	5.0	5.7	39	7.1	8.2	95	11.2	12.8
20	5.1	5.9	40	7.2	8.3	100	11.4	13.2

SUNRISE AND SUNSET 38°N

JANUARY			MAY			SEPTEMBER		
Date	Rises	Sets	Date	Rises	Sets	Date	Rises	Sets
1	07 16	16 51	1	05 04	18 51	3	05 31	18 27
6	07 17	16 56	6	04 59	18 55	8	05 35	18 19
11	07 16	17 00	11	04 54	19 00	13	05 40	18 12
16	07 15	17 05	16	04 49	19 04	18	05 44	18 04
21	07 12	17 11	21	04 45	19 08	23	05 48	17 56
26	07 09	17 16	26	04 42	19 12	28	05 53	17 48
31	07 06	17 22	31	04 40	19 16			

FEBRUARY			JUNE			OCTOBER		
5	07 01	17 27	5	04 38	19 19	3	05 57	17 41
10	06 56	17 33	10	04 37	19 22	8	06 02	17 33
15	06 50	17 39	15	04 37	19 24	13	06 06	17 26
20	06 44	17 44	20	04 37	19 26	18	06 11	17 19
25	06 38	17 49	25	04 38	19 26	23	06 16	17 12
			30	04 40	19 27	28	06 21	17 06

MARCH			JULY			NOVEMBER		
2	06 31	17 54	5	04 43	19 26	2	06 26	17 00
7	06 24	17 59	10	04 46	19 25	7	06 32	16 55
12	06 16	18 04	15	04 49	19 22	12	06 37	16 51
17	06 09	18 09	20	04 53	19 19	17	06 43	16 47
22	06 01	18 14	25	04 57	19 14	22	06 48	16 44
27	05 53	18 18	30	05 01	19 11	27	06 53	16 42

APRIL			AUGUST			DECEMBER		
1	05 46	18 23	4	05 05	19 06	2	06 58	16 41
6	05 38	18 27	9	05 09	19 01	7	07 02	16 40
11	05 31	18 32	14	05 14	18 55	12	07 07	16 41
16	05 24	18 37	19	05 18	18 48	17	07 10	16 42
21	05 17	18 41	24	05 23	18 42	22	07 12	16 44
26	05 10	18 46	29	05 27	18 34	27	07 15	16 47

Vertical sextant angles

FOR FINDING DISTANCE OFF

Miles	49ft 15m	66ft 20m	82ft 25m	98ft 30m	115ft 35m	131ft 40m	148ft 45m	164ft 50m	180ft 55m	197ft 60m
0.1	4°38'	6°10'	7°41'	9°13'	10°42'	12°11'	13°39'	15°07'	16°32'	17°57'
0.2	2 19	3 05	3 52	4 38	5 24	6 10	6 56	7 41	8 27	9 12
0.3	1 33	2 04	2 35	3 05	3 36	4 07	4 38	5 09	5 39	6 10
0.4	1 10	1 33	1 56	2 19	2 42	3 05	3 29	3 52	4 15	4 38
0.5	0 56	1 14	1 33	1 51	2 10	2 28	2 47	3 05	3 24	3 42
0.6	0 46	1 02	1 17	1 33	1 48	2 04	2 19	2 35	2 50	3 05
0.7	0 40	0 53	1 06	1 20	1 33	1 46	1 59	2 13	2 26	2 39
0.8	0 35	0 46	0 58	1 10	1 21	1 33	1 44	1 56	2 08	2 19
0.9	0 31	0 41	0 52	1 02	1 12	1 22	1 33	1 43	1 53	2 04
1.0	0 28	0 37	0 46	0 56	1 05	1 14	1 24	1 33	1 42	1 51
1.1	0 25	0 34	0 42	0 51	0 59	1 07	1 16	1 24	1 33	1 41
1.2	0 23	0 31	0 39	0 46	0 49	1 02	1 10	1 17	1 25	1 33
1.3	0 21	0 29	0 36	0 43	0 50	0 57	1 04	1 11	1 19	1 26
1.4	0 20	0 27	0 33	0 40	0 46	0 53	1 00	1 06	1 13	1 20
1.5	0 19	0 25	0 31	0 37	0 43	0 49	0 56	1 02	1 08	1 14
1.6	0 17	0 23	0 29	0 35	0 41	0 46	0 52	0 58	1 04	1 10
1.7	0 16	0 22	0 27	0 33	0 38	0 44	0 49	0 55	1 00	1 06
1.8	0 15	0 21	0 26	0 31	0 36	0 41	0 46	0 52	0 57	1 02
1.9	0 15	0 20	0 24	0 29	0 34	0 39	0 44	0 49	0 54	0 59
2.0	0 14	0 19	0 23	0 28	0 32	0 37	0 42	0 46	0 51	0 56
2.1	0 13	0 18	0 22	0 27	0 31	0 35	0 40	0 44	0 49	0 53
2.2	0 13	0 17	0 21	0 25	0 30	0 34	0 38	0 42	0 46	0 51
2.3	0 12	0 16	0 20	0 24	0 28	0 32	0 36	0 40	0 44	0 48
2.4	0 12	0 15	0 19	0 23	0 27	0 31	0 35	0 39	0 43	0 46
2.5	0 11	0 15	0 19	0 22	0 26	0 29	0 33	0 37	0 41	0 44
2.6	0 11	0 14	0 18	0 21	0 25	0 29	0 32	0 36	0 39	0 43
2.7	0 10	0 14	0 17	0 21	0 24	0 27	0 31	0 34	0 38	0 41
2.8	0 10	0 13	0 17	0 20	0 23	0 27	0 30	0 33	0 36	0 40
2.9	0 10	0 13	0 16	0 19	0 22	0 26	0 29	0 32	0 35	0 38
3.0	0 09	0 12	0 15	0 19	0 22	0 25	0 28	0 31	0 34	0 37
3.1	0 09	0 12	0 15	0 18	0 21	0 24	0 27	0 30	0 33	0 36
3.2	0 09	0 12	0 15	0 17	0 20	0 23	0 26	0 29	0 32	0 35
3.3	0 08	0 11	0 14	0 17	0 20	0 22	0 25	0 28	0 31	0 34
3.4	0 08	0 11	0 14	0 16	0 19	0 22	0 25	0 27	0 30	0 33
3.5	0 08	0 11	0 13	0 16	0 19	0 21	0 24	0 27	0 29	0 32
3.6	0 08	0 10	0 13	0 15	0 18	0 21	0 23	0 26	0 28	0 31
3.7	0 08	0 10	0 13	0 15	0 17	0 21	0 23	0 25	0 28	0 30
3.8	0 07	0 10	0 12	0 15	0 17	0 20	0 22	0 24	0 27	0 29
3.9	0 07	0 10	0 12	0 15	0 17	0 19	0 21	0 24	0 26	0 29
4.0	0 07	0 09	0 12	0 14	0 16	0 19	0 21	0 23	0 26	0 28
4.1	0 07	0 09	0 11	0 14	0 16	0 18	0 20	0 23	0 25	0 27
4.2	0 07	0 09	0 11	0 14	0 15	0 18	0 20	0 23	0 24	0 27
4.3	0 06	0 09	0 11	0 13	0 15	0 17	0 19	0 22	0 24	0 26
4.4	0 06	0 08	0 11	0 13	0 15	0 17	0 19	0 21	0 23	0 25
4.5	0 06	0 08	0 10	0 12	0 14	0 16	0 19	0 21	0 23	0 25
4.6	0 06	0 08	0 10	0 12	0 14	0 16	0 18	0 20	0 22	0 24
4.7	0 06	0 08	0 10	0 12	0 14	0 16	0 18	0 20	0 22	0 24
4.8	0 06	0 08	0 10	0 12	0 14	0 15	0 17	0 19	0 21	0 23
4.9	0 06	0 08	0 09	0 11	0 13	0 15	0 17	0 19	0 21	0 23
5.0	0 06	0 07	0 09	0 11	0 13	0 15	0 17	0 19	0 20	0 22

Miles	213ft 65m	230ft 70m	246ft 75m	262ft 80m	279ft 85m	295ft 90m	312ft 95m	328ft 100m	344ft 105m	361ft 110m
0.1	19°20′	20°42′	22°03′	23°22′	24°39′	25°56′	27°09′	28°22′	29°34′	30°42′
0.2	9 57	10 42	11 27	12 11	12 55	13 39	14 23	15 07	15 50	16 32
0.3	6 40	7 11	7 41	8 12	8 42	9 12	9 42	10 12	10 42	11 12
0.4	5 01	5 24	5 47	6 10	6 33	6 56	7 18	7 41	8 04	8 27
0.5	4 01	4 19	4 38	4 56	5 15	5 33	5 51	6 10	6 28	6 46
0.6	3 21	3 36	3 52	4 07	4 22	4 38	4 53	5 09	5 24	5 39
0.7	2 52	3 05	3 19	3 32	3 45	3 58	4 11	4 25	4 38	4 51
0.8	2 31	2 42	2 54	3 05	3 17	3 29	3 40	3 52	4 03	4 15
0.9	2 14	2 24	2 35	2 45	2 55	3 05	3 16	3 26	3 36	3 47
1.0	2 01	2 10	2 19	2 28	2 38	2 47	2 56	3 05	3 14	3 24
1.1	1 50	1 58	2 07	2 15	2 23	2 32	2 40	2 49	2 57	3 05
1.2	1 41	1 48	1 56	2 04	2 11	2 19	2 27	2 35	2 42	2 50
1.3	1 33	1 40	1 47	1 54	2 01	2 08	2 16	2 23	2 30	2 37
1.4	1 26	1 33	1 39	1 46	1 53	1 59	2 06	2 13	2 19	2 26
1.5	1 20	1 27	1 33	1 39	1 45	1 51	1 58	2 04	2 10	2 16
1.6	1 15	1 21	1 27	1 33	1 39	1 44	1 50	1 56	2 02	2 08
1.7	1 11	1 16	1 22	1 27	1 33	1 38	1 44	1 49	1 55	2 00
1.8	1 07	1 12	1 17	1 22	1 28	1 33	1 38	1 43	1 48	1 53
1.9	1 03	1 08	1 13	1 18	1 23	1 28	1 33	1 38	1 43	1 47
2.0	1 00	1 05	1 10	1 14	1 19	1 24	1 28	1 33	1 37	1 42
2.1	0 57	1 02	1 06	1 11	1 15	1 20	1 24	1 28	1 33	1 37
2.2	0 55	0 59	1 03	1 07	1 12	1 16	1 20	1 24	1 29	1 33
2.3	0 52	0 56	1 01	1 05	1 09	1 13	1 17	1 21	1 25	1 29
2.4	0 50	0 54	0 58	1 02	1 06	1 10	1 13	1 17	1 21	1 25
2.5	0 48	0 52	0 56	0 59	1 03	1 07	1 11	1 14	1 18	1 22
2.6	0 46	0 50	0 54	0 57	1 01	1 04	1 08	1 11	1 15	1 19
2.7	0 44	0 48	0 51	0 55	0 58	1 02	1 05	1 09	1 12	1 16
2.8	0 43	0 46	0 50	0 53	0 56	1 00	1 03	1 06	1 10	1 13
2.9	0 42	0 45	0 48	0 51	0 54	0 58	1 01	1 04	1 07	1 10
3.0	0 40	0 43	0 46	0 49	0 53	0 56	0 59	1 02	1 05	1 08
3.1	0 39	0 42	0 45	0 48	0 51	0 54	0 57	1 00	1 03	1 06
3.2	0 38	0 41	0 44	0 46	0 49	0 52	0 55	0 58	1 01	1 04
3.3	0 37	0 39	0 42	0 45	0 48	0 51	0 53	0 56	0 59	1 02
3.4	0 35	0 38	0 41	0 44	0 46	0 49	0 52	0 55	0 57	1 00
3.5	0 34	0 37	0 40	0 42	0 45	0 48	0 50	0 53	0 56	0 58
3.6	0 34	0 36	0 39	0 41	0 44	0 46	0 49	0 52	0 54	0 57
3.7	0 33	0 35	0 38	0 41	0 43	0 45	0 48	0 50	0 53	0 55
3.8	0 32	0 34	0 37	0 39	0 42	0 44	0 46	0 49	0 51	0 54
3.9	0 31	0 33	0 36	0 38	0 40	0 43	0 45	0 48	0 50	0 52
4.0	0 30	0 32	0 35	0 37	0 39	0 42	0 44	0 46	0 49	0 51
4.1	0 29	0 32	0 34	0 36	0 38	0 41	0 43	0 45	0 48	0 50
4.2	0 29	0 31	0 33	0 35	0 38	0 40	0 42	0 44	0 46	0 49
4.3	0 28	0 30	0 32	0 35	0 37	0 39	0 41	0 43	0 45	0 47
4.4	0 27	0 30	0 32	0 34	0 36	0 38	0 40	0 42	0 44	0 46
4.5	0 27	0 29	0 31	0 33	0 35	0 37	0 39	0 41	0 43	0 45
4.6	0 26	0 28	0 30	0 32	0 34	0 36	0 38	0 40	0 42	0 44
4.7	0 26	0 28	0 30	0 32	0 34	0 36	0 38	0 39	0 41	0 43
4.8	0 25	0 27	0 29	0 31	0 33	0 35	0 37	0 39	0 41	0 43
4.9	0 25	0 27	0 28	0 30	0 32	0 34	0 36	0 38	0 40	0 42
5.0	0 24	0 26	0 28	0 30	0 32	0 33	0 35	0 37	0 39	0 41

Miles	377ft 115m	394ft 120m	410ft 125m	427ft 130m	443ft 135m	459ft 140m	476ft 145m	492ft 150m	509ft 155m	525ft 160m
0.1	31°50′	32°56′	34°01′	35°04′	36°05′	37°05′	38°03′	39°00′	39°56′	40°49′
0.2	17 15	17 57	18 39	19 20	20 02	20 42	21 23	22 03	22 42	23 22
0.3	11 42	12 11	12 41	13 10	13 39	14 09	14 38	15 07	15 35	16 04
0.4	8 49	9 12	9 35	9 57	10 20	10 42	11 04	11 27	11 49	12 11
0.5	7 05	7 23	7 41	7 59	8 18	8 36	8 54	9 12	9 30	9 48
0.6	5 55	6 10	6 25	6 40	6 56	7 11	7 26	7 41	7 56	8 12
0.7	5 04	5 17	5 30	5 44	5 57	6 10	6 23	6 36	6 49	7 02
0.8	4 26	4 38	4 49	5 01	5 12	5 24	5 35	5 47	5 58	6 10
0.9	3 57	4 07	4 17	4 28	4 38	4 48	4 58	5 09	5 19	5 29
1.0	3 33	3 42	3 52	4 01	4 10	4 19	4 29	4 38	4 47	4 56
1.1	3 14	3 22	3 31	3 39	3 47	3 56	4 04	4 13	4 21	4 29
1.2	2 58	3 05	3 13	3 21	3 29	3 36	3 44	3 52	3 59	4 07
1.3	2 44	2 51	2 58	3 05	3 13	3 20	3 27	3 34	3 41	3 48
1.4	2 32	2 39	2 46	2 52	2 59	3 05	3 12	3 19	3 25	3 32
1.5	2 22	2 28	2 35	2 41	2 47	2 53	2 59	3 05	3 12	3 18
1.6	2 13	2 19	2 25	2 31	2 37	2 42	2 48	2 54	3 00	3 05
1.7	2 06	2 11	2 16	2 22	2 27	2 33	2 38	2 44	2 49	2 55
1.8	1 59	2 04	2 09	2 14	2 19	2 24	2 29	2 35	2 40	2 45
1.9	1 52	1 57	2 02	2 07	2 12	2 17	2 22	2 26	2 31	2 36
2.0	1 47	1 51	1 56	2 01	2 05	2 10	2 15	2 19	2 24	2 28
2.1	1 42	1 46	1 50	1 55	1 59	2 04	2 08	2 13	2 17	2 21
2.2	1 37	1 41	1 45	1 50	1 54	1 58	2 02	2 07	2 11	2 15
2.3	1 33	1 37	1 41	1 45	1 49	1 53	1 57	2 01	2 05	2 09
2.4	1 28	1 32	1 37	1 41	1 44	1 48	1 52	1 56	2 00	2 04
2.5	1 25	1 29	1 33	1 36	1 40	1 44	1 48	1 51	1 55	1 59
2.6	1 22	1 26	1 29	1 33	1 36	1 40	1 43	1 47	1 51	1 54
2.7	1 19	1 22	1 26	1 29	1 33	1 36	1 40	1 43	1 47	1 50
2.8	1 16	1 20	1 23	1 26	1 29	1 33	1 36	1 39	1 43	1 46
2.9	1 14	1 17	1 20	1 23	1 26	1 30	1 33	1 36	1 39	1 42
3.0	1 11	1 14	1 17	1 20	1 24	1 27	1 30	1 33	1 36	1 39
3.1	1 09	1 12	1 15	1 18	1 21	1 24	1 27	1 30	1 33	1 36
3.2	1 07	1 10	1 12	1 15	1 18	1 21	1 24	1 27	1 30	1 33
3.3	1 05	1 07	1 10	1 13	1 16	1 19	1 22	1 24	1 27	1 30
3.4	1 03	1 06	1 08	1 11	1 14	1 16	1 19	1 22	1 25	1 27
3.5	1 01	1 04	1 06	1 09	1 12	1 14	1 17	1 20	1 22	1 25
3.6	0 59	1 02	1 04	1 07	1 10	1 12	1 15	1 18	1 20	1 22
3.7	0 58	1 00	1 03	1 05	1 08	1 10	1 13	1 15	1 18	1 20
3.8	0 56	0 59	1 01	1 03	1 06	1 08	1 11	1 13	1 16	1 18
3.9	0 55	0 57	0 59	1 02	1 04	1 07	1 09	1 11	1 14	1 16
4.0	0 53	0 56	0 58	1 00	1 03	1 05	1 07	1 10	1 12	1 14
4.1	0 52	0 54	0 57	0 59	1 01	1 03	1 06	1 08	1 10	1 12
4.2	0 51	0 53	0 55	0 57	1 00	1 02	1 04	1 06	1 08	1 11
4.3	0 49	0 52	0 54	0 56	0 58	1 00	1 03	1 05	1 07	1 09
4.4	0 49	0 51	0 53	0 55	0 57	0 59	1 01	1 03	1 05	1 07
4.5	0 47	0 49	0 52	0 54	0 56	0 58	1 00	1 02	1 04	1 06
4.6	0 46	0 48	0 50	0 52	0 54	0 56	0 59	1 01	1 03	1 05
4.7	0 45	0 47	0 49	0 51	0 53	0 55	0 57	0 59	1 01	1 03
4.8	0 44	0 46	0 48	0 50	0 52	0 54	0 56	0 58	1 00	1 02
4.9	0 44	0 45	0 47	0 49	0 51	0 53	0 55	0 57	0 59	1 01
5.0	0 43	0 45	0 46	0 48	0 50	0 52	0 54	0 56	0 58	0 59

Miles	541ft 165m	558ft 170m	574ft 175m	591ft 180m	607ft 185m	623ft 190m	640ft 195m	656ft 200m	673ft 205m	689ft 210m
0.1	41°42′	42°33′	43°23′	44°12′	44°58′	45°44′	46°29′	47°12′	47°54′	48°35′
0.2	24 01	24 39	25 17	25 55	26 32	27 09	27 46	28 22	28 58	29 33
0.3	16 32	17 01	17 29	17 57	18 25	18 53	19 20	19 48	20 15	20 42
0.4	12 33	12 55	13 17	13 39	14 01	14 23	14 45	15 07	15 28	15 50
0.5	10 06	10 24	10 42	11 00	11 18	11 36	11 54	12 11	12 29	12 47
0.6	8 27	8 42	8 57	9 12	9 27	9 42	9 57	10 12	10 27	10 42
0.7	7 15	7 28	7 41	7 54	8 07	8 20	8 33	8 46	8 59	9 12
0.8	6 21	6 33	6 44	6 56	7 07	7 18	7 30	7 41	7 53	8 04
0.9	5 39	5 49	6 00	6 10	6 20	6 30	6 40	6 51	7 01	7 11
1.0	5 05	5 15	5 24	5 33	5 42	5 51	6 01	6 10	6 19	6 28
1.1	4 38	4 46	4 55	5 03	5 11	5 20	5 28	5 36	5 45	5 53
1.2	4 15	4 22	4 30	4 38	4 46	4 53	5 01	5 09	5 16	5 24
1.3	3 55	4 02	4 09	4 17	4 24	4 31	4 38	4 45	4 52	4 59
1.4	3 39	3 45	3 52	3 58	4 05	4 11	4 18	4 25	4 31	4 38
1.5	3 24	3 30	3 36	3 42	3 49	3 55	4 01	4 07	4 13	4 19
1.6	3 11	3 17	3 23	3 29	3 34	3 40	3 46	3 52	3 57	4 03
1.7	3 00	3 05	3 11	3 16	3 22	3 27	3 33	3 38	3 44	3 49
1.8	2 50	2 55	3 00	3 05	3 11	3 16	3 21	3 26	3 31	3 36
1.9	2 41	2 46	2 51	2 56	3 01	3 05	3 10	3 15	3 20	3 25
2.0	2 33	2 38	2 42	2 47	2 52	2 56	3 01	3 05	3 10	3 15
2.1	2 26	2 30	2 35	2 39	2 43	2 48	2 52	2 57	3 01	3 05
2.2	2 19	2 23	2 28	2 32	2 36	2 40	2 44	2 49	2 53	2 57
2.3	2 13	2 17	2 21	2 25	2 29	2 33	2 37	2 41	2 45	2 50
2.4	2 08	2 11	2 15	2 19	2 23	2 27	2 31	2 35	2 38	2 42
2.5	1 56	2 06	2 10	2 14	2 17	2 21	2 25	2 28	2 32	2 36
2.6	1 58	2 01	2 05	2 08	2 12	2 16	2 19	2 23	2 26	2 30
2.7	1 53	1 57	2 00	2 04	2 07	2 11	2 14	2 17	2 21	2 24
2.8	1 49	1 53	1 56	1 59	2 03	2 06	2 09	2 13	2 16	2 19
2.9	1 46	1 49	1 52	1 55	1 58	2 02	2 05	2 08	2 11	2 14
3.0	1 42	1 45	1 48	1 51	1 54	1 58	2 01	2 04	2 07	2 10
3.1	1 39	1 42	1 45	1 48	1 51	1 54	1 57	2 00	2 03	2 06
3.2	1 36	1 39	1 41	1 44	1 47	1 50	1 53	1 56	1 59	2 02
3.3	1 33	1 36	1 38	1 41	1 44	1 47	1 50	1 52	1 55	1 58
3.4	1 30	1 33	1 36	1 38	1 41	1 44	1 46	1 49	1 52	1 55
3.5	1 27	1 30	1 33	1 35	1 38	1 41	1 43	1 46	1 49	1 51
3.6	1 25	1 28	1 30	1 33	1 35	1 38	1 41	1 43	1 46	1 48
3.7	1 23	1 25	1 28	1 30	1 33	1 35	1 38	1 40	1 43	1 45
3.8	1 21	1 23	1 25	1 28	1 30	1 33	1 35	1 38	1 40	1 43
3.9	1 19	1 21	1 23	1 26	1 28	1 30	1 33	1 35	1 38	1 40
4.0	1 17	1 19	1 21	1 24	1 26	1 28	1 30	1 33	1 35	1 37
4.1	1 15	1 17	1 19	1 21	1 24	1 26	1 28	1 30	1 33	1 35
4.2	1 13	1 15	1 17	1 20	1 22	1 24	1 26	1 28	1 31	1 33
4.3	1 11	1 13	1 16	1 18	1 20	1 22	1 24	1 26	1 28	1 31
4.4	1 10	1 12	1 14	1 16	1 18	1 20	1 22	1 24	1 26	1 29
4.5	1 08	1 10	1 12	1 14	1 16	1 18	1 20	1 22	1 25	1 27
4.6	1 07	1 09	1 11	1 13	1 15	1 17	1 19	1 21	1 23	1 25
4.7	1 05	1 07	1 09	1 11	1 13	1 15	1 17	1 19	1 21	1 23
4.8	1 04	1 06	1 08	1 10	1 12	1 13	1 15	1 17	1 19	1 21
4.9	1 02	1 04	1 06	1 08	1 10	1 12	1 14	1 16	1 18	1 20
5.0	1 01	1 03	1 05	1 07	1 09	1 11	1 12	1 14	1 16	1 18

Tide prediction

INTRODUCTION

High water is the maximum height reached by each rising tide, and low water is the minimum height reached by each falling tide. If you sail in tidal waters, you should be aware of the amount of rise from low to high water and the force and direction of the normal tidal current. This information can be found in tide tables which give the times and heights of high and low tides at several selected points for a full year at a time. However, these are just predictions; a strong wind or a serious change in the barometric pressure at the time of the high or low tide, and the amount of tidal rise or fall may be considerably different from the forecast.

Tide tables The following pages contain examples of typical tide tables and their accompanying explanations. These are taken from Tables 1 and 2 of *Tide Table 1981* which is published by the US Department of Commerce, National Oceanic and Atmospheric Administration, National Ocean Survey. This publication is available from the National Ocean Survey, Rockville, Maryland, 20852 and and also be purchased at many marine stores.

Pages 38–42 explain the use of the Daily Tide Prediction Table—Table 1—and show parts of that table relating to Galveston, Texas and Tampico Harbor, Mexico. This is followed, on pages 43–47, by an explanation of Table 2—the Table of Tidal Differences and Other Constants—which is illustrated by the part of the table giving data for various points around the coast of Maine.

State of the tide To figure tide you should use a reference point near your location. If you have a time for the predicted high or low, you can use the following procedure to make what is generally a reliable prediction of the state of the tide at a time between its high and low.

Take the amount of tidal fluctuation in feet and divide it into twelfths. For example, if the charted high water is 6.0 feet and the low water datum of soundings is 0.0, the tidal fluctuation is 6 feet, and each twelfth is 0.5 feet or half a foot.

Then:

Time low water	**Tide** 0 feet [datum]
1 hour after low, add 1/12	$\frac{1}{2}$ foot above datum
2 hours after low, add 3/12	$1\frac{1}{2}$ feet above datum
3 hours after low, add 6/12	3 feet above datum
4 hours after low, add 9/12	$4\frac{1}{2}$ feet above datum
5 hours after low, add 11/12	$5\frac{1}{2}$ feet above datum
6 hours after low, add 12/12	high water

How to use tide tables

DAILY TIDE PREDICTIONS – TABLE 1

This table contains the predicted times and heights of the high and low waters for each day of the year at a number of places which are designated as *reference stations*. By using tidal differences from Table 2, one can calculate the approximate times and heights of the tide at many other places which are called subordinate stations. Instructions on the use of the tidal differences are found in the explanation of Table 2.

High water is the maximum height reached by each rising tide, and low water is the minimum height reached by each falling tide. High and low waters can be selected from the predictions by the comparison of consecutive heights. Because of diurnal inequality at certain places, however, there may be a difference of only a few tenths of a foot between one high water and low water of a day, but a

GALVESTON (Galveston Channel), TEXAS, 1981
Times and Heights of High and Low Waters

OCTOBER

Day	Time h m	Height ft	m	Day	Time h m	Height ft	m	Day	Time h m	Height ft	m
1 Th	0454	1.5	0.5	16 F	0006	1.3	0.4	1 Su	0112	1.3	0.
	1148	0.6	0.2		0433	1.6	0.5		0344	1.4	0.
	1859	1.6	0.5		1201	0.1	0.0		1222	0.3	0.1
					1954	1.9	0.6		2113	1.6	0.5
2 F	0015	1.2	0.4	17 Sa	0111	1.4	0.4	2 M	1309	0.3	0.1
	0459	1.5	0.5		0454	1.6	0.5		2227	1.6	0.5
	1224	0.5	0.2		1253	0.0	0.0				
	2008	1.5	0.5		2117	1.9	0.6				
15 Th	0413	1.6	0.5	30 F	0339	1.4	0.4	15 Su	0124	1.3	0.
	1111	0.2	0.1		1110	0.3	0.1		0406	1.4	0.
	1840	1.9	0.6		1904	1.6	0.5		1235	-0.3	-0.
									2108	1.8	0.
				31 Sa	0013	1.3	0.4				
					0343	1.4	0.4				
					1145	0.3	0.1				
					2003	1.6	0.5				

NOVEMBER

Time meridian 90° W. 0000 is midnight. 1200 is noon.
Heights are referred to Gulf Coast Low Water which is the chart datum of soundings.
On days when the tide is diurnal, high water has an approximate stand of about 7 hours.
Predictions are for beginning of stand.

marked difference in height between the other high water and low water. It is essential, therefore, in using the tables to note carefully the heights as well as the times of the tides.
Time The kind of time used for the predictions at each reference station is indicated by the time meridian at the bottom of each page. Daylight saving time is not used.
Datum The datum from which the predicted heights are reckoned is the same as that used for the charts of the locality. The datum for the Atlantic coast of the United States is mean low water. For foreign coasts a datum approximating to mean low water springs, Indian spring low water, or the lowest possible low water is generally used. The depression of the datum below mean sea level for each of the reference stations is given on the preceding page of the volume.

DECEMBER

Day	Time h m	Height ft	m	Day	Time h m	Height ft	m	Day	Time h m	Height ft	m
6	1331	-0.2	-0.1	1	1241	-0.1	0.0	16	0320	0.8	0.2
M	2211	1.7	0.5	Tu	2135	1.4	0.4	W	0603	0.9	0.3
									1407	-0.2	-0.1
									2212	1.2	0.4
7	1437	0.0	0.0	2	1330	0.0	0.0	17	0426	0.7	0.2
u	2314	1.6	0.5	W	2221	1.3	0.4	Th	0746	0.8	0.2
									1506	0.0	0.0
									2248	1.1	0.3
0	1158	-0.1	0.0	15	0211	0.9	0.3	30	0132	0.7	0.2
M	2043	1.4	0.4	Tu	0451	1.0	0.3	W	0349	0.8	0.2
					1313	-0.4	-0.1		1221	-0.4	-0.1
					2127	1.3	0.4		2036	1.1	0.3
								31	0221	0.7	0.2
								Th	0501	0.8	0.2
									1309	-0.3	-0.1
									2105	1.0	0.3

Depth of water The nautical charts published by the United States and other maritime nations show the depth of water as referred to a low water datum corresponding to that from which the predicted tidal heights are reckoned. To find the actual depth of water at any time the height of the tide should be added to the charted depth. If the height of the tide is negative—that is, if there is a minus sign [−] before the tabular height—it should be subtracted from the charted depth. For any time between high and low water, the height of the tide may be estimated from the heights of the preceding and following tides, or Table 3 may be used.

Variation in sea level Changes in winds and barometric conditions cause variations in sea level from day to day. In general, with onshore winds or a low barometer the

TAMPICO HARBOUR (Madero). MEXICO, 1981
Times and Heights of High and Low Water

January				January				February		
Day	Time	Height		Day	Time	Height		Day	Time	Heigh
	h m	ft	m		h m	ft	m		h m	ft
1 Th	0518 1418	0.5 1.6	0.2 0.5	16 F	0510 1432	0.1 1.8	0.0 0.5	1 Su	0558 1521	0.2 1.8	0 0
2 F	0552 1506	0.4 1.7	0.1 0.5	17 Sa	0603 1522	-0.1 1.9	0.0 0.6	2 M	0640 1547	0.1 1.8	0. 0.
14 W	0331 1201 1545 1933	0.5 1.5 1.4 1.5	0.2 0.5 0.4 0.5	29 Th	0344 1357	0.6 1.5	0.2 0.5	14 Sa	0452 1424	0.1 1.9	0 0.
15 Th	0424 1334	0.3 1.7	0.1 0.5	30 F	0429 1429	0.4 1.6	0.1 0.5	15 Su	0552 1506	0.1 1.9	0. 0.
				31 Sa	0516 1448	0.3 1.7	0.1 0.5				

Time meridan 90 W. 0000 is midnight. 1200 is noon.
Heights are referred to the chart datum of soundings.

heights of both the high and low waters will be higher than
predicted while with offshore winds or a high barometer
they will be lower. There are also seasonal variations in
sea level, but these variations have been included in the
predictions for each station. At ocean stations the seasonal
variation in sea level is usually less than half a foot.

At stations on tidal rivers the average seasonal variation
in river level due to freshets and droughts may be
considerably more than a foot. The predictions for these
stations include an allowance for this seasonal variation
representing average freshet and drought conditions.
Unusual freshets or droughts, however, will cause the
tides to be higher or lower, respectively, than predicted.
Number of tides There are usually two high and two low
waters in a day. Tides follow the Moon more closely than

MARCH

Day	Time h m	Height ft	m	Day	Time h m	Height ft	m	Day	Time h m	Height ft	m
16 M	0645 1539	0.1 1.9	0.0 0.6	1 Su	0433 1405	0.5 1.8	0.2 0.5	16 M	0540 1417 1941 2158	0.4 1.9 1.6 1.7	0.1 0.6 0.5 0.5
17 Tu	0734 1606 2048 2352	0.2 1.8 1.6 1.7	0.1 0.5 0.5 0.5	2 M	0527 1427	0.4 1.9	0.1 0.6	17 Tu	0636 1442 1937 2341	0.5 1.8 1.5 1.7	0.2 0.5 0.5 0.5
				14 Sa	0322 1310	0.4 2.0	0.1 0.6	29 Su	0229 1223	0.7 1.9	0.2 0.6
				15 Su	0435 1345	0.4 2.0	0.1 0.6	30 M	0342 1255	0.6 1.9	0.2 0.6
								31 Tu	0448 1320 1920 2136	0.6 1.9 1.5 1.6	0.2 0.6 0.5 0.5

they do the Sun, and the lunar or tidal day is about 50 minutes longer than the solar day. This causes the tide to occur later each day, and a tide that has occurred near the end of one calendar day will be followed by a corresponding tide that may skip the next day and occur in the early morning of the third day. Thus on certain days of each month only a single high or a single low water occurs. At some stations, during portions of each month the tide becomes diurnal—that is, only one high and one low water will occur during the period of a lunar day.

Relation of tide to current In using these tables of tide predictions it must be borne in mind that they give the times and heights of high and low waters and *not* the times of turning of the current or slack water. For stations on the outer coast there is usually but little difference between the time of high or low water and the beginning of ebb or flood current, but for places in narrow channels, landlocked harbors, or on tidal rivers, the time of slack water may differ by several hours from the time of high or low water stand. The relation of the times of high and low water to the turning of the current depends upon a number of factors, so that no simple or general rule can be given. For the predicted times of slack water reference should be made to the tidal current tables published by the National Ocean Survey in two separate volumes, one for the Atlantic coast of North America and the other for the Pacific coast of North America and Asia.

Typical tide curves The variations in the tide from day to day and from place to place are illustrated on the opposite page by the tide curves for representative ports along the Atlantic and Gulf coasts of the United States. It will be noted that the range of tide for stations along the Atlantic coast varies from place to place but that the type is uniformly semidiurnal with the principal variations following the changes in the Moon's distance and phase. In the Gulf of Mexico, however, the range of tide is uniformly small but the type of tide differs considerably. At certain ports such as Pensacola there is usually but one high and one low water a day while at other ports such as Galveston the inequality is such that the tide is semidiurnal around the times the Moon is on the Equator but becomes diurnal around the times of maximum north or south declination of the Moon. In the Gulf of Mexico, consequently, the principal variations in the tide are due to the changing declination of the Moon. Key West, at the entrance to the Gulf of Mexico, has a type of tide which is a mixture of semidaily and daily types. Here the tide is semidiurnal but there is considerable inequality in the heights of high and low waters. By reference to the curves it will be seen that where the inequality is large there are times when there is but a few tenths of a foot difference between high water and low water.

Tidal differences

AND OTHER CONSTANTS – TABLE 2

The publication of full daily predictions is necessarily limited to a comparatively small number of stations. Tide predictions for many other places, however, can be obtained by applying certain differences to the predictions for the reference stations in Table 1—Daily Tide Predictions. Table 2 lists the places called 'subordinate stations' for which such predictions can be made and the differences or ratios to be used. These differences or ratios are to be applied to the predictions for the proper reference station which is listed in Table 2 in bold face type above the differences for the subordinate station. The stations in this table are arranged in geographical order. The index at the end of the volume will assist in locating a particular station.

Caution The time and height differences listed in this table are average differences derived from comparisons of simultaneous tide observations at the subordinate location and its reference station. Because these figures are constant, they cannot provide for the daily variances of the actual tide. Therefore, it must be realized that although the application of the time and height differences will generally provide reasonably accurate approximations, they cannot result in as accurate predictions as those for the reference stations which are based upon much longer periods of analyses and which do provide for daily variances. In addition, at subordinate stations where the tide is chiefly diurnal, the tide correctors are intended primarily to be used to approximate the times and heights of the higher high and the lower low waters. When the lower high water and higher low water at the reference station are nearly the same height, great reliance should not be placed on the calculated corresponding tides at the subordinate station.

Time difference To determine the time of high water or low water at any station listed in this table there is given in the columns headed 'Differences, Time' the hours and minutes to be added to or subtracted from the time of high or low water at some reference station. A plus [+] sign indicates that the tide at the subordinate station is later than at the reference station and the difference should be added, a minus [−] sign that it is earlier and should be subtracted.

To obtain the tide at a subordinate station on any date apply the difference to the tide at the reference station for that same date. In some cases, however, to obtain an am tide it may be necessary to use the preceding day's pm tide at the reference station, or to obtain a pm tide it may be necessary to use the following day's am tide. For example, if a high water occurs at a reference station at 2200 on July 2, and the tide at the subordinate station occurs 3 hours later, then high water will occur at 0100 on July 3 at the subordinate station. For the second case, if a high

No	PLACE	POSITION	
		Lat	Lon
		^{o} N $^{'}$	^{o} W
	MAINE		
	Time meridian, 75°W		
	Mount Desert Island		
709	Salsbury Cove	44 26	68 1
711	Bar Harbor	44 23	68 1
713	Southwest Harbor	44 16	68 1
715	Mount Desert	44 22	68 2
717	Bass Harbor	44 14	68 2
719	Pretty Marsh Harbor	44 20	68 2
	Blue Hill Bay		
721	Union River	44 30	68 2
723	Blue Hill Harbor	44 24	68 3
725	Allen Cove	44 18	68 3
727	Mackerel Cove	44 10	68 2
729	Burnt Coat Harbor, Swans Island	44 09	68 2
	MAINE, Penobscot Bay		
	Eggemoggin Reach		
731	Naskeag Harbor	44 14	68 3
733	Center Harbor	44 16	68 3
735	Sedgwick	44 18	68 38
736	Isle Au Haut	44 04	68 38
737	Head Harbor, Isle Au Haut	44 01	68 37
739	Kimball Island	44 04	68 3
741	Oceanville, Deer Isle	44 12	68 38
743	Stonington, Deer Isle	44 09	68 40
745	Northwest Harbor, Deer Isle	44 14	68 41
747	Matinicus Harbor	43 52	68 5
749	Vinalhaven, Vinalhaven Island	44 03	68 5
751	Iran Point, North Haven Island	44 08	68 52
753	Pulpit Harbour, North Haven Island	44 09	68 53
755	Castine	44 23	68 48
757	Pumpkin Island, South Bay	44 25	68 44
	Penobscot River		
759	Fort Point	44 28	68 49
761	Bucksport	44 34	68 48
763	South Orrington	44 42	68 49
765	Hampden	44 45	58 50
767	Bangor	44 48	68 46
769	Belfast	44 26	69 00
771	Camden	44 12	69 03
773	Rockland	44 06	69 06
775	Owls Head	44 06	69 03
777	Dyer Point, Weskeag River	44 02	69 07

DIFFERENCES				RANGES		
Time		Height		Mean	Spring	MEAN TIDE LEVEL
High water	Low water	High water	Low water			
h m	h m	feet	feet	feet	feet	feet

on, PORTLAND, p 32

-0 15	-0 12	+1.6	0.0	10.6	12.2	5.3
-0 22	-0 16	+1.5	0.0	10.5	12.1	5.2
-0 22	-0 12	+1.2	0.0	10.2	11.7	5.1
-0 16	-0 08	+1.6	0.0	10.6	12.2	5.3
-0 18	-0 11	+0.9	0.0	9.9	11.3	5.0
-0 13	-0 13	+1.2	0.0	10.2	11.7	5.1
-0 09	-0 08	+1.4	0.0	10.4	11.9	5.2
-0 13	-0 08	+1.1	0.0	10.1	11.6	5.0
-0 12	-0 12	+1.3	0.0	10.3	11.8	5.1
-0 20	-0 13	+1.0	0.0	10.0	11.5	5.0
-0 23	-0 13	+0.5	0.0	9.5	10.8	4.7
-0 16	-0 14	+1.2	0.0	10.2	11.6	5.1
-0 13	-0 07	+1.1	0.0	10.1	11.5	5.0
-0 11	-0 06	+1.2	0.0	10.2	11.7	5.1
-0 23	-0 19	+0.3	0.0	9.3	10.7	4.7
-0 20	-0 20	+0.1	0.0	9.1	10.4	4.6
-0 20	-0 20	+0.6	0.0	9.6	10.9	4.8
-0 18	-0 17	+1.1	0.0	10.1	11.5	5.0
-0 18	-0 17	+0.7	0.0	9.7	11.0	4.8
-0 12	-0 12	+1.1	0.0	10.1	11.5	5.0
-0 17	-0 12	0.0	0.0	9.0	10.4	4.5
-0 13	-0 06	+0.3	0.0	9.3	10.7	4.6
-0 13	-0 13	+0.5	0.0	9.5	10.8	4.8
-0 13	-0 15	+0.8	0.0	9.8	11.L	4.9
-0 04	-0 01	+0.7	0.0	9.7	11.1	4.8
+0 11	+0 29	+1.3	0.0	10.3	11.7	5.1
-0 06	-0 05	+1.3	0.0	10.3	11.8	5.1
-0 02	-0 01	+2.0	0.0	11.0	12.5	5.5
+0 01	+0 04	+3.3	0.0	12.3	14.0	6.1
+0 02	+0 06	+3.8	0.0	12.8	14.6	6.4
+0 04	+0 13	+4.1	0.0	13.1	14.9	6.5
-0 08	-0 01	+1.0	0.0	10.0	11.5	5.0
-0 12	-0 06	+0.6	0.0	9.6	10.9	4.8
-0 16	-0 10	+0.7	0.0	9.7	11.2	4.8
-0 16	-0 13	+0.4	0.0	9.4	10.7	4.7
-0 10	-0 10	+0.6	0.0	9.6	10.9	4.8

water at a reference station occurs at 0200 on July 17, and the tide at the subordinate station occurs 5 hours earlier, the high water at the subordinate station will occur at 2100 on July 16. The necessary allowance for change in date when the international date line is crossed is included in the time differences. In such cases use the same date at the reference station as desired for the subordinate station as explained above.

The results obtained by the application of the time differences will be in the kind of time indicated by the time meridian shown above the name of the subordinate station. Summer or daylight saving time is not used in the tide tables.

Height differences The height of the tide, referred to the datum charts, is obtained by means of the height differences or ratios. A plus [+] sign indicates that the difference should be added to the height at the reference station and a minus [−] sign that it should be subtracted. All height differences, ranges, and levels in table 2 are in feet but may be converted to meters by the use of Table 7.

Ratio For some stations height differences would give unsatisfactory predictions. In such cases they have been omitted and one or two ratios are given. Where two ratios are given, one in the 'height of high water' column and one in the 'height of low water' column, the high waters and low waters at the reference station should be multiplied by these respective ratios. Where only one is given, the omitted ratio is either unreliable or unknown.

For some subordinate stations there is given in parentheses a ratio as well as a correction in feet. In those instances, each predicted high and low water at the reference station should first be multiplied by the ratio and then the correction in feet is added to or subtracted from each product as indicated.

As an example, at Port of Spain, Trinidad, the values in the time and height difference columns in Table 2 are gives as − 0 44, − 1 12, and [*0.31 + 1.4] as referred to the reference station at Punta Gorda, Venezuela. If we assume that the time predictions in column (1) below are those of Punta Gorda on a particular day, application of the time and height corrections in columns (2) and (3) would result in the tide predictions for Port of Spain in column (4).

(1)		(2)	(3)	(4)		
Time	Height	Time	Height	Time	Height	
h/m	ft	Corrections	Corrections	h/m	ft	meters
		h/m				
0326	0.6	− 1 12	× 0.31 + 1.4	0214	1.6	0.5
0900	5.1	− 0 44	× 0.31 + 1.4	0816	3.0	0.9
1608	− 0.3	− 1 12	× 0.31 + 1.4	1456	1.3	0.4
2148	5.4	− 0 44	× 0.31 + 1.4	2104	3.1	0.9

Range The *mean range* is the difference in height between mean high water and mean low water. The *spring range* is the average semidiurnal range occurring semimonthly as the result of the Moon being new or full. It is larger than the mean range where the type of tide is either semidiurnal or mixed, and is of no practical significance where the type of tide is diurnal. Where the tide is chiefly of the diurnal type the table gives the *diurnal range*, which is the difference in height between mean higher high water and mean lower low water.

Datum The datum of the predictions obtained through the height differences or ratios is also the datum of the largest scale chart for the locality. To obtain the depth at the time of high or low water, the predicted height should be added to the depth on the chart unless such height is negative [—], when it should be subtracted. To find the height at times between high and low water see Table 3. On some charts the depths are given in meters and in such cases the heights of the tide can be reduced to meters by the use of Table 7. The chart datum for the east coast of the United States and for a part of the West Indies is *mean low water*. For the rest of the area covered by these tables the datums generally used are approximately *mean low water*, *mean low water springs*, *Indian spring low water*, or the *lowest possible low water*.

Mean Tide Level [Half Tide Level] The mean tide level is a plane midway between mean low water and mean high water. Tabular values are reckoned from chart datum.

Note Dashes are entered in the place of data which are unknown, unreliable, or not applicable.

This section is taken from *Tide Table 1981* which is published by the US Department of Commerce, National Oceanic and Atmospheric Administration, National Ocean Survey. This publication is for sale by the National Ocean Survey, Rockville, Maryland, 20852 and can also be purchased in many marine stores.

Time zones

The standard time zone system is based on the division of the world into 24 zones, each of 15° longitude. The 'zero' time zone is centered at the Greenwich meridian, and the standard time of this zone is Greenwich Mean Time. The 12th time zone is divided by the 180th meridian and designated as plus 12 and minus 12 zones: the half of the zone in *west* longitude is numbered *plus* 12; the half in *east* longitude is numbered *minus* 12. All other time zones are designated by numbers representing the number of hours by which the standard time of each zone differs from GMT.

Some countries, islands and island groups find it impractical, because of local conditions, irregular boundaries, etc., to maintain time according to the fixed time zones. In these cases, zones are normally modified by law. Some countries find it convenient to modify standard

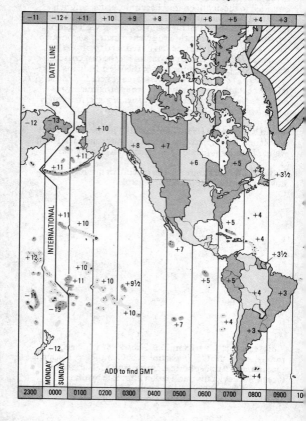

time for part of the year, particularly during the summer, in order to prolong daylight hours in the evening. This is accomplished by adopting the standard time of the zone immediately to the eastward. This 'fast time' is called 'Daylight Saving Time' or 'Summer Time'.

In the United States all states, except Arizona and Hawaii, keep Daylight Saving Time from the last Sunday in April to the last Sunday in October. The change being made at 0200 hours local time.

The International Date Line is a hypothetical line [approximating the 180th meridian] fixed by international agreement as the place where travelers must change the calendar date by one day. Crossing the International Date Line going to the *West* the date is *advanced* one day. Crossing it traveling *East* the date becomes one day earlier.

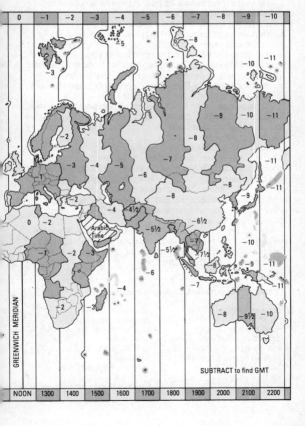

This chapter describes techniques that are used regularly in yacht navigation. It is not intended to be a complete guide to the subject and yachtsmen seeking one are advised to read one of the many books on the subject.

Magnetic variation This is the difference between Magnetic and True bearings. The variation is said to be west if Magnetic north is west of True north and *vice versa*. To convert a Magnetic course or bearing to a True one

ADD the variation if it is EAST;
SUBTRACT the variation if it is WEST.

To convert a True course or bearing to a Magnetic one

Add the variation if it is WEST;
SUBTRACT the variation if it is EAST.

The amount and direction of variation changes gradually with time and varies according to your position on the globe. A chart gives the variation for a particular area as it was at the time the chart was produced, together with the approximate annual increase or decrease. Large scale charts may be marked with isogonic lines, joining places of equal variation and showing the variation in different areas.

On many charts the inner ring of the compass rose gives Magnetic bearings. Provided that it is reasonably up-to-date you can work straight from the Magnetic ring when plotting Magnetic courses or bearings.

Compass deviation This is the difference between a Magnetic course and the reading on the steering compass. The amount and direction of deviation varies from boat to boat and according to which way the boat is pointing. In wood or GRP boats the amount of deviation may be negligible. If not, there should be a deviation card which lists Magnetic courses in one column and the equivalent compass courses in the other.

A check for deviation can be made by sighting along the centreline of the boat with a hand bearing compass from a position free of magnetic interference. The readings of the two compasses are then compared.

Coastal Navigation Equipment

Steering compass checked for deviation	**Barometer**
Hand bearing compass	**Binoculars** best size is 7×50
Sextant sometimes useful inshore	**Charts** of every area you may visit
Echo sounder and lead line	**Tide tables**
Log towed type or hull-mounted	**Pilot books** and light lists
Direction finder	**Log book**
Radar	**Parallel rules** or plotting instrument
Clock	**Dividers** and compasses
	Pencils with eraser and sharpener

Tide and current Information about the rate [speed] and set [direction] of tidal streams is found on tidal stream charts. Some ordinary charts also carry information about tidal streams at specified points. On these, compass directions given for tidal streams refer to the True compass and give the point the tide is flowing *toward*. Rates are in knots. Information on ocean currents is given on the appropriate charts.

When navigating close to land be careful of the effect of tidal inset. This is the tendency of a stream flowing parallel to the coast to set toward the shore as it passes a bay which may carry you closer to land than you expect.

Leeway angle This is determined by hull shape, course, and wind and sea conditions. The allowance for it has to be an approximation based on your experience of a particular boat. A rough idea of the angle can be gained by taking the bearing of the boat's wake and comparing this bearing with the compass course.

Surface drift, which may occur after the wind has been blowing strongly in one direction for a time and reach a speed of a knot or more, is likely to be encountered only in the open ocean.

Distance run This is found by comparing successive log readings. Towed logs tend to over-read in a headwind and under-read with a strong following wind. They also tend to under-read if the boat is moving slowly.

Distances on a chart, if there is no mileage scale, are measured from the latitude scale [1 minute of latitude = 1 nautical mile].

Charts A nautical chart is a graphic representation of navigable portions of the Earth's surface. It shows the depth of water by numerous soundings, and sometimes by depth curves, the shoreline of adjacent land, topographic features that may serve as landmarks, aids to navigation, dangers, and other information of interest to the navigator.

Designed as a work sheet on which courses may be plotted and positions ascertained, it assists the navigator in avoiding dangers and is one of the most essential and reliable aids available.

A complete index of chart symbols can be found in Appendix K of Bowditch's *American Practical Navigator*.

Chartwork Symbols

⊙ **Fix.** The size of the circle shows roughly the area of uncertainty

→ **Wake course.** Boat's course relative to the water

+ **Dead reckoning position.** Allowing for course steered and distance run only

⇝ **Track.** Boat's course relative to land

△ **Estimated position.** Allowing for tide or current and leeway, in addition to the above

⋙ **Tidal stream** or current

→ **Position line**

⇜⇝ **Transferred position line**

Course to steer

LAYING A COURSE

This procedure is used to find out what to steer by the boat's compass—the Course to Steer—in order to make good a given course relative to land—the Required Course. The course will hold good as long as there is no change in any of the relevant variables, such as a change in the speed or direction of the tidal stream.

The steps below include adjustments for tide or current, leeway angle, magnetic variation and compass deviation. Depending on circumstances, some of these adjustments may not be necessary and can be left out.

1 Required Course This is drawn on the chart to show the course that you wish to make good relative to land.

2 Tide or current From any suitable point [A] on the Required Course lay off a second line in the direction of the stream of current and measure off along it the distance [AB] that the water will travel in an hour (or any other convenient period of time). Setting the dividers to the distance that the boat will travel in the same time, find the point [C] on the Required Course which is that distance from B.

3 Magnetic variation Read off the bearing of BC on the Magnetic rose on the chart. If working from the True rose convert the course to Magnetic by applying the variation.

4 Leeway angle This is allowed to *windward* of BC. Add or subtract the angle, as appropriate, from the course just found. This gives you the Course to Steer, as shown below. In practice, there is no need to draw it on the chart.

5 Compass deviation If there is a deviation card look up the equivalent compass course.

This is the course that the helmsman should steer.

Note that a tidal stream or current makes no difference to the Course to Steer unless it is setting at an angle to the required course. If it is setting parallel to your course it affects the distance made good relative to land [AC] but has no effect on the Course to Steer.

On a short passage it is often possible to work out courses to steer in advance of setting sail. This is generally easier than waiting until you are at sea when the motion of the boat makes plotting more laborious.

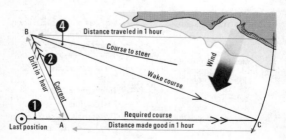

Estimated position

POSITION FINDING BY DEAD RECKONING

In the absence of a more reliable way of determining your position it can be estimated from the Course Steered and distance run since your last known or estimated position, making allowance for the effects of leeway and tide or current. The position thus obtained is commonly called an Estimated Position [EP].

The procedure below takes into account Course Steered, compass deviation, magnetic variation, leeway angle, distance run and tide or current. Depending on circumstances, some of these factors may not be relevant and can be ignored.

1 Course Steered This is the course by the boat's steering compass that the helmsman estimates he/she has been steering.

2 Compass deviation If there is a deviation card look up the equivalent Magnetic course.

3 Leeway angle This is allowed to *leeward* of the Course Steered. Add or subtract the angle, as appropriate.

4 Magnetic variation Working from the Magnetic rose on the chart lay off the course just found from your last position [X]. If working from the True rose first convert the course to True by applying the variation.

5 Distance run This is the difference between the present log reading and the log reading at the time of your last position. Measure off the distance [XY] along the new course line.

6 Tide or current From Y lay off a line in the direction of the tide or current and measure off along it the distance [YZ] that the water has traveled since the time of your last position.

The point Z is your Estimated Position.

An EP is as accurate only as the assumptions on which it is based. However, a good EP may well be more reliable than an indifferent fix.

A dead reckoning [DR] position is plotted in the same way as an EP, but omitting steps 4 and 6 [i.e. from Course Steered and distance run only]. It is therefore easier to plot but less informative than an EP.

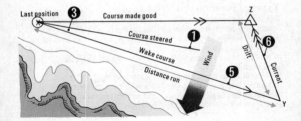

Obtaining a fix

INTRODUCTION

A fix is normally more accurate than an estimated position, so it is usually to be preferred to one. However, like an estimated position, a fix is as reliable only as the information on which it is based. You should assess its accuracy before placing too much reliance upon it.

Position lines are lines somewhere along which the boat is known to lie. They may be 'circles of position', as they are in the case of a distance off, or straight lines. At least two position lines are needed for a fix and the fix is more reliable if it can be confirmed by a third one. There is no reason why position lines of different types should not be crossed to produce a fix.

Although by itself it is not enough to fix your position exactly, a single position line can also be very valuable, since it limits the number of possible positions where you may be. In this way it may tell you whether you are clear of a particular danger or it may help to confirm your estimated position.

Angle of cut When objects are chosen for a fix they should be chosen so that the resulting position lines form a good angle with one another. In the case of two position lines 90° is ideal; for three 60° or 120° when one of the objects lies on the opposite side of the boat to the others.

Transits are the most reliable form of position line because they can be drawn straight on to the chart without the need of any instruments. For use at long range, however, the two objects forming the transit must be well separated.

Bearings should be taken of objects as near to the boat as possible. Objects on land are preferable to floating objects like buoys for visual bearings. Indeterminate features like headlands are not usually suitable.

Radar can detect objects only within its visual horizon. This means that it may pick up hills some distance inland long before it detects the nearby low-lying coastline. Radar is usually more accurate in providing ranges than it is in providing bearings.

Soundings seldom give a clear position line and are often highly ambiguous. However, they are extremely useful in darkness or fog, and may help to confirm a fix that has been obtained by other methods.

Types of position line

Transit formed by two objects or lights in line one behind the other
Compass bearing of an object or light taken with a hand bearing compass
DF bearing of a radio beacon taken with a direction finder
Rising or dipping distance of a light when it is level with the horizon
Vertical sextant angle formed by an object of known height

Horizontal sextant angle formed by two objects or lights
Celestial position line obtained from observation with a sextant
Radar range of an object appearing on a radar screen
Radar bearing of an object appearing on a radar screen
Soundings taken by echo sounder or lead line

Fix by cross bearings

THREE-POINT FIX

If two or more objects or lights marked on the chart
are visible you can find your position by taking bearings
of them with a hand bearing compass. With the aid of a
radio direction finder similar bearings can be taken using
radio beacons.

Two objects or beacons alone can be used but the
resulting fix is less reliable than that obtained by using three
bearings or more.

1 Take the bearings of all the objects or beacons in
quick succession.
2 Convert the bearings to True by applying the variation
if working from the True rose on the chart. Alternatively,
you can work from the Magnetic rose.
3 Plot the bearings on the chart.

The meeting point of the bearings is your position.

It is desirable to take all the bearings in quick
succession because your position is normally changing
as you take them.

If more than two bearings are used they rarely meet
at a single point. The size of the 'cocked hat' which they
form gives some indication of the accuracy of the fix.
Your position is not necessarily within the cocked hat but
it is likely to be in the same general area. It is prudent to
assume that you are on the side closest to danger.

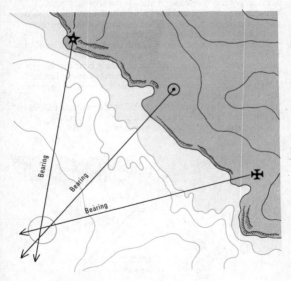

Running fix

POSITION FINDING FROM A SINGLE OBJECT

Even if there is only one object or light suitable for a bearing you can still obtain a reasonably accurate fix by taking two separate bearings of it at different times, provided you can plot your course between the two times accurately. The same technique can be used to obtain a fix from a pair of celestial observations taken at different times [see pages 62 and 63].

Since this method relies on there being a fairly substantial change in the bearing of the object it is mainly useful when sailing parallel to the coast.

1 Take the first bearing of the object. Note the time and log reading.
2 Steer a straight course until the bearing of the object has changed substantially.
3 Take the second bearing of the object. Note the time and log reading again.
4 Plot both bearings on the chart.
5 Plot your course made good between the times of the two bearings as you would for an EP [see page 53], starting from any convenient point on the first bearing.
6 Transfer the first bearing by drawing a line parallel to it through the end of your course plot.

The meeting point of the transferred bearing and the second bearing is your position.

Note that the reliability of the fix depends not only on accuracy of the bearings but also on the accuracy with which you plot your course. The method is exactly the same as for plotting an EP except that you begin at an arbitrary point anywhere along the first bearing.

It is not in fact necessary for both the bearings to be of the same object. If a pair of objects are not in view simultaneously a conventional fix by cross bearings is impossible. But by transferring a bearing of one object to a time when the other object is visible it is possible to obtain a fix by the method above.

A better indication of the reliability of a running fix can be obtained by taking three bearings of an object and transferring two of them to the time of the third.

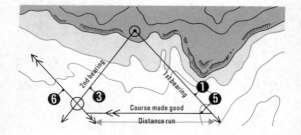

Rising & dipping distance of lights

FINDING DISTANCE OFF AT NIGHT

When approaching or departing from land at night you can find your distance off at the moment when the light of a lighthouse appears or disappears over the horizon, without having to plot anything on a chart, by using the Distance of Sea Horizon table on page 32. Your distance away from the object is equal to the total of the distance of the horizon from the lighthouse and the distance of the horizon from your eye level. A fix can be obtained if the bearing of the light is taken at the same time.

1 Take the bearing of the light at the moment when it is level with the horizon.
2 Find the distance off from the Distance of Sea Horizon table by adding the distance of sea horizon [A] for your height of eye above sea level to that [B] for the height of the light. The combined total is your distance off.
3 Plot the bearing on the chart and measure off the distance off along it.

The point thus found is your position.

Take great care to identify the light correctly. The rising and falling of the boat on a swell can interfere with the pattern of light flashes when the light is level with the horizon.

Make sure, too, that the light really is over the horizon and not out of sight for some other reason. The 'loom' of the light should be visible above the horizon when the light itself is not. When the light is exactly level with the horizon you should be able to make it appear and disappear by raising or lowering the level of your eye. This method of determining distance off is less accurate in rough weather when the exact moment that the light is level with the horizon may be hard to define.

The height of the light of a lighthouse is printed alongside it on the chart. This is the height above MHWS. If the tide is lower the extra height should be allowed for when using the Distance of Sea Horizon table. However, since failure to do so will give you a position nearer to the lighthouse than you really are, the resultant error may be looked upon as an added safety margin.

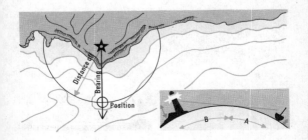

Vertical sextant angle

FINDING DISTANCE OFF WITH A SEXTANT

In daylight, when an object of known height, such as a lighthouse, and the shoreline immediately below it are visible you can find your distance off, without having to plot anything on a chart, by using a sextant and the Vertical Sextant Angle table on pages 33–36.

A good fix can be obtained if the bearing of the object is taken at the same time.

1 Adjust the sextant until the reflected image of the top of the object is level with the shoreline.
2 Read the sextant and correct the reading for index error, if necessary.
3 Take an accurate bearing of the object with a hand bearing compass.
4 Find the distance off from the Vertical Sextant Angle table. Look down the column for the height of the object until you come to the appropriate sextant angle, then read the distance off in the left hand column.
5 Plot the bearing on the chart and measure off the distance along it.

The point thus found is your position.

Note that you must be able to see the shoreline immediately below the object as well as the object itself. This means that if your height of eye is, say, 7ft [2.1m], it is not possible to measure the vertical sextant angle if your distance off is more than 3 miles because at such distances the shoreline is not visible because it is beyond the horizon.

The height of an object, if given, is printed alongside it on the chart. This is the height above MHWS. If the tide is lower the extra height should be allowed for when using the Vertical Sextant Angle table. However, since failure to do so will give you a position nearer to the object than you really are, this may be looked upon as an added safety margin.

In the case of a lighthouse, the height given on the chart is the height of the center of the lantern. So the sextant angle should be taken of that, *not* of the top of the tower.

A vertical sextant angle is also useful if you wish to make sure that you keep a certain distance away from an object. In that case set the sextant to the required angle in advance.

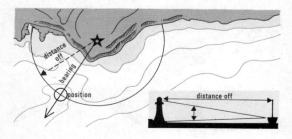

Horizontal sextant angle

OBTAINING A FIX WITH A SEXTANT

If three objects or lights marked on the chart are visible you can often obtain a good fix by measuring the angles between them with a sextant. The instrument must be held on its side and it may be easier to see the objects with the telescope removed.

The quickest way to plot the fix is with a station pointer but it can also be done using a piece of tracing paper. There are also various ways of plotting the fix geometrically.

1 Adjust the sextant until the image of, say, the left-hand object is level with the middle one.
2 Read the sextant and correct the reading for index error if necessary.
3 Repeat the operation for the right-hand pair of objects.
4 Set the arms of the station pointer to the appropriate angles and slide it around on the chart until it fits the positions of all three objects.

A pencil mark through the hole in the center of the station pointer marks your position.

The objects should be chosen so that the middle one is either roughly on a line between the other two or on the same side of it as you are. One of the objects may even be on the opposite side of the boat to the other two. Both the angles should be greater than 30°. It is essential that your position and those of the objects do not all lie on one circle.

If you do not have a station pointer you can draw the two angles on a piece of tracing paper. Slide the paper around until the lines fit the positions of the objects on the chart seen through it, then press through the paper with a sharp point to mark your position.

One method of plotting the fix geometrically using only a ruler and a protractor is to draw a straight line between both pairs of objects, then draw a line at right-angles to each of these lines seaward from both the outside objects. Now draw lines from the middle object to meet them at the angles for each pair of objects you obtained using the sextant. Draw a line between the apexes of the two triangles and drop a perpendicular from it, to pass through the middle object. Your position is at the base of the perpendicular.

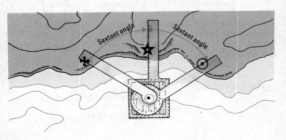

Calculators in navigation

TYPES AND THEIR USE

Within the past decade, electronic calculators have become increasingly popular and useful to navigators. The use of a calculator can save valuable time when making calculations for a navigational fix, particularly using a celestial body.

Although most modern calculators are extremely accurate, a calculated fix is only as accurate as the sight you take and the operation of your calculator. In addition, with some navigational problems, such as the calculation of Set and Drift, the results must be plotted. Therefore, it is just as easy to plot the information on to the chart in the first place. Nevertheless, when used to solve appropriate problems, the right calculator is an asset. Every navigator will find, among the many excellent models of calculator available on the market, one to suit his or her needs and budget.

Two basic types of calculator may be used for navigational purposes:
● **Scientific calculators** generally have algebraic, trigonometric, logarithmic, and exponential, as well as the usual arithmetic, functions. The functions required for navigational purposes are: $+$, $-$, $\times$, $\div$, sin, cos, tan, and an inverse [sometimes called arc] key for obtaining sec, cosec, and cot. Also, it is useful to have three memories or stores, and a key that converts degrees, minutes, and seconds into degrees and decimal parts of a degree.

A scientific calculator should be considered only as an aid, and not a substitute for a sound understanding of, and an ability to solve, navigational problems. To make calculations you need to know the correct formulas. These can be found in Bowditch's *The American Navigator*.
● **Pre-programmed and programmable calculators** vary in sophistication, from the simplicity of a scientific calculator to the complexity of a specialized computer. Their chips [minature electronic circuits] are programmed either during manufacture or at any time by the user. Some give a printed as well as a visual display. Depending on their sophistication, these calculators can store data, such as *The Nautical Almanac* and the tables in Bowditch, and will refer to such data as programmed, without the user's intervention. Pre-programmed and programmable calculators are fast and simple to use. They require little or no mathematical expertise but, again, their use should not be a substitute for a sound understanding of the principles involved. Probably the most sophisticated navigational calculator available is the Plath Navicomp, which is pre-programmed for all functions and has a built-in chronometer and nautical almanac.

Popular models

Tamaya NC-2	Texas Instruments 59
Tamaya NC-77	Hewlett-Packard 41C
Texas Instruments 58	Plath Navicomp

Celestial navigation

INTRODUCTION

Celestial navigation enables you to find out your position anywhere on the sea. Although it is mainly used offshore where other forms of navigation are not practicable, it can also be useful on coastal passages.

The tables in Chapter 1 of this almanac and the working methods on the following pages are concerned with obtaining position lines from the sun, which is the celestial body most commonly used by the yacht navigator.

Finding the sextant altitude of the sun This is the angle formed between the sun and the horizon which is measured with the sextant. The Sun Altitude Correction table [page 31] is for the *lower limb* of the sun [the lower edge of the sun's disc] and so it is that which must be aligned with the horizon when taking a sight. The table includes the correction for the sun's semidiameter.

A good practice for sights other than noon sights is to take a series of three sights and work the first two. If they do not correspond closely, work the third to find out which is in error.

Do not take sights when the altitude is less than about 10°

Timing sights Noon sights do not have to be timed although you need to know the time of local noon in order to know when to take them. Other sights must be timed to the nearest second as you take them.

The times for GHA and declination in the monthly tables [pages 6–29] are GMT. Normally, the chronometer will be on GMT wherever you are. If not, you will have to convert the time of your sights to GMT. For the times of broadcast time signals *see* Time ticks [page 87].

Tables All the information needed for finding latitude by a noon sight is contained in this almanac. Since much of it changes annually it is essential to have an almanac for the current year. Other sun sights require, in addition, a normal set of sight reduction tables for air or marine navigation. These have to be bought only once because they do not become out of date.

Index error This is what the sextant actually reads when it should read 0° and a correction for it must be applied to any sextant altitude. Index error can be measured at any time by aligning the reflected image of the horizon with the real horizon through the sextant. If the reading is 'on the arc' the correction is *subtracted* from the sextant altitude; if it is 'off the arc' it is *added*.

Fixes from celestial navigation To obtain a fix from a single celestial body like the sun it is necessary to obtain two position lines at different times and transfer the first one to the time of the second, exactly as for a running fix [*see* page 56]. As with any other fix, the position lines must make a good angle of 'cut' which means the sights must be separated by several hours.

You can also combine a position line from the sun with, say, a DF bearing if you are within range of a suitably placed radio beacon.

Noon sight
FINDING LATITUDE FROM THE SUN

This technique for finding your latitude requires only a
sextant and tables included in this almanac. The working
of the sight is straightforward and no plotting on the chart is
necessary. The only restriction is that you must know your
approximate longitude and the sight must be taken at local
noon, when the sun is at its highest point.

1 Find the time of local noon Look up the time of the
sun's meridian passage at Greenwich for the relevant day in
the bottom right-hand corner of the appropriate monthly
table [pages 6–29]. The time of local noon will be four
minutes *earlier* for each whole degree of longitude if you
are east of Greenwich meridian and four minutes *later* if
you are west of it.
2 Find the sextant altitude when the sun is at its highest
point. Keep the sun's lower limb aligned with the horizon
until it starts to fall. The sextant reading will then give the
maximum altitude.
3 Find the true altitude Three corrections have to be
applied—for index error [*see* page 61], dip of sea horizon and
the altitude correction. The last two are found from the
tables on page 31. The correction for dip is *subtracted* from
the sextant altitude. The altitude correction is *added* to it.
4 Find the zenith distance by subtracting the true
altitude from 90°.
5 Find the declination of the sun at local noon from the
relevant monthly table [pages 6–29]. As local noon is likely
to fall somewhere within one of the two-hourly periods, the
declination will be between the two figures shown. However,
you can estimate the correct figure for an intermediate time
simply enough.
6 Find the latitude by adding or subtracting the
declination from the zenith distance. If your latitude and the
declination are both north or both south you *add* the
declination to the zenith distance; if one is north and the
other south, you *subtract*.

The result is your latitude.

If you do not know the exact time of local noon it is possible
to find out by taking sights continuously until the sun is
observed to begin falling. The sextant reading will then give
the maximum altitude as above.

As well as being simple a noon sight is usually the most
accurate way of obtaining a single position line from the sun.

The method of finding latitude by noon sight is less
satisfactory when the sun's altitude is very great [i.e. close
to 90°] as it is near the tropics in summer. A slight change
in the working of step 6 is necessary if you are between the
equator and the sun's geographical position. Then latitude
equals declination *minus* zenith distance.

If you wish to obtain a fix it is a common and useful
practice to combine the latitude found at noon with a position
line from a sun sight taken in the morning or afternoon.

Sun sights
OTHER THAN NOON SIGHTS

This is the method to use at all times other than local noon.
The working is slightly more complicated than for a noon
sight and the sights must be accurately timed. Instructions
for finding the tabulated altitude and azimuth will be found
in the sight reduction tables.

1 Find the sextant altitude A method which reduces the
risk of error is described on page 61. All sights must be
timed exactly.

2 Find the true altitude The method is the same as for a
noon sight described on the opposite page.

3 Find the Greenwich hour angle of the sun for the time
of the sight, using the monthly tables [pages 6–29] and the
Sun GHA Correction table [page 30].

4 Determine the assumed position This should be as
near as possible to your estimated position, except that the
assumed latitude must be a whole number of degrees and the
assumed longitude must make the LHA a whole number of
degrees [see next step].

5 Find the local hour angle of the sun. This is the GHA
plus or minus your assumed longitude. *Add* the longitude
if it is east; *subtract* it if it is west. The answer must be a whole
number of degrees.

6 Find the declination of the sun at the time of the sight
by the method used opposite.

7 Find the tabulated altitude and azimuth These are
obtained from the sight reduction tables which you enter
with your assumed latitude, declination and LHA as
computed in steps 4, 5 and 6 above.

8 Find the intercept This is the difference between the
tabulated altitude and the true altitude. Convert it to
nautical miles [1 minute = 1 nautical mile].

9 Plot the position line on the chart. Mark the assumed
position and draw the azimuth through it [note that the
azimuth is a *True* bearing]. From the assumed position
measure off the intercept distance, *towards* the sun if the
true altitude is greater than the tabulated altitude, *away* from
the sun if the true altitude is smaller. Draw a line at right-
angles to the azimuth at this point.

This is your position line.

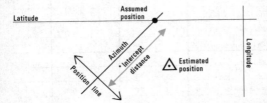

Work forms

FOR CELESTIAL NAVIGATION

Work forms are used, in conjunction with sight reduction tables and *The Nautical Almanac*, for the calculation of observations of celestial bodies. They are designed to simplify the work of the navigator and reduce the chance of

		M (W/O/G/T/m compass diagram)	M (W/m compass diagram)	M (W/m compass diagram)
	Star	KOCHAB		
	DR Latitude N S	36° 51′ N	° ′	°
	DR Longitude E W	124 20 W		
TIME	Date (Local)	3 DEC		
	Watch Time	06 h 11 m 54 s	h m s	h
	Watch Error F−, S+	+3 16		
	Zone Time	06 15 10		
	Zone Descr. E−, W+	+8		
	GMT	14 15 10		
	Date (Greenwich)	3 DEC		
LHA ♈	GHA ♈ (hrs)	282° 30′	° ′	°
	GHA increment (m:s)	3 48		
	GHA ♈	286 18		
	Asmd Longitude E+, W−	124 18 W		
	LHA ♈	162 00′	00′	
ALTITUDE	Index Corr. Off+, On−	° −01 ′	° ′	°
	Dip Corr. (9′) −	−03		
	Sum + −	−04		
	Hs (Sext. Alt.)	43 09		
	App. Alt.	43 05		
	Alt. Corr. + −	−01		
	Ho (Obs. Alt.)	43 04		
H.O. 249 VOL. I	Hc (Comp. Alt.) (Table)	43 15		
	a (Alt. Diff.) A T	A 11		
	Zn (Azimuth) (Table)	019°		
	Prec. & Nut. Corr. mi (Table 5) °	2 120°		
	Asmd Latitude N S	37° 00′ N	° 00′	°
	Asmd Longitude EW	124 18 W		

N. Lat. { L.H.A. greater than 180°......Zn=Z
        { L.H.A. less than 180°.........Zn=360°−Z

S. Lat. { L.H.A. greater than 180°......Zn=180°−Z
        { L.H.A. less than 180°.........Zn=180°+Z

error. The forms published by Davis Instruments Corporation—parts of which are shown on these pages–are accompanied by step-by-step instructions and are useful to those learning navigation as well as experienced navigators.

Celestial Body		SUN ☉		
DR Latitude N S		36 ° 51 S	° '	
DR Longitude E W		124 ° 20 W		
TIME Date (Local)		3 DEC		
Watch Time		11 h 15 m 24 s	h m s	h
Watch Error F–, S+		+ 3 16		
Zone Time		11 18 40		
Zone Descr. E–, W+		+8		
G M T		19 18 40		
Date (Greenwich)		3 DEC		
DEC. and L H A v (P ☾) +–		—		
GHA (hrs)		107 ° 24 '	° '	
GHA increment (m:s)		4 40		
v corr. / SHA		— '		
G H A		112 09		
Asmd Longitude E+, W–		124 09 W		
L H A		348 00 '	00 '	
d (P ☉ ☾) +–		+0.3		
Dec. (hrs) N S		22 ° 12.5	° '	
d corr. +–		—		
Declination N S		22 12 5		
ALTITUDE Index Corr. Off+, On–		9 01 '	° '	
Dip Corr. (9) –		– 03		
Sum +–		– 04		
Hs (Sext. Alt.)		71 30		
App. Alt.		71 26		
H.P. ☾ (Horiz. Par.)		+ (—) –	+ ( ) –	+ (
Alt. Corr. +–		+16		
Add'l Alt. Corr. +–				
Sum +–		+16 '	° '	
App. Alt.		71 26		
Ho (Obs. Alt.)		71 42		
H.O. 249 VOL. II & III Tab. Dec. NS		22 ° 00' S	° '	
Dec. Diff.		12 '		
d (Table) +–		+ 50		
Hc (Table)		71 ° 46 '	° '	
Correction +–		+ 10		
Hc (Comp. Alt.)		71 56		
Ho (Obs. Alt.)		71 42		
a (Alt. Diff.) A T		A 14		
Z (Table)		142		
Zn* (Azimuth)		038°		
Asmd Latitude N S		37 ° 00 'S	° 00 '	
Asmd Longitude E W		124 09 W		

* N. Lat. { L.H.A. greater than 180°......Zn=Z   { L.H.A. less than 180°...........Zn=360°–Z   S. Lat. { L.H.A. greater than 180°......Zn=180°–Z   { L.H.A. less than 180°...........Zn=180°+Z

Radio direction finding

POSITION FINDING FROM RADIO BEACONS

A radio direction finder enables you to obtain a position line or a fix up to 75 miles from land, depending on the range of the radio beacon. DF bearings are plotted on the chart in the same way as visual bearings and can be used for all types of fix.

1 Tune the receiver to the right frequency. Switch on the beat frequency oscillator or switch to 'navigate'.
2 When the beacon is heard adjust the tuning to obtain a clear signal.
3 Rotate the antenna while the beacon is transmitting the continuous note, until the null [position where it cannot be heard] is found.
4 Read the bearing on the compass in the middle of the null position.

This is the bearing of the radio beacon.

With a permanently mounted DF antenna the 360° scale beneath it usually gives the bearing relative to the vessel's head. This has to be compared with the course by the steering compass in order to determine the Magnetic bearing of the radio beacon.

Note that a null occurs when the antenna is pointing directly *away* from the beacon, as well as directly toward it. If it is not obvious which way the beacon lies take a second bearing farther along your course and then compare these two bearings.

Signal characteristics Most marine radio beacons are arranged in groups, all transmitting on the same frequency but in sequence so that only one is transmitting at any one time. Individual signals last one minute and the whole sequence takes six minutes, after which it is repeated. The signals of each beacon take the following form:
● Call sign in Morse Code repeated four times
● Continuous note for 25 seconds
● Call sign repeated once or twice
Beacons in groups of less than six may transmit more than once every six minutes. Beacons not in a group may transmit continuously or at regular intervals within a six-minute cycle.

Errors in DF bearings may arise in the following circumstances, when not too much reliance should be placed upon them:
● When the signal passes obliquely over the coast, not at right-angles to it
● At night and especially around sunset and sunrise. This error is less likely at ranges of less than 25 miles
● When the beacon is behind high ground
● When the beacon is beyond its listed range
● When there is a continuous metal lifeline round the boat
● When the bearing is about 45° off the bow or stern

Navigational radio beacons
UNITED STATES

The following table lists radio beacons generally suitable
for radio direction finding purposes. When choosing
beacons for direction finding bearings, you should be
aware of possible sources of error [*see* opposite page].
Aeronautical radio beacons like marine radio beacons,
broadcast a characteristic signal at a fixed frequency. Their
assigned frequencies are normally from 200 to 415 kHz
whereas the frequencies for marine radio beacons are
normally from 285 to 325 kHz. Aeronautical radio beacons
not within the marine radio beacon band are not listed.

Beacon	Characteristic	Range [miles]	Frequency [kHz]	Notes
Ohio				
Fairport Harbor West Breakwater Lt Marker Radiobeacon	series of 0.5 second dashes	Local use only	318	a
ATLANTIC COAST				
Maine				
West Quoddy Head Lt Stn	WQ ·—— — ——··	20	308	
Great Duck Island Lt Stn	GD ——·—···	50	286	
Matinicus Rock Lt Stn	MR —— ·—·	20	314	
Marina Island Fog Signal Stn	MI —— ··	100	286	
Cuckolds Lt Stn Marker	CU —·—· ··—	10	320	
Halfway Rock Lt Stn	HR ···· ·—·	10	291	
Portland Lighted Horn Buoy 'P'	PH ·——· ····	30	301	
Massachusetts				
Eastern Point Lt Stn	EP · ·——·	10	325	
Lynnfield Aeronautical	SEW ··· · ·——	100	382	
Boston Lighted Horn Buoy 'B'	BH —··· ····	30	304	
Scituate Harbor Marker	SH ··· ····	10	295	
Cape Cod Breakwater Lt Stn	CC —·—· —·—·	20	318	
Highland Lt Radiobeacon	HI ···· ··	100	286	
Catham Lt Stn	CH —·—· ····	20	311	
Brant Point Lt Marker	BP —··· ·——·	10	325	
Nantucket Shoals Lightship	NS —· ···	100	286	
Nobska Point Lt Stn	NP —· ·——·		291	
New Bedford East Barrier Lt Stn	NB —· —···	10	322	
Cleveland Ledge Lt Stn	CL —·—· ·—··	20	308	
Buzzards Bay Entrance Lt Stn	BB —··· —···	20	314	
Block Island Southeast Lt Stn	BI —··· ··	20	301	
Connecticut				
Saybrook Breakwater Lt Marker	SB ··· —···	10	320	
Rhode Island				
Brenton Reef Lt	BR —··· ·—·	10	295	
Point Judith Lt Stn	PJ ·——· ·———	10	325	
New York				
Montauk Point Lt Stn	MP —— ·——·	125	286	
Little Gull Island Lt Stn	J ·———	15	306	
Stratford Shoal Lt Stn	P ·——·	20	295	
Execution Rocks Lt Stn	K —·—	15	286	
Shinnecock Lt Marker	SN ··· —·	20	311	
Fire Island Lt Stn	RT ·—· —	15	291	

Beacon	Characteristic	Range [miles]	Frequency [kHz]	Notes
				a
South Buffalo South Side	B ━ ···	60	322	
Jones Inlet Marker	JI ·━━━ ··	10	319	
Kennedy Aeronautical	JF ·━━━ ··━·	25	373	
Ambrose Lt Stn	T ━	125	286	
Scotlan Lighted Horn Buoys Marker	S ···	10	294	
Rockaway Inlet Marker	RI ·━· ··	10	326	
New Jersey				
Manasquan Inlet	MI ━━ ··	20	308	
Barnegat Inlet Marker	BI ━··· ··	20	322	
Atlantic City Marker	AC ·━ ━·━·	15	316	
Cape May Marker	CM ━·━· ━━	10	325	
Five Fathom Bank Lighted Horn Buoy 'F'	F ··━·	10	312	
Delaware				
Cape Henlopen	HL ···· ·━··	125	298	
Indian River Inlet Marker	IR ·· ·━·	10	308	
Delaware Lighted Horn Buoy 'D'	D ━··	10	319	
Maryland				
Ocean City Inlet Marker	OC ━━━ ━·━·	10	293	
Virginia				
Wachapreague Inlet Marker	WI ·━━ ··	10	324	
Chesapeake Lt Stn	CO ━·━· ━━━	50	290	
North Carolina				
Diamond Shoal Lt Stn	DS ━·· ···	50	321	
Hatteras Inlet Lt Stn	HI ···· ··	30	309	
Cape Lookout	CL ━·━· ·━··	125	298	
Oak Island Lt Stn	OA ━━━ ·━	70	298	
Frying Pan Shoals Lt Stn	FP ··━· ·━━·	50	290	
South Carolina				
Georgetown Lt Stn	F ··━·	30	310	
Charleston Lt Stn [Sullivan's I]	S ···	125	298	
Georgia				
Tybee Lt Stn	TR ━ ·━·	125	317	
Florida				
Jacksonville Aeronautical	JA ·━━━ ·━	100	344	
St John's Lt Stn	R ·━·	125	306	
Cape Canaveral Lt Stn	Z ━━··	125	313	
Jupiter Inlet Lt Stn	J ·━━━	125	294	
Palm Beach Aeronautical	PB ·━━· ━···	50	356	
Hillsboro Inlet Lt Stn	Q ━━·━	25	299	
Miami	U ··━	100	322	
Marathon Aeronautical	MTH ━━ ━ ····		260	
Fish Hook Aeronautical	FIS ··━· ·· ···	100	332	
Dry Tortugas Lt Stn	OE ━━━ ·	130	286	
Egmont Key Lt Stn	H ····	170	310	
Cape San Blas Lt Stn	W ·━━	125	320	
Pensacola Aeronautical	PKZ ·━━· ━·━ ━━··	100	326	
Alabama				
Mobile Point [Rear Range] Lt Stn	C ━·━·	125	300	
Louisiana				
Mississippi River-Gulf Outlet Approach Lighted Horn Buoy 'NO' Marker	series of 0.5 second dashes	10	294	
South Pass West Jetty Lt Stn	M ━━	50	314	
Southwest Pass Entrance Lt Stn	OT ━━━ ━	125	307	
Southwest Pass Entrance Lt Stn	J4 ·━━━ ━ ····━ [twice]	5	287	
Calcasieu	UT ··━ ━	150	323	
Texas				
Sabine Pass	F ··━·	50	310	
Galveston	G ━━·	125	296	
Galveston Lt Stn	J5 ·━━━ ━ ····· [twice]	5	286	
Freeport Marker	R ·━·	20	290	

Beacon	Characteristic	Range [miles]	Frequency [kHz]	Notes
Aransas Pass Lt Stn	Z —— · ·	125	304	
Brazos Santiago [Padre I] Lt Stn	PIL · —— · · · · · —— · · ·	175	314	
PACIFIC COAST				
California				
Point Loma Lt Stn	L · —— · ·	150	302	
Los Angeles Harbor Lt Stn	A · —	70	302	
Point Arguello Lt Stn	O —— ——	150	302	
Point Loma Lt Stn Calibration Radiobeacon	Y2 —· —— · · —— · —— [twice]	10	480	
Mission Bay North Jetty Marker	MB —— —— · · · ·	15	317	
San Clemente Island Aeronautical	NUC —· · · —— — · — · N —·		350	
Oceanside Lt 6 Marker	OC —— —— — · — ·	10	323	
Avalon Harbor Marker	AV · — · · · —	10	307	
Dana Point Breakwater Lt 5	DP —· · · — — · ·	15	292	
Newport Bay West Jetty Lt 3 Marker	NE —· ·	15	285	
Long Beach Harbor Lt Stn	LB · —· · —· · ·	10	296	
Los Angeles Harbor Lt Stn	M2 —— · · —— · —— [twice]	10	480	
Redondo Beach West Jetty Lt 3	RB · —· —· · ·	15	319	
Marina Del Rey Lt 3 Marker	MR —— · — ·	10	289	
Channel Islands Harbor South Jetty Lt 2 Marker	CI —· — · · · ·	10	308	
Anacapa Island Lt Stn Marker	AN · — —·	10	323	
Ventura Marina South Jetty Lt 2	VM · · · — ——	15	314	
Santa Barbara Marker	SB · · · —· · ·	10	294	
San Luis Obispo Lt Stn	SL · · · · —· ·	20	288	
Morro Bay West Breakwater Lt Stn	series of 0.5 second dashes	15	310	b
Piedras Blancas Lt Stn Marker	PB · —— · · —· · ·	15	296	
Point Sur Lt Stn	S · · ·	50	322	
Pigeon Point Lt Stn	PI · —— · · · ·	40	286	
Point Pinos Lt Stn	P · —— ·	10	290	
Mass Landing Harbor Entrance Lt Stn	ML —— · —· ·	10	298	
Santa Cruz Breakwater Lt Stn	SC · · · — · — ·	10	294	
Farallon Stn	F · · —·	50	314	
San Francisco Approach Lighted Horn Buoy	SF · · · · · —·	17	305	
Bonita Point Lt Stn	series of 0.5 second dashes	10	296	c
Point Blunt Lt Stn	N2 —· · · —— —— [twice]	10	310	
Point Reyes Lt Stn	R · —·	10	292	
Bodega Head Radiobeacon	BO —· · · —— ——	20	325	
Point Arena Lt Stn	A · —	50	320	
Blunts Reef Lighted Horn Buoy 'B'	BR —· · · · —·	15	286	
Humboldt Bay	H · · · ·	50	300	
Trinidad Head	TR —· —·	15	292	
St George Reef Lt Stn	SG · · · —— · Long dash	20	310	
Chetlo River Entrance	B —· · · Long dash	20	296	

Sequence Unless otherwise noted, all broadcasts are continuous.
Notes
a Operates during navigation season
b Unreliable east of 306 degrees to the shore
c Vessels are requested to calibrate during daylight hours and to be sure to signal the station when calibration is completed.

The following rules are based on the International
Regulations for Preventing Collisions at Sea [1972] and are
substantially abridged. Yachtsmen should also be familiar
with the full text of the regulations.

Narrow channels Keep as near to the starboard [right]
side as practicable. A boat less than 65ft [20m] long or a
sailing boat must not impede a vessel that can navigate
safely only within the channel. You should never anchor in a
narrow channel.

Traffic separation schemes Avoid crossing the traffic
lanes if practicable. If you have to cross them, do so at
right angles and never tack in them.

Action by give-way vessel In any situation, the boat that
has to give way should take action as soon as possible and
make it substantial enough to be readily apparent to the
other vessel. If necessary, she should slow down or stop.

Action by stand on vessel In any situation, the boat that
has right of way should hold her course and speed, unless
it becomes apparent that the other vessel is not taking the
appropriate action or the only way of averting a collision is
to take avoiding action herself.

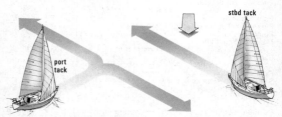

Vessels on opposite tacks The vessel on port tack should give way to the one on
starboard tack, either by tacking herself or passing astern.

Vessels on the same tack The vessel which is to windward should give way to the
vessel to leeward, either by luffing up or passing astern.

Vessels on opposite tacks The boat that has the wind on her port [left] side must keep out of the way of the one with the wind on her starboard [right] side, unless the latter is overtaking. On port tack, if you are uncertain whether a boat to windward is on the starboard tack or not you must keep out of her way. Do not cross ahead.
Vessels on the same tack When both boats have the wind on the same side the one which is the farther to windward must keep out of the way of the other, unless the latter vessel is being overtaken by the former.
Keep out of the way of any vessel which is restricted in her ability to maneuver or engaged in fishing.

Vessels approaching head-on must both alter course to starboard and pass to the right of one another. If you are in doubt whether such a situation exists you must assume it does and act accordingly.
Vessels on converging courses The boat that has the other on its starboard [right] side must keep out of the way, unless the other is overtaking.
Keep out of the way of any vessel that is for any reason restricted in its ability to maneuver, for example, a vessel engaged in fishing, or a sailing vessel.

Overtaking Notwithstanding any of the rules above, a vessel that is overtaking another must keep out of her way throughout the maneuver.

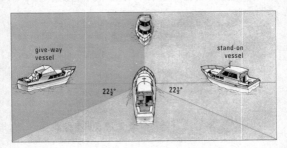

Vessels on converging courses The vessel in the dark sector should keep out of the way of the boat in the center. The vessel in the light sector has right of way. In the case of a vessel approaching head-on both vessels should alter course to starboard.

Overtaking All the vessels in the dark sector should keep out of the way of the vessel in the center.

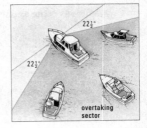

Shapes and sound signals

INTERNATIONAL REGULATIONS

Shapes are exhibited by day. Except where their position has a special significance, as described below, they should be hoisted wherever they can best be seen.
Sound signals in restricted visibility are used whenever conditions dictate, by day or night.
Maneuvering and warning signals are for use by power-driven vessels. Except for the last two, they are used only by vessels in sight of one another.

For purposes of these regulations a sailing yacht under power is regarded as a power-driven vessel, with the exception that when 'motor-sailing' she should display an inverted cone as described below.

Shapes

- Vessel proceeding under sail when also propelled by machinery [i.e. motor-sailing]
- Vessel engaged in fishing. Vessels under 65.6ft [20m] long may exhibit a basket instead
- Nets or gear extending more than 164yds [150m]. Exhibited in addition to the above, the position of the cone indicates the direction of the gear

- Vessel towing or being towed when length of tow exceeds 219yds [200m]
- Vessel at anchor. The ball is exhibited over her fore part
- Vessel aground. Exhibited in addition to those for a vessel at anchor
- Vessel engaged in dredging or underwater operations. The side with the two diamonds is where it is safe to pass

Sound signals in restricted visibility

- ▬ ▬ Power-vessel making way
- ▬ ▬ Power-vessel under way but not making way through the water
- ▬ •• Vessel not under command, vessel restricted in her ability to maneuver, vessel constrained by her draft, sailing vessel, vessel engaged in fishing, vessel towing or pushing
- ▬ ••• Vessel being towed

- Vessel at anchor. In the case of a vessel more than 328ft [100m] long the bell is rung in the fore part of the vessel and followed by 5-second sounding of a gong aft
- • ▬ • Warning signal to an approaching vessel made in addition to the signal above

Vessel aground

Maneuvering and warning signals

- • I am altering course to starboard
- •• I am altering course to port
- ••• I am operating astern propulsion
- ▬ ▬ • I intend to overtake you on your starboard [right] side
- ▬ ▬ ••• I intend to overtake you on your port [left] side

- ▬ • ▬ • Agreement [by vessel about to be overtaken]
- •••• I am in doubt whether you are taking sufficient action to avoid a collision
- ▬ Vessel approaching a bend or obstruction to vision
- ▬ Answer [by vessel approaching the other way]

Lights

INTERNATIONAL REGULATIONS

All vessels must show the correct lights at night and at other times when visibility is restricted, whether at anchor or under way.

Masthead light is a fixed white light over the fore-and-aft centerline of the vessel which is visible from ahead round to an angle of $22\frac{1}{2}°$ abaft the beam on both sides.

Sidelights are red and green lights visible on the port and starboard sides respectively from directly ahead to an angle of $22\frac{1}{2}°$ abaft the beam.

Sternlight is a white light placed as near the stern as possible and visible astern from an angle of $22\frac{1}{2}°$ abaft the beam on either side.

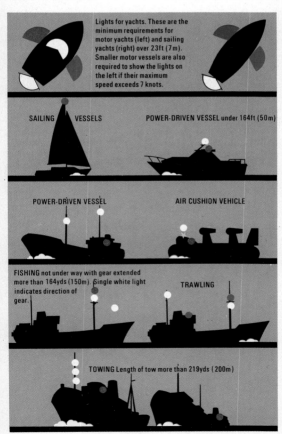

Lights for yachts. These are the minimum requirements for motor yachts (left) and sailing yachts (right) over 23ft (7m). Smaller motor vessels are also required to show the lights on the left if their maximum speed exceeds 7 knots.

SAILING VESSELS

POWER-DRIVEN VESSEL under 164ft (50m)

POWER-DRIVEN VESSEL

AIR CUSHION VEHICLE

FISHING not under way with gear extended more than 164yds (150m). Single white light indicates direction of gear.

TRAWLING

TOWING Length of tow more than 219yds (200m)

Vessels under 65.6ft [20m] **long** may have sidelights combined in one lantern on the centerline.

Vessels under 39.4ft [12m] long may have sidelights and sternlight combined in one lantern at the top of the mast. Vessels under 23ft [7m] long should carry sidelights and sternlight if practicable. If not there must be a torch or other white light ready to be shone in time to prevent collision.

Vessels under 164ft [50m] long are not obliged to carry a second masthead light. Vessels under 23ft [7m] long with a maximum speed of less than 7 knots may show a single all-round white light instead of other lights. If possible they should also have sidelights.

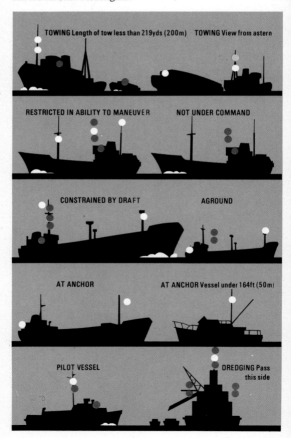

Aids to navigation

MARKING SYSTEMS

There are Intracoastal Waterway markers [along the Atlantic and Gulf coasts] and state markers within certain state areas [such as crowded inlets and lakes]. However, these marker systems are generally compatible.

Intracoastal Waterway aids to navigation are distinguished by a special yellow border or other yellow mark. On this waterway, black markers are on the port and red markers on the starboard side of the channel entering from north and east and traversed to south and west respectively.

State "Regulatory Markers" use international orange geometric shapes with a white background on a sign or buoy.

Navigable waters except ICW and Western Rivers

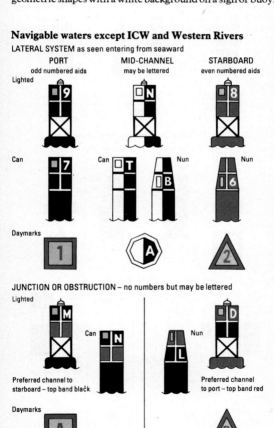

The Intracoastal Waterway
LATERAL SYSTEM as seen entering from N and E – proceeding to S and W

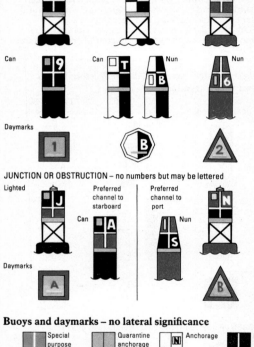

PORT
odd numbered aids

MID-CHANNEL
may be lettered

STARBOARD
even numbered aids

Lighted

Can

Daymarks

JUNCTION OR OBSTRUCTION – no numbers but may be lettered

Lighted

Preferred channel to starboard

Preferred channel to port

Daymarks

Buoys and daymarks – no lateral significance

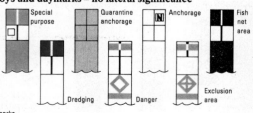

Special purpose

Quarantine anchorage

Anchorage

Fish net area

Dredging

Danger

Exclusion area

Daymarks

On Western Rivers
As seen entering from seaward

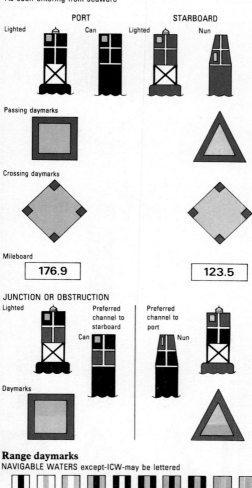

PORT
Lighted Can

STARBOARD
Lighted Nun

Passing daymarks

Crossing daymarks

Mileboard

176.9

123.5

JUNCTION OR OBSTRUCTION

Lighted Preferred channel to starboard Can

Preferred channel to port Nun Lighted

Daymarks

Range daymarks
NAVIGABLE WATERS except-ICW-may be lettered

INTRACOASTAL WATERWAY-may be lettered

Dual purpose marking

WHERE ICW AND OTHER WATERWAYS COINCIDE

When following the ICW from New Jersey through Texas, the triangular mark should be kept to starboard and the square to port, regardless of the color of the aid on which they appear.

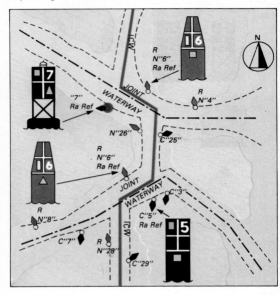

DUAL PURPOSE BUOYS

DUAL PURPOSE DAYMARKS

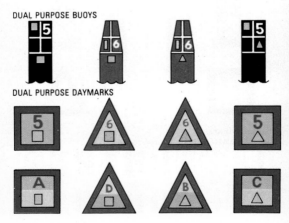

State marking system

MARKERS AND BUOYS

Regulatory markers

DANGER

CONTROLLED AREA

Buoys used to display regulatory markers – may show white light
may be lettered

BOAT EXCLUSION AREA

INFORMATION

Cardinal system

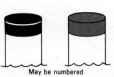

May be lettered
Do not pass between
buoy and nearest shore

May be numbered
Pass to North
or East of buoy

Pass to South
or West of buoy

Lateral system

MOORING
BUOY

PORT

STARBOARD

LOOKING UPSTREAM

SIGNALS AND SIGNALING
Code flags
INTERNATIONAL

Code flags are generally hoisted one below the other in groups of up to four which read from top to bottom. A gap of 6ft [2m] is left between groups when more than one is hoisted on a single halyard. Flag signaling is normally used only for code signals but words may also be spelt out letter by letter in the normal way.

Answering pendant is hoisted halfway up the halyard when a signal is first seen and is raised to the top when it has been received and understood. The sender hoists it fully to indicate the end of a signal, which the receiver acknowledges in the same way. It is also used to indicate a decimal point.

Substitute flags are used if a letter or numeral occurs more than once in a group and the sender does not have another set of flags. The first substitute stands for the first flag in the group, the second for the second, and the third for the third.
Code flag 'A' While [generally] flag signaling does not impinge much on the cruising yachtsman, particular attention should be paid to vessels, large and small, flying code flag 'A' or a rigid replica of it. This means that diving operations are in progress and you should keep clear.

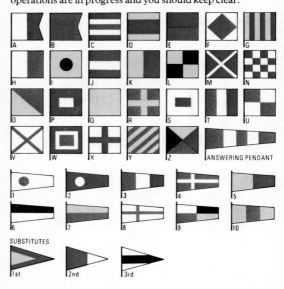

Morse Code

INTERNATIONAL

Morse code is generally transmitted with an Aldis lamp, torch or other light source. It can be used for code signals or to send messages in plain language. Sound signaling is not recommended, except for single-letter code signals or in an emergency. It is potentially dangerous to use sound signaling in crowded waters or in fog, except for that prescribed by the International Regulations for Preventing Collisions at Sea [*see* page 72].

Morse can also be transmitted by flag or arm signaling in the same way as semaphore, a dot being indicated by raising both arms vertically and a dash by extending them sideways. However, this is a very slow method of signaling.

The procedure signals at the bottom of the page are used when sending Morse by flashing light.

General call [call for unknown station] is used to attract the attention of the receiver.
Answering signal is repeated until the sender ceases the general call and/or the receiver is ready to receive the message.
Word received signal is made at the end of each word or code group provided the receiver is sure that he/she has received it correctly. It not he/she waits for it to be repeated.
Erase signal is made immediately the sender realises that he/she has made a mistake. The receiver acknowledges with the same signal whereupon the sender repeats the word or group correctly.

Morse code

A	· —		N	— ·		1	· — — — —
B	— · · ·		O	— — —		2	· · — — —
C	— · — ·		P	· — — ·		3	· · · — —
D	— · ·		Q	— — · —		4	· · · · —
E	·		R	· — ·		5	· · · · ·
F	· · — ·		S	· · ·		6	— · · · ·
G	— — ·		T	—		7	— — · · ·
H	· · · ·		U	· · —		8	— — — · ·
I	· ·		V	· · · —		9	— — — — ·
J	· — — —		W	· — —		0	— — — — —
K	— · —		X	— · · —			
L	· — · ·		Y	— · — —			
M	— —		Z	— — · ·			

End of message $\overline{AR}$	· — · — ·
Waiting signal $\overline{AS}$	· — · · ·
Full stop or decimal point $\overline{AAA}$	· — · — · —

Signals for flashing lights transmission

General call $\overline{AA}$, etc.	· — · —
Answering signal $\overline{TTTTTT}$	— — — — — —
Word received signal T	—
Erase signal $\overline{EEEEEE}$	· · · · · ·

Code signals

INTERNATIONAL

The following signals may be made by any signaling method. Their meanings are understood internationally.

Single-letter signals Each letter of the alphabet, except for 'R', is a complete signal when transmitted individually by any signaling method. For a complete list of these signals and their meanings, which are either very urgent or are in common use, *see* front endpaper.

Procedure signals are used to facilitate the business of sending and receiving messages. In addition to those listed below, there are other procedure signals peculiar to particular signaling methods.

Two-letter signals These signals are also useful but are less commonly needed than single-letter ones. A selection of two-letter signals likely to be useful is listed below.

Procedure signals

AA	All after . . . *Used after RPT means* Repeat all after . . .
AB	All before . . . *Used after RPT means* Repeat all before . . .
AR	*Ending signal, or end of transmission or signal.*
AS	*Waiting signal, or period.*
BN	All between . . . and . . . *Used after RPT means* Repeat all between . . . and . . .
CS	What is the name or identity signal of your vessel [*or* station]?
DE	From . . . *Used to precede the name or identity signal of the calling station or vessel.*
NO	Negative [No *or* The significance of the previous group should be read in the negative]. *When used in voice transmission the pronunciation should be 'No'.*
OK	*Acknowledging a correct repetition or* It is correct.
R	Received *or* I have received your last signal.
RQ	*Interrogative or* The significance of the previous group should be read as a question.
RPT	*Repeat signal.* I repeat *or* Repeat what you have sent *or* Repeat what you have received.
WA	Word or group after . . . *Used after RPT means* Repeat word or group after . . .
WB	Word or group before . . . *Used after RPT means* Repeat word or group before . . .

Two-letter signals

AC	I am abandoning my vessel.
AG	You should abandon your vessel as quickly as possible.
AH	You should not abandon your vessel.
AL	I have a physician on board.
AN	I need a physician.
BR	I require a helicopter urgently.
CB	I require immediate assistance.
CB7	I require immediate assistance; I have sprung a leak.
CJ	Do you require assistance?
CK	Assistance is not [*or* is no longer] required by me [*or* vessel indicated].

CV	I am unable to give assistance.
DV	I am drifting.
EF	SOS/MAYDAY has been canceled.
FA	Will you give me my position?
GW	Man overboard. Please take action to pick him up.
JL	You are running the risk of going aground.
JM	You are running the risk of going aground at low water.
KF	I require a tug.
LO	I am not in my correct position *to be used by a light vessel.*
LX	The canal is clear.
LY	The canal is not clear.
MC	There is an uncharted obstruction in the channel/fairway. You should proceed with caution.
NB	There is fishing gear in the direction you are heading.
NC	I am in distress and require immediate assistance.
NE	You should proceed with great caution.
NF	You are running into danger.
NG	You are in a dangerous position.
NH	You are clear of all danger.
PD	Your navigation light(s) is (are) not visible.
PI	You should maintain your present course.
PJ	I cannot maintain my present course.
PK	I cannot steer without assistance.
PM	You should follow in my wake [*or* wake of vessel indicated].
PP	Keep well clear of me.
PS	You should not come any closer.
QD	I am going ahead.
QI	I am going astern.
QQ	I require health clearance.
QT	You should not anchor. You are going to foul my anchor.
QU	Anchoring is prohibited.
QX	I request permission to anchor.
RF	Will you lead me to a safe anchorage?
RU	Keep clear of me; I am maneuvering with difficulty.
RV2	You should proceed into port.
RY	You should proceed at slow speed when passing me [*or* vessels making this signal].
SO	You should stop your vessel instantly.
UG	You should steer in my wake.
UH	Can you lead me into port?
UM	The harbor is closed to traffic
UP	Permission to enter harbor is urgently requested. I have an emergency case.
YG	You appear not to be complying with the traffic separation scheme.
YU	I am going to communicate with your station by means of the International Code of Signals.
YZ	The words which follow are in plain language.
ZD1	Please report me to Coast Guard, New York.
ZD2	Please report me to Lloyds, London.
ZL	Your signal has been received but not understood.

VHF radiotelephony
PROCEDURES

For radio distress, urgency and security procedures *see* page 101. The procedures below are for normal communications between yachts and shore stations or other vessels.

Always bear in mind that VHF channels are shared between hundreds of users, so keep communications short and to the point.

Calling a coast radio station Initial contact is made on Channel 16, except for some continental stations which are called on their working frequency. There is no need to use your call sign unless there is a possibility of confusion or the coast station needs it for charging a telephone call, etc. The name of the station called or the yacht calling should not be repeated more than three times. Once contact is established it should not be necessary to say it more than once. When calling give an indication of the channels at your disposal which are also working channels of the coast station.

The following procedure is for a yacht wishing to make a telephone call to a number on shore. The same procedure may be used, with appropriate modifications, for a telegram, request for a weather forecast, etc.

> **Marine Operator, Marine Operator, Marine Operator. This is Shearwater. One telephone call please. I have Channels 4 and 28. Over.**

The coast station replies on Channel 16:

> **Shearwater. This is Marine Operator. Channel 28 and stand by. Over.**

To this the yacht answers, still on Channel 16:

> **Marine Operator. This is Shearwater. Channel 28. Over.**

The yacht then switches to Channel 28 and waits for the coast station to call:

> **Shearwater. This is Marine Operator. What number do you want? Over.**

The yacht replies giving her call sign:

> **Marine Operator. This is Shearwater. Call sign Mike Alfa Delta Charlie. I have a call for Southampton 66821. I say again Southampton 66821. Over.**

The coast station will answer:

> **Shearwater. This is Marine Operator. Stand by.**

The yacht now waits for the connection to be made when the coast station will call again on the same frequency.

Calling another vessel Initial contact is made on Channel 16 before switching to an intership channel:

> **Fulmar, Fulmar, Fulmar. This is Shearwater. Channel 6. Over.**

The other vessel replies on Channel 16:

> **Shearwater. This is Fulmar. Roger Channel 6. Over.**

At this point both vessels switch to the agreed channel.

Traffic lists contain the names or call signs of vessels for which there are messages. They are transmitted by coast stations at certain times every day, on a normal working frequency and are preceded by an announcement on Channel 16. If there is traffic for you, you should contact the coast radio station in the normal way.

Phonetic alphabet

This may be used for transmissions in plain language or code. The syllables underlined should be stressed.

A	Alfa	<u>al</u> fah
B	Bravo	<u>brah</u> voh
C	Charlie	<u>char</u> lee or <u>shar</u> lee
D	Delta	<u>dell</u> tah
E	Echo	<u>eck</u> oh
F	Foxtrot	<u>foks</u> trot
G	Golf	golf
H	Hotel	hoh <u>tell</u>
I	India	<u>in</u> dee ah
J	Juliet	<u>jew</u> lee ett
K	Kilo	<u>key</u> loh
L	Lima	<u>lee</u> mah
M	Mike	mike
N	November	no <u>vem</u> ber
O	Oscar	<u>oss</u> cah
P	Papa	pah <u>pah</u>
Q	Quebec	keh <u>beck</u>
R	Romeo	<u>row</u> me oh
S	Sierra	see <u>air</u> rah
T	Tango	<u>tang</u> go
U	Uniform	<u>you</u> nee form or
		<u>oo</u> nee form
V	Victor	<u>vik</u> tah
W	Whiskey	<u>wiss</u> key
X	Xray	<u>ecks</u> ray
Y	Yankee	<u>yang</u> key
Z	Zulu	<u>zoo</u> loo

Should it be necessary, for clarity, to spell out a word; you should use the proword 'I spell' after pronouncing the word and proceed to spell the word using the phonetic alphabet thus:

Yacht, I spell,
Yankee Alfa Charlie Hotel Tango,
Yacht.

Prowords

The following procedure words are commonly used to facilitate radiotelephone communication.

Acknowledge Have you received and understood my message?

Affirmative Yes, or permission granted.

All before . . . , all after . . . Used to identify part of a message to be repeated.

Correction . . . An error has been made. The correct version is . . .

Go ahead Proceed with your message.

How do you read? Can you understand what I am saying?

I say again . . . I am repeating the following . . .

I spell . . . Used before spelling out a word

Negative No.

Out My transmission is over and I do not expect a reply.

Over My transmission is over and I expect a reply.

Received Acknowledgment of receipt of a message.

Read back Please repeat the whole message.

Repeat . . . I am repeating the following word[s] which are important . . .

Roger Message received and understood.

Say again Please repeat.

Seelonce [Silence] All stations keep silence and await instructions.

Wait Used when receiver cannot reply at once. May be followed by a number to indicate the number of minutes' waiting to expect.

Numerals

When transmitted by radiotelephone numerals should be pronounced in the following way. Numbers above 9 should be transmitted digit by digit. Thus 21 is spoken as 'two one'.

1	wun	6	six
2	too	7	<u>sev</u> en
3	tree	8	ait
4	<u>fow</u> er	9	<u>nin</u> er
5	fife	0	zero

VHF channels
CALLING, INTERSHIP AND PUBLIC CORRESPONDENCE

The VHF channels listed at the bottom of the page have been allocated for the purposes shown. The allocation is not necessarily exclusive. In addition to the allocations mentioned below, certain channels have been designated for communications relating to port operations and ship movements, which are mainly of concern to larger vessels.

Distress, safety and calling channel This is generally used for making initial contact with a ship or shore station before transferring to the appropriate working channel. Apart from calling, it is *never* used for traffic other than distress or urgency communications. Some European coast radio stations prefer initial contact to be made on their working channel. French stations are unlikely to answer anything but distress calls on Channel 16.

Intership channels Channel 6 is the primary intership channel and it is also used for search and rescue communications between ships and aircraft. Yachtsmen should not use channel 6 if it is being used for this purpose. Of the other intership frequencies, Channels 8, 70, 72 and 77 are preferable to the rest which are allocated for other purposes as well as intership communications.

Public correspondence channels for communicating with shore stations are obtained after initial contact has been made with Marine Operator on Channel 16.

Small craft safety channel Apart from any other uses, Channel 67 is used in the UK for the exchange of safety communications between small craft and the coastguard service in situations that do not justify the use of distress or urgency procedures.

Marina channel In the UK Channel M is used for communication between yachts and marinas or yacht clubs which have their own VHF stations. It may also be used for controlling club rescue boats and for communications between the committee boat and the shore during a regatta.

Allocation	Channel	MHz
Distress, safety and calling	16	156.800
Marine Operator	16	156.800
Small craft safety	67	156.375
Marina Channel	M	157.850
Intership	6	156.300
	8	156.400
	9	156.450
	10	156.500
	13	156.650
	67	156.375
	69	156.475
	70	156.625
	72	156.625
	73	156.675
	77	156.875

Time ticks
NATIONAL BUREAU OF STANDARDS SERVICES

The usual method of determining radio chronometer error and daily rate is by radio time signals, or time ticks. Most maritime nations broadcast time signals several times daily from one or more stations, and a vessel equipped with a radio receiver normally has no difficulty in obtaining a time tick anywhere in the world.

The National Bureau of Standards [NBS] broadcasts time signals continuously from stations WWV [near Fort Collins, Colorado] and WWVH [Kekaha-Kawai, Hawaii] on frequencies 2.5, 5, 10, 15 and 20 MHz, and also on 25 MHz from Fort Collins only. For the hourly broadcast format of these stations *see* chart below. The NBS also broadcasts from its low frequency station WWVB at Fort Collins.

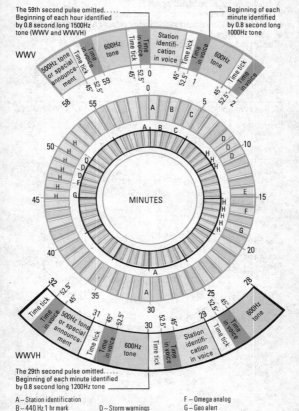

A – Station identification
B – 440 Hz 1 hr mark
C – NBS reserved
D – Storm warnings
E – Propagation forecasts
F – Omega analog
G – Geo alert
H – No audio tone

5 WEATHER FORECASTS
Continuous broadcasts

The National Weather Service VHF-FM stations listed
below broadcast continuously, 24 hours a day. The
broadcast contents vary but, in general, contain:
- Description of the weather patterns affecting the
broadcast area, including coastal waters.
- Regional and state forecasts with outlook for the third day.
- Marine forecasts and warnings for coastal waters.
- Observations from selected National Weather Service
and Coast Guard stations.
- Radar summaries and reports.
- Local weather observations and forecasts.
- Special bulletins and summaries concerning severe weather.
- Tide reports.

The broadcast tapes are up-dated every 3 to 6 hours.

City	Station	Frequency/MHz	City	Station	Frequency/MHz
Ellsworth, Me	KEC-93	162.40	Tampa, Fla	KHB-32	162.55
Portland, Me	KDO-95	162.55	West Palm Beach, Fla	KEC-50	162.40
Boston, Mass	KHB-35	162.40	New Orleans, La	KHB-43	162.55
Hyannis, Mass	KEC-73	162.55			
New York, NY	KWO-35	162.55	*Baton Rouge, La	KHB-46	162.45
New London, Conn	KHB-47	162.40	Mobile, Ala	KEC-61	162.55
Lewes, Del	WXJ-94	162.55	Pensacola, Fla	KEC-86	162.40
Philadelphia, Pa	KIH-28	162.475	Brownsville, Texas	KHB-33	162.55
Atlantic City, NJ	KHB-38	162.40	Corpus Christi, Texas	KHB-41	162.55
Baltimore, Md	KEC-83	162.40	Galveston, Texas	KHB-40	162.55
Washington, DC	KHB-36	162.55	Lake Charles, La	KHB-42	162.55
Salisbury, Md	KEC-92	162.40			
Norfolk, Va	KHB-37	162.55	Crescent City/ Brookings	KIH-37	162.55
Cape Hatteras, NC	HIG-77	162.55	Pt. Arena, Calif	KIH-30	162.40
Charleston, SC	KHB-29	162.55	San Luis Obispo, Calif	KIH-31	162.55
Jacksonville, Fla	KHB-39	162.55	Redwood City, Calif	KHB-49	162.55
Myrtle Beach, SC	KEC-95	162.40	Monterey, Calif	KEC-49	162.40
New Bern, NC	KEC-84	162.40	Eureka, Calif	KEC-82	162.40
Savannah, Ga	KEC-85	162.40	Sacramento, Calif	KEC-57	162.40
Wilmington, NC	KHB-31	162.55	Astoria, Ore	KEC-91	162.40
Daytona Beach, Fla	KIH-26	162.40	Coos Bay, Ore	KIH-32	162.40
Key West, Fla	KIH-25	162.40	Eugene, Ore	KEC-42	162.40
Miami, Fla	KHB-34	162.55	Neah Bay, Wash	KIH-36	162.55
Panama City, Fla	KGG-67	162.55	Newport, Ore	KIH-33	162.55
Tallahassee, Fla	KIH-24	162.40	Portland, Ore	KIG-98	162.55
			Seattle, Wash	KHB-60	162.55

* On the hour and at 10 minute intervals thereafter, 24 hours a day.

Weather bulletins

The following stations broadcast marine weather forecasts and warnings by marine radiotelephone stations on the frequencies and at the times shown.

Location	Station	Frequencies [kHz/MHz]	Broadcast times [local]
Boston, Mass	NMF [USCG]	2670 [A3H] † 2670 [A3H] ‡ 157.1 MHz [ch 22]	0540 1740 2340* Warnings at 1140 and on receipt
	WOU [Tel Co]	2450 [A3H] 2506 [A3H] +2566 [A3H]	0520 0620 1120 1720 2320 [warnings on receipt and on odd hours].
	KCD-817 [Tel Co]	161.9 MHz [ch 26]	
New York, NY	WOX [Tel Co]	+2482 [A3H] 2522 [A3H] 2590 [A3H]	0715 1215 1915 [warnings on receipt and 15 minutes past odd hours]
New York, NY [Shinnecock]	NMY-41 [USCG]	2670 [A3H] 2670 [A3J]	May 15 – Oct 15: 0420 0720 1020 1320 1620 1920
		† 2670 [A3H] ‡ 157.1 MHz [ch 22]	Warnings on receipt
Cape May, NJ	NMK [USCG]	2670 [A3J]	0600 1800* May 15 – Oct 15: 0445 0745 1045 1345 1645 1945
		† 2670 [A3J] ‡ 157.1 MHz [ch 22]	Warnings on receipt
Ocean Gate, NJ	WAQ [Tel Co]	2558 [A3H]	0715 1915 [warnings on receipt and 15 minutes past odd hours]
	WOO [AT & T]	∅ 4390.2 [A3A] ∅ 8557.6 [A3A] ∅ 13175.5 [A3A] ∅ 17321.5 [A3A] ∅ 22657 [A3A]	0800 2000 [offshore waters; New England waters; West Central North Atlantic]
Washington, DC	NMH [USCG]	∅ 4393.4 [A3J] ∅ 6521.8 [A3J] ∅ 8760.8 [A3J]	0500 2300* [offshore waters; New England waters; West Central North Atlantic]
		∅ 6521.8 [A3J] ∅ 8760.8 [A3J] ∅ 13144 [A3J]	1100 1700* [same forecasts as above]
Norfolk, Va	WGB [Tel Co]	+2450 [A3H] 2538 [A3H]	0000 0600 1200 1800 [warnings on receipt]
Portsmouth, Va	NMN [USCG]	† 2670 [A3J] ‡ 157.1 MHz [ch 22]	Warnings at 0020 1220* and on receipt
		#4393.4 [A3J] #6521.8 [A3J] #8760.8 [A3J]	0500 2300* [offshore waters; New England waters; West Central and Southwest North Atlantic]
		#6521.8 [A3J] #8760.8 [A3J] #13144 [A3J]	1100 1700* [same forecasts as above]
		4428.8 [A3J] 6506.4 [A3J] 8765.4 [A3J] 13113.2 [A3J]	0500 1100 1700 [offshore waters] Carrier frequency
Fort Macon, NC	NMN-37 [USCG]	2670 [A3J] † 2670 [A3J] 2670 [A3H] ‡ 157.1 MHz [ch 22]	0630 1200* Warnings on receipt
		2670 [A3H] ‡ 2670 [A3H] ‡ 157.1 MHz [ch 22]	0600 1200* Warnings on receipt

Location	Station	Frequencies [kHz/MHz]	Broadcast times [local]
Charleston, SC	NMB [USCG]	† 2670 [A3H]	1120 2320* [warnings on receipt]
		‡ 157.1 MHz [ch 22]	0600 1200 1700* [warnings on receipt]
	WJO [Tel Co]	2566 [A3H]	0715 1915 [warnings on receipt and on even hours thereafter]
Jacksonville, Fla	WNJ [Tel Co]	2566	0700 1900 [warnings on receipt and on odd days]
Mayport, Fla	NMA-10 [USCG]	† 2670 [A3H]	0120 0820 1020 1320* [warnings on receipt]
		‡ 157.1 MHz [ch 22]	0610 1210 1710* [warnings on receipt]
		† 2670 [A3J]	0120 1320* [warnings on receipt]
		‡ 157.1 MHz [ch 22]	0710 0910 1210 1710 [warnings on receipt]
Miami, Fla	WOM [AT & T]	#4428.6 [A3J] #8792.8 [A3J]	0700 2300 [offshore waters: West Central North Atlantic; Caribbean Sea; Gulf of Mexico]
		#4422.2 [A3J] #8796 [A3J]	0000 0600 [same forecasts as above]
	WDR [Tel Co]	+2442 2490 +2514	0715 1915 [warnings on receipt and on odd hours]
Miami Beach, Fla	NCF [USCG]	† 2670 [A3J]	1050 2250* [warnings on receipt]
		‡ 157.1 MHz [ch 22]	0730 0830 1230 1730* [warnings on receipt]
Key West, Fla	NOK [USCG]	‡ 157.1 MHz [ch 22]	0700 1200 1700 [warnings on receipt]
St Petersburg, Fla	NMA-21 [USCG]	† 2670 [A3J]	0920 2220 [warnings on receipt]
		‡ 157.1 MHz [ch 22]	0750 0950 1250 1750 [warnings on receipt]
Tampa, Fla	WFA [Tel Co]	2466 [A3H] +2550 [A3H]	0700 1900 [warnings on receipt and even hours]
Mobile, Ala	WLO	2572 161.9 MHz	On odd hours
New Orleans, La	NMG	2670	0350 0550 0750 1150 1350 1550 1750 2350
	WAK	2482 2558 2598	0800 2300
Corpus Christi, Tex	KCC	2538	0600 1800 and on request
Galveston, Tex	KQP	2530	0000 1200
	NOY	2670	0320 0520 0720 1120 1320 1520 1720 2320
Port Isabel, Tex	NCH	2670	0700 1100 1700
Swan Island	WSG	2738	1105 and on request
Eureka, Calif	KOE [Tel Co]	2450 [A3H] 2506 [A3H]	0845 1345 2045 [warnings on receipt and on odd hours]
Humboldt Bay, Calif	NMC-11 [USCG]	2670 [A3J] 157.1 MHz [ch 22]	0700 1900 0745 1545
Monterey, Calif	NMC-6 [USCG]	157.1 MHz [ch 22] † 2670 [A3J]	0745 1545 Warnings only 0730 1930
San Francisco, Calif	KLH	2450 [A3H] 2506 [A3H]	0830 1330 2030
	NMC [USCG]	2670 [A3J] 157.1 MHz [ch 22]	0730 1100 1530

Location	Station	Frequencies [kHz/MHz]	Broadcast times [local]
Astoria, Ore	KFX [Tel Co]	2598 [A3H] † 2442 [A3H]	0915 2115
	NMW [USCG]	2670 [A3H]	0930 2130
Coos Bay, Ore	KTJ [Tel Co]	2566 [A3H]	0930
	NOE [USCG]	2670 [A3J]	0415
Port Angeles, Wash	NOW [USCG]	2670 [A3J]	0945 2145
Seattle, Wash	KOW [Tel Co]	2522 [A3H] † 2482 [A3H]	0900 2100
	NMW-43 [USCG]	2670 [A3J]	0915

* Broadcast 1 hour later during Daylight Saving Time
† Preceded by announcement on 2182 kHz
‡ Preceded by announcement on 156.8 MHz [ch 16]
+ Used during daytime only

Weather bulletins for the Caribbean

Ft Lauderdale	WAVS [religious station]	1190	0725 Florida and Bahama waters
Cap Haitian	4 VEH [religious station]	1030 [AM dial] 6.12 [short 9.77 wave] 11.835	0700 [after news] Southern area of Bahamas, Haiti and Dominican Rep
Montserrat	Radio Antilles	930 [AM dial]	1230 1830 [after local news]. Monserrat waters 1240 1840 [after international news] Caribbean; Atlantic E of Caribbean; Southwest North Atlantic
Miami, Fla High Seas Radio	WOM[1]	4363.6 8722.0 13116.3	1230 Southwest North Atlantic, Caribbean Sea, Gulf of Mexico
		4391.5 8731.3 13122.5	1330 GMT [forecasts as above]
		4407.0 8746.8	2230 GMT [forecasts as above]
		4425.6 8793.3	2330 GMT [forecasts as above]
Portsmouth, VA	NMN [USCG] offshore forecast[1]	4428.7 6506.4 8765.4	0400 1000[2] West Central and Southwest North Atlantic; Caribbean Sea; Gulf of Mexico
		6506.4 8765.4 13113.2	1600[3] 2200[2] [forecasts as above]
	NMN Highseas forecast	4428.7 6506.4 8765.4	0530 Gale and storm warnings. Atlantic west 35°W; Southwest North Atlantic; Caribbean Sea; Gulf of Mexico
		6506.4	1130 2330 [as above]
		8765.4	1130 1730 2330 [as above]
		13113.2	[as above]
		17307.2	1730 [as above]

[1]SSB transmission, BFO switch needed to unscramble
[2]includes New England waters forecast and the Gulfstream location
[3]includes New England waters forecast

Beaufort Scale

WIND FORCES

0 **Calm** Sea like a mirror.

1 **Light air** Ripples with the appearance of scales are formed but without foam crests.
Wind speed 1–3 knots.

2 **Light breeze** Small wavelets, short but pronounced. Crests have a glassy appearance and do not break.
Wind speed 4–6 knots, Wave height 0.48ft [0.15m].

3 **Gentle Breeze** Large wavelets. Crests begin to break. Foam of glassy appearance. Occasional white horses.
Wind speed 7–10 knots, Wave height 1.92ft [0.60m].

4 **Moderate Breeze** Small waves, becoming longer; fairly frequent white horses.
Wind speed 11–16 knots, Wave height 3.20ft [1m].

5 **Fresh Breeze** Moderate waves, taking a more pronounced long form; many white horses are formed [chance of some spray].
Wind speed 17–21 knots, Wave height 5.76ft [1.80m].

6 **Strong breeze** Large waves begin to form; the white foam crests are more extensive [probably some spray].
Wind speed 22–27 knots, Wave height 9.60ft [3.00m].

7 **Near gale** Sea heaps up and white foam from breaking waves begins to be blown in streaks along the direction of the wind.
Wind speed 28–33 knots, Wave height 12.80ft [4.00m].

8 **Gale** Moderately high waves of greater length; edges of crests begin to break into spindrift. The foam is blown in well-marked streaks along the direction of the wind.
Wind speed 34–40 knots, Wave height 17.60ft [5.50m].

9 **Strong gale** High waves. Dense streaks of foam along the direction of the wind. Crests of waves begin to topple, tumble and roll over. Spray may affect visibility.
Wind speed 41–47 knots, Wave height 22.40ft [7.00m].

10 **Storm** Very high waves with long overhanging crests. The resulting foam in great patches is blown in dense white streaks along the direction of the wind. On the whole the surface of the sea takes a white appearance. The tumbling of the sea becomes heavy and shocklike. Visibility affected.
Wind speed 48–55 knots, Wave height 28.80ft [9.00m].

11 **Violent storm** Exceptionally high waves. [Small and medium ships might for a time be lost to view behind the waves]. The sea is completely covered with long white patches of foam lying along the direction of the wind. Everywhere the edges of the wave crests are blown into froth. Visibility affected.
Wind speed 56–63 knots, Wave height 36.16ft [11.30m].

Weather forecasts by telephone

UNITED STATES

National Weather Service Office telephone numbers which give forecasts – usually round-the-clock – are listed below.

Maine
Portland 207-775-7781
Massachussetts
Boston 617-567-4670
617-569-3700*
617-569-3701**
Rhode Island
Providence 401-738-1211*
401-737-6820**
Connecticut
Hartford 203-623-3888*
New York
Buffalo 716-632-1319
New York 212-399-5561
Rochester 716-235-0240*
716-328-7391
Syracuse 315-455-6641*
315-455-6601*
New Jersey
Atlantic City 609-646-6400*
Newark 201-624-8118
Trenton 609-393-8951
Pennsylvania
Philadelphia 215-627-5575*
Delaware
Wilmington 302-328-7596*
Maryland
Baltimore 301-761-5380
District of Columbia
Washington 202-920-3820*
202-899-3210**
Virginia
Norfolk 804-853-3013*
Richmond 804-222-7411*
North Carolina
Durham 919-683-8306
Hatteras 919-995-2321
Raleigh 919-787-4856
Wilmington 919-763-3491*

South Carolina
Charleston 803-744-3207*
Columbia 803-794-2409
Georgia
Savannah 912-964-0234*
Florida
Apalachicola 904-653-9318
Daytona Beach 904-252-3112
904-252-5575*
Fort Myers 813-332-5595*
Jacksonville 904-757-1110
904-757-3311*
Key West 305-296-2011*
Lakeland 904-682-4221
Miami 305-665-0429
305-661-5065*
Orlando 305-857-1910
Pensacola 904-453-2188
Tallahassee 904-576-6318
904-576-7151*
Tampa 813-645-2506*
West Palm Beach 305-689-4013*
Alabama
Mobile 205-342-2458*
Louisiana
Lake Charles 318-477-5285
318-478-4810*
Baton Rouge 504-355-4823*
New Orleans 504-525-8831
504-522-2686*
Texas
Beaumont-Port
Arthur 713-722-1152*
Brownsville 512-546-5378*
Corpus Christi 512-888-8111*
Galveston 713-765-9579*
Houston 713-228-4427*
Victoria 713-575-1782

*Recorded **Recorded May 15 to October 15

Visual warning signals

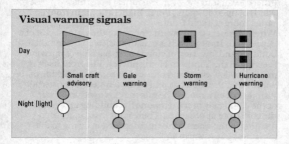

Day

Small craft advisory | Gale warning | Storm warning | Hurricane warning

Night [light]

Weather charts

INTERPRETATION

While it is possible to make some predictions on the basis of a single weather chart, it is necessary to have information about the movement and development of pressure systems in order to forecast the weather accurately for a particular area.

In temperate latitudes of both Northern and Southern Hemispheres the weather is largely determined by the procession of high and low pressure areas which move around the world in an easterly direction. Pressure systems in both hemispheres take basically the same form, except that depressions and anticyclones in the south are mirror images of those in the north in that the circulation of winds around them is reversed.

Depressions are areas of low pressure which, with their attendant fronts and troughs, are responsible for most of the bad weather experienced by the yachtsman in temperate latitudes. The circulation of winds around a depression is counterclockwise in the Northern Hemisphere and clockwise in the Southern. The direction of movement of the depression as a whole is generally parallel to the isobars in the warm sector. The speed of movement may vary between 60 knots and completely stationary, if blocked by a stationary ridge of high pressure in its path.

Anticyclones or ridges of high pressure are generally associated with settled, though not necessarily sunny, weather. The wind near the center of an anticyclone tends to be slight, increasing as you move outward. The circulation of winds around an anticyclone is clockwise in the Northern Hemisphere and counterclockwise in the Southern. Large anticyclones are often slow-moving, becoming completely stationary at times. Smaller ones and ridges of high pressure between depressions may move at 30 or 40 knots.

Isobars joining places of equal barometric pressure appear on the weather chart as concentric rings around depressions and anticyclones. Wind direction is roughly parallel to the isobars, though angled slightly inward around a depression and outward around an anticyclone. Wind speeds are proportional to the spacing of the isobars—the closer the spacing, the stronger the wind. A pressure difference of four mb over 35 nautical miles may give rise to winds of up to 40 knots [Force Eight] at a warm front and rather more at a cold front.

Warm front is the forward frontier of the warm sector of a depression. Its approach is usually indicated by a gradual build-up and lowering of cloud, and a backing of the wind [veering in the Southern Hemisphere]. The front itself is marked by low cloud and rain and a veering or backing of the wind. After the front has passed the temperature rises but visibility deteriorates. The rain may give way to drizzle or the cloud may break temporarily, building up again as the cold front approaches. There is often a danger of fog forming in the warm sector of a depression owing to the moistness of the warm air.

Cold front is the forward frontier of the colder air following the warm sector of a depression. Its approach is usually indicated by a build-up of cloud. The front itself is marked by low cloud and heavy rain, often with violent squalls, and a veer of the wind to the west or northwest [backing west or southwest in the Southern Hemisphere]. After the front has passed, the weather may be showery but visibility improves. Strong winds may continue for several hours, even increasing for a time although the barometer is rising.

Occluded front The cold front of a depression advances faster than the warm front, gradually decreasing the size of the warm sector. An occlusion is formed when the cold front overtakes the warm front, and lifts the warm air off the earth's surface. The signs of an approaching occluded front are similar to those of a warm front but there is no warm sector behind it. Sometimes a new center of low pressure develops at the apex of the remaining warm sector. The occluded front is then on the other side of the depression and begins to move around it like a third front, usually with cold front characteristics.

Secondary 'wave' depression may form along the trailing end of a cold front. It has the same characteristics as normal depressions and may cause the wind to back [veer in the Southern Hemisphere] and freshen again after the first cold front has passed.

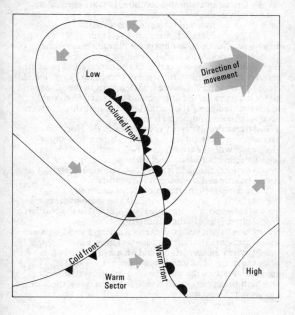

Weather indicators

FORECASTING BY OBSERVATION

In the absence of an official forecast, or to supplement an official forecast, you can tell a good deal about the likely development of the weather in your own area from the barometer and your own observations. Of course, these forecasting methods are by no means infallible and too much reliance should not be placed upon them.

Barometric pressure Rapid changes of pressure usually indicate strong winds. A rise or fall of eight mb or more within three hours is often followed by a gale, perhaps in four to eight hours time. A less rapid change of, say, five mb may indicate strong winds of less than gale force.

A falling barometer is a sign of an approaching depression but the worst of the wind may not come until the barometer has began to rise again.

> First rise after low
> Foretells a stronger blow.

Gales with a rising barometer are usually more squally than gales with a falling barometer.

Normal barometric pressures vary from area to area but if the barometer is lower than normal, and steady or falling, unsettled weather is indicated. If the barometer is high, and steady or rising, settled weather may be expected.

Clouds are useful weather indicators. For a description of seven different cloud types and their implications *see* pages 98–99. Cirrus and cumulus combinations are particularly noteworthy in this respect.

> Mackerel skies and mares' tails
> Make tall ships carry low sails.

In general, clouds becoming lower indicate bad weather. If the lower clouds [or wind] are moving at an angle to high cloud a change of weather can be expected. When you stand with your back to the wind or oncoming lower clouds, if the upper cloud is moving from left to right the change will be for the worse; if the upper cloud is moving from right to left the change will be for the better. These directions are reversed for the Southern Hemisphere.

Wind direction As a very rough rule, in the Northern Hemisphere the wind backs [changes direction counter-clockwise] with the approach of bad weather and veers [changes direction clockwise] with the coming of an improvement, although it may not come immediately. The reverse is true in the Southern Hemisphere.

You can also tell the direction of the center of a depression from that of the wind. If you stand with your back to the wind, low pressure is on your left in the Northern Hemisphere [right in the Southern].

Sunsets A bright yellow sunset often means wind, a pale yellow sunset rain, and a pink sunset fair weather. A 'high' sunset, when the sun sets behind a bank of clouds, often gives warning of bad weather, assuming the cloud is approaching from the west. Conversely, when the sun's rays light the upper clouds after it has gone below the horizon the sky to the west must be clear.

Deteriorating weather is often preceded by some or all of these signs, indicating the approach of a depression.
● Barometer falling.
● Feathery cirrus at high altitude ['mares' tails'], followed by cirrostratus, then altostratus becoming a thick gray sheet of cloud.
● Haloes round sun or moon. Later, a watery-looking sun, finally disappearing altogether.
● Wind backing gradually [veering in the Southern Hemisphere].

Improving weather when a depression has passed is often preceded by these signs.
● Barometer rising steadily.
● Low stratus breaking up and giving way to small cumulus or stratocumulus.
● Wind veering [backing in the Southern Hemisphere]. However, if the wind moderates rapidly, then begins to back once more [veer in the Southern Hemisphere], and the barometer starts falling again, be prepared for a secondary depression following the first one.

Good weather can be expected to continue under these circumstances.
● Barometer high, and steady or rising slowly.
● Small fleecy cumulus ['fair weather cumulus']. Cirrus dissolving at high altitude.
● Light easterly winds.

Sea fog is formed when relatively warm, moist air comes into contact with a relatively cool sea. In winter and spring the water is normally coldest inshore, so that is where fog forms; in summer and fall the pattern is reversed. Fog also forms over cold ocean currents and where tidal streams stir up cold water from below the surface. Sea fog may persist even in winds of Force Six and may not disperse until the arrival of a cold front.

'Radiation fog' which forms over land sometimes drifts out over the coast, but it tends to be lifted as it comes into contact with the sea and so is less of a hazard.

Sea breezes occur when the heating of the air over land, often marked by small cumulus clouds, draws in air from the relatively cool sea. Such winds reach their peak in the afternoon and die away toward evening. Sea breezes may attain Force Four but do not generally occur if the general wind is Force Five or more. They are a summer phenomenon in temperate latitudes.

At night the sea breeze may be replaced by a 'land breeze' but this wind is not usually so marked.

Other local winds Winds tend to be influenced quite substantially by the lie of the coastline, being channeled up estuaries or around headlands and often becoming more concentrated in strength. When blowing roughly parallel to the coast, or at a slight angle onto it, the wind often increases in strength within about ten miles of land. This is especially marked on the edges of an anticyclone.

Cloud types

IDENTIFICATION AND INTERPRETATION

Other factors must be taken into consideration when interpreting cloud formations, apart from the mere appearance of the cloud itself.

Sequence Do not rely solely on the cloud pattern at a single time. Cirrus followed by cirrostratus [*see* below] often precedes a depression, but cirrus or cirrocumulus may also be visible when a depression has passed and better weather is on the way.

Wind direction at sea level, unless it is a sea breeze, is important when interpreting cirrus [*see* page 96].

High cloud developments are often not visible because of the presence of cloud at a lower level.

Cirrus 'Mares' tails'. High wispy clouds often early warning of bad weather if followed by build-up of cloud, but wind direction is important. Cirrus dissolving means an improvement.

Cirrostratus with solar halo. Bad weather sign, especially if it follows the above. The larger the halo, the sooner the onset of bad weather.

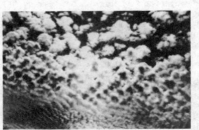

Altocumulus White and gray, formed in round masses, often partly fibrous. Sometimes a sign of rain, especially when masses break off higher than the rest; these can indicate thunderstorms.

Altostratus Gray cloud sheet formed by cirrostratus thickening. Usually followed by rain, it resembles stratus without its blackness.

Nimbostratus with fractostratus below. May follow cirrostratus. Often accompanies rain and strong winds.

Cumulonimbus with characteristic anvil-shaped top. Thunder cloud bringing heavy rain and perhaps violent squalls. Such clouds may mark isolated storms or may indicate an approaching front.

Cumulus Small fluffy clouds, as here, are a fair weather sign. Build-up of small cumulus over land in the morning may bring sea breezes later. If they grow large, thundery showers can follow.

6 SAFETY AT SEA
Distress Signals
INTERNATIONAL

Distress signals proper [*see* inside front cover] should be used when a vessel or person is in imminent and serious danger and requires immediate assistance from other vessels or the shore. The illustrations below are of other types of signals for use in emergencies at sea. For radiotelephone distress and urgency signals, *see* page 101.

    All vessels are obliged to render assistance where possible to vessels in distress. Distress signals should not be used if the situation does not justify it.

International distress signals *See* inside front cover. These are the signals prescribed in the Collision Regulations. They may be made either separately or together.

Other distress signals Although not official, these are generally recognized to indicate distress and may be useful if other signaling methods are not available.

Aids to identification from the air may be used to attract the attention of aircraft to a vessel in distress.

Answering signals may be made by other vessels or rescue services to show that a distress signal has been seen and assistance will be given as soon as possible.

Requests for assistance These signals may be used when a situation does not warrant a distress signal proper.

Other distress signals
Ensign hoisted upside down

Ensign made fast high in the rigging

Piece of clothing attached to an oar or spar held up in the air

Aids to identification from the air
Piece of ORANGE material with a BLACK square and circle on it

Dye marker in the sea

Answering signals
ORANGE smoke signal or three combined light and sound signals fired at one minute intervals, by day

Three WHITE star rockets fired at one minute intervals, by night

Requests for assistance
International Code Flag V meaning 'I require assistance'

●●●▬ Above signal in Morse Code

VHF distress signals
DISTRESS AND URGENCY PROCEDURES

Distress calls are made when a vessel or person is in imminent and serious danger, and requires immediate assistance. They take priority over all other communications. If the situation does not warrant use of the distress call but you have a very urgent message concerning the safety of a vessel or person, you should use the urgency call. Urgency calls take priority over all other communications except distress calls.

An urgency call would be appropriate, for example, in the case of complete engine failure in a boat which depended on motor propulsion, assuming that there was no immediate danger. It would be used if medical advice was urgently required, in which case a coast station would put you in contact with a hospital.

To send a distress message All distress messages are transmitted on Channel 16 [156.800 MHz] unless you are unable to make contact on that frequency. The first part of the procedure is the distress call, which may be preceded by the two-tone alarm signal if your set is equipped to make it. A distress call from the yacht 'Albatross' would take the following form:

**Mayday, Mayday, Mayday.
This is Albatross, Albatross, Albatross.**

The call is followed by the actual distress message which should give the yacht's position [either as a bearing *from* a well known point or as a latitude and longitude], nature of her distress, assistance required and any other information which might assist rescuers.

Mayday. Albatross. One nine five Breton Tower six miles. Holed below waterline. Require lifeboat or helicopter. Will fire distress rocket at intervals. Over.

If there is not an immediate reply the call and message are repeated until one is received. If there is no acknowledgment on Channel 16 you should try any other frequency on which people might be listening.

To send an urgency message Urgency messages are normally transmitted on Channel 16 unless you are unable to make contact on that frequency. The message takes the following form:

Pan Pan, Pan Pan, Pan Pan. Hello all stations, Hello all stations, Hello all stations. This is Albatross, Albatross, Albatross. One three zero Galley Head four miles. Complete engine failure. Drifting east at one knot. Require tow urgently. Over.

In the case of a long urgency message or one requiring a long reply, such as a request for medical advice, the call only is transmitted on Channel 16, together with an indication of the working frequencies available for transmitting the message.

Pan Pan, Pan Pan, Pan Pan. Castle Hill Coast Guard, Castle Hill Coast Guard, Castle Hill Coast Guard. This is Albatross, Albatross, Albatross. Have long urgency message for you. Channel 25. Over.

If you hear a distress signal your reaction should be determined by your ability to help and whether there are others better able to help than you are. There are three courses open to you:

● You can acknowledge the signal. This means that you intend to go to the aid of the vessel in distress. You should pause before acknowledging if you think that there are others in the vicinity who are better placed to help.

● You can relay the signal. This is what you should do if you are not in a position to help but do not hear an acknowledgement by another station. Alternatively, you may hear an acknowledgement, or may acknowledge the signal yourself, but consider that further help is required from stations who have not heard the signal.

● You can keep silence but stay tuned to Channel 16 and await developments. This is what you should do if there is acknowledgement from another station better placed to help than you are and you have no cause to relay the signal.

To acknowledge a distress message An acknowledgement of the following form should be transmitted as quickly as possible, unless you are allowing time for another station to acknowledge.

> **Mayday. Albatross, Albatross, Albatross. This is Petrel, Petrel, Petrel. Received. Mayday.**

As soon as possible after sending this signal a yacht acknowledging a distress call should send a message giving her position, the speed at which she is proceeding towards the vessel in distress and her estimated time of arrival.

> **Mayday. Albatross, Albatross, Albatross. This is Petrel, Petrel, Petrel. My position two five five, Breton Tower ten miles. Speed nine knots. Will reach you at approximately Two Zero Three Zero. Over.**

To relay a distress message the following call is made. It is essential to make it clear that the vessel in distress is not your own.

> **Mayday relay, Mayday relay, Mayday relay. This is Petrel, Petrel, Petrel. Mayday. Albatross. One nine five Breton Tower six miles. Holed below waterline. Require lifeboat or helicopter. Will fire distress rocket at intervals. Over.**

This signal should not be acknowledged by another vessel unless she is in a position to give assistance.

Radio silence When a distress call has been made all normal communications on Channel 16 are suspended. If a station interferes with distress traffic the station controlling it may impose radio silence, using the expression 'Seelonce Mayday'. At a later stage it may be considered possible to allow restricted working. This is conveyed by the expression 'Pru-donce' [Prudence]. When the distress traffic has ceased radio silence is lifted by the controlling station, using the expression 'Seelonce Feenee' [Finis].

First aid

TREATMENT OF INJURIES AND AILMENTS

The procedures on the following pages are for the treatment of ailments and injuries in the absence of medical assistance. Serious, or potentially serious, cases should be landed and taken to hospital as quickly as possible. If necessary, use distress signals to summon medical aid. Medical advice can also be obtained by radiotelephone [see page 101].

The subjects discussed are listed below with the pages on which they can be found.

Procedure to follow in the event of an accident resulting in an unconscious victim.

1 Summon assistance, if possible.
2 Do not move the victim if there is a risk of broken bones, unless it is to remove him/her from danger of further injury.
3 If the victim is not breathing, check for a pulse [under the angle of the jaw beside the windpipe].
• If there is a pulse, ensure that the air passage is clear and give artificial respiration if necessary [see page 104].
• If there is no pulse, give external cardiac massage *and* artificial respiration [see pages 104-105].
4 If the victim is breathing, check for fractures and bleeding.
• If bleeding is severe, it must be stopped [see page 106] before fractures are treated.
• If bleeding is not severe, then fractures should be immobilized [see page 107] before wounds are treated.

First Aid Kit

Adhesive plaster	Aspirin/acetaminophen
Adhesive transparent	[to relieve pain]
waterproof tape	Aluminum hydroxide
Bandages [triangular and crepe]	[for indigestion]
Cotton wool	Antihistamine cream
Dressings [sterile non-adhesive]	[for stings and bites]
Gauze packs	Anti-seasickness tablets
Safety pins	Antiseptic solution
Scissors and tweezers	Calamine lotion [for sunburn]
Space blanket	Diarrhea remedy
Thermometer	Talampicillin [for infection]

Artificial respiration by mouth-to-mouth resuscitation should be applied when the casualty shows no sign of breathing. The following procedure should be used.

1 Check that the air passage is clear. Remove potential obstructions [dentures, vomit etc.]
2 Place the casualty on his/her back on a hard surface.
3 Lift the neck, tilt the head back and pinch the nose between finger and thumb. Take a deep breath and cover the casualty's mouth with your mouth.
4 Blow steadily into the mouth until the lungs inflate and the chest has risen visibly.
5 Take away your mouth.

Look to see if the casualty's chest falls [i.e. he/she is exhaling through the mouth]. If this does *not* happen the passage must be blocked and should be cleared before the operation can be repeated. If this *does* happen repeat the operation every five or six seconds until spontaneous breathing is restored.
   If injury makes sealing the casualty's mouth impossible, close his/her mouth and blow through the nose.
   If this whole procedure clearly is not working [i.e. the causalty's color remains blue-gray], check that the heart is beating, and if not rap the breastbone sharply with the side of your fist to start the heart beating. Loosen the casualty's clothing and start external cardiac massage [*see* next page].

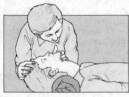

Support the casualty's neck and shoulders. Push the chin back and press the forehead down.

Pinch the casualty's nose and blow into his/her mouth until the chest rises.

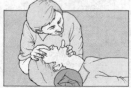

Take a deep breath and repeat the blowing sequence six times rapidly and then about every six seconds.

External cardiac massage is necessary as a means of restarting the natural heartbeat when it has failed. The procedure is as follows.

1 Lift the casualty's legs if possible, until they are vertical so that the blood will run back to the heart.
2 Kneel at the casualty's left shoulder.
3 Place the heel of one hand on the bottom of the casualty's breastbone [not the ribs]. Place your other hand on top of this one.
4 Jerk your whole weight onto your hands very briefly, keeping the arms straight.
5 Repeat every two seconds until the heart starts beating rhythmically again. Continue giving artificial respiration at the rate of two breaths for 15 compressions.

An unconscious adult's breastbone must be depressed only by one and a half inches. More pressure may result in rib-fracture. Treatment should be continued until the heartbeat is properly restored and a steady pulse can be felt. If strong breathing is restored, remove any damp clothing from the casualty, keeping him/her warm and massaging the limbs to restore circulation. If the casualty is able to swallow, give him/her a warm nonalcoholic drink. Keep the casualty warm and under observation for up to 24 hours. As serious complications may arise, even after apparent recovery, you should obtain medical assistance as soon as possible.

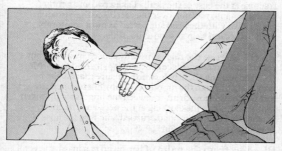

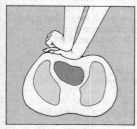

Kneeling at the casualty's side, place the heel of one hand over the lower end of the breastbone. Place your other hand on top.

Briefly jerk your weight on to your hands. Repeat this action, which compresses the heart [left], every two seconds until the casualty's heart beats regularly on its own.

Bleeding can almost always be stopped effectively by the application of direct pressure on the wound. The procedures for wounds of different kinds are dealt with individually in the following sections.

Slight bleeding Place the casualty at rest and clean the wound from the middle outwards. Place a dressing on the wound, if necessary with a pad, and bandage firmly, but not tightly, in position. If possible elevate the wounded area, supporting it in this position.

Severe bleeding Remove any visible alien matter [except impalements] from the wound with a dressing. Press on the affected area with your hand or a piece of clean cloth to close the broken blood vessels. This is effective in most cases after five or ten minutes. If the area is large, close the wound by pressing its edges gently but firmly together. Place the casualty lying down in a comfortable position. Elevate the wounded area, supporting it in this position. Place a dressing on the wound and press firmly down. Cover the wound with a pad and secure with a firm bandage, ensuring that both dressing and pad extend beyond the sides of the wound. If bleeding does not stop, apply more dressings and pads on top of the original ones, bandaging more firmly. Obtain medical help as soon as possible.

Bleeding from the ear may be a sign that there is a fracture at the base of the skull. Take a pad and gently bandage it into position over the ear. Place the casualty lying down with the head supported as most comfortable. Obtain medical help as soon as possible.

Bleeding from the nose is usually caused by a blow but can be spontaneous. Place the casualty sitting down with the head leaning slightly forward. Ensure that he/she is breathing through the mouth. Get him/her to pinch the soft part of the nose firmly between the fingers for up to ten minutes. Loosen the clothing at the neck and the chest. Ensure that the clot is not disturbed, and that the nose is not blown for several hours.

Bleeding from the palm of the hand can involve several blood vessels. Press directly on the wounded area. Raise the affected arm and place a dressing on the wound. Place a pad over the dressing. Make a fist of the fingers over the pad. Bind the fist firmly with a triangular bandage. Support the arm in a sling.

Bleeding from the scalp should be treated by the application of a pad over a sterile dressing. The bleeding may be stopped only after up to 30 minutes of this treatment, when the wound should be covered with a large dressing. Stitches may prove to be necessary, so medical assistance should be obtained.

Fractures should be dealt with as follows. Ensure that bleeding and asphyxia are dealt with first. Treat the casualty without moving him/her, except where to do so would endanger life; in such a case move the casualty as little as possible before treating. Support the injured part with a splint or something rigid until the fracture has been immobilized. Immobilization can be achieved by the use of body bandages or [where movement of the casualty is unavoidable] by splint and bandages.

Sprains [wrenched or torn ligaments and tissues connected with joints] manifest themselves by swelling and bruising about the joint and cause pain when the joint is used; they should be treated as follows. Place the joint in a position the casualty finds comfortable and support it there. Carefully remove any covering from the joint. Apply pressure over it by either surrounding it with a layer of cotton wool and bandaging it up firmly or applying a cold compress to it. Treat all doubtful cases as fractures.

Dislocations occur when a joint is prevented from functioning smoothly by the displacement of one of the bones meeting there. Movement of the joint is severely restricted and can be extremely painful. Treatment of the dislocation itself should be left to a medical expert, but an arm should be put into a sling and the pain controlled with acetaminophen tablets until medical assistance is reached.

Bandages should be firm enough to prevent undue movement but not so as to interfere with circulation. Skin surfaces should be separated with pads to avoid chafing before they are bandaged together. Check every 15 minutes to ensure that swelling has not made the bandages too tight.

Splints should be rigid, of sufficient length to immobilize joints above and below the break, and wide enough to fit on the limb. Clothing need not be removed; splints can be applied over it. Articles useful as splints include broom handles, oars, spars and even firmly folded magazines.

Burns and scalds should be treated as follows. Place the affected area under cold running water. Remove any clothing from the affected area. Place the casualty in a lying position. Cover the affected area with a dressing. Provide casualty with a little water at intervals. Do *not* apply ointments, oil dressings or lotions. Do *not* burst blisters or breathe over the affected area. Many burns and scalds require medical assistance, since all but minor injuries cause shock.

Eye injuries Chemicals in the eye must be washed out with cold fresh, or if necessary salt, water. Cover the eye with a nonadhesive dressing. In the case of a blow to the eye lie the casualty down and cover the eye with a dressing. Obtain medical help as soon as possible.

Shock may be caused by severe bleeding, recurrent vomiting, heart failure etc. and is characterized by the casualty's turning very pale, sweating profusely and feeling giddy, nauseous and thirsty. The casualty should be placed in a lying position. Deal with his/her injury before attempting to deal with shock. Keep his/her head low, raising the lower limbs. Loosen clothing from the neck, chest and waist. Moisten his/her lips with water. Cover with a blanket or a sheet, ensuring that a record is kept of the pulse and respiration rate. Do *not* use hot water bottles, or allow the casualty to drink. Do *not* allow him/her to move about unless absolutely necessary.

Poison can be inhaled, swallowed or absorbed and its effects should be treated as follows. If the casualty is conscious, ask him/her what happened. If the lips are burned, give the casualty drinking water. If the casualty is unconscious, ensure that he/she can breathe; if not, begin artificial respiration. Obtain medical assistance as soon as possible, giving all particulars of the incident to the physician, together with any vomited matter and, if possible, any sample of the poison.

Abdominal pains, vomiting and shock can be associated with surgical emergencies, in which case they should be treated by a physician as soon as possible. Place the casualty in a lying position, putting a pillow under the knees. Allow neither food nor drink.

Rupture often manifests itself as a painless swelling, sometimes accompanied by vomiting. Reassure the casualty, place him/her in a lying position, supporting the head and shoulders and bending and supporting the knees. Do *not* touch the swelling.

Stitches can be cured by rest, but if this has no effect, give the casualty sips of hot water. Rub the affected parts of the abdomen gently.

Winding is usually the result of a blow in the solar plexus [upper part of the abdomen]; it can cause the casualty to faint, or even to collapse. The casualty should be placed in the recovery position. His/her clothing should be loosened from the neck, chest and waist. Gently massage the casualty just below the breastbone.

Food poisoning is caused by a variety of germs in food. Vomiting and diarrhea are the symptoms and the casualty feels cold and clammy. Watery drinks should be given to the sufferer, even if he/she is vomiting. No food should be given. The casualty should be made to rest in a comfortable position in a well ventilated place. After six hours or so the casualty should begin to recover; plenty of drinks and a light diet should then be administered.

Minor stomach upsets can be caused by excessive eating or anxiety. They usually disappear after a few hours, but can be treated as follows. The casualty should be given a hot strong drink or a cup of hot salty bouillon. He/she should be allowed to eat only dry toast or salty soda crackers. Apply a hot water bottle to the casualty's abdomen. If the pain persists, medical attention should be sought.

Concussion is not readily diagnosable by lay people, as skull fracture can easily be mistaken for it; if in doubt, treat the casualty as carefully as if the skull were fractured. Concussion usually occurs after a blow on the head, a fall or a blow on the jaw, and temporarily disturbs the working of the brain. It should be treated as follows. Ensure that the air passage is clear of mucus, blood and loose teeth. Loosen clothing from the neck, chest and waist. Ensure that the casualty gets fresh air to breathe. If breathing stops, employ techniques of artificial respiration [*see* page 104]. If breathing is satisfactory, place the casualty in the recovery position [*see* page 105] with the head flat or flopped forward so that vomit and other secretions can drain easily from the mouth. Cover casualty with a blanket and try to obtain medical assistance. Do *not* give liquid to an unconscious person. Do *not* leave the casualty unattended.

Asphyxia is commonly caused by a lack of oxygen in the blood due to the inability to breathe, or because the heart and lungs are not functioning effectively; it can be treated as follows. Check to see that the casualty is breathing. If he/she is not, start artificial respiration without delay [*see* page 104]. The speed at which this treatment can be started is the single most important factor in the treatment of asphyxia, but treatment may have to be continued until the casualty is able to receive medical attention; the cerebral cortex [the brain center for speech etc.] is quickly affected by asphyxia and can be irreparably damaged by only five minutes' oxygen deprivation.

Exposure cases should be wrapped in a warm blanket and given warm drinks, ideally sweetened condensed milk. It is important to take the casualty's age into account; young adults can be quickly warmed, older casualties should be heated more gradually.

Seasickness is more easily prevented than cured. Heavy meals and alcohol should be avoided before sailing. Seasickness pills should be taken one hour before sailing. Treatment consists of getting the casualty's feet off the floor, keeping him/her warm and ensuring that he/she gets enough fresh air and frequent small amounts of liquid. Keep anyone vomiting over the side attached by a safety harness and ensure that he/she vomits to leeward.

Many people who are affected by seasickness at the start of a voyage become immune as time passes.

Man overboard

DRILL FOR RECOVERING PERSON IN WATER

1 Throw a lifebuoy The horseshoe type is best. In
darkness or poor visibility it should for preference be one
with an automatic light.
2 Alert everyone on board by shouting 'Man overboard'
and get them all on deck.
3 Keep the person in sight at all times if possible. Have
one crew member watching the person continuously and
pointing toward him/her.
4 Get back to the person as quickly as possible. Sort
out a rope and anything else you may need to get him/her
back on board.

If the spinnaker is up you may not be able to turn
back immediately. In that case note your compass
course while it is being lowered so that you can sail back
in exactly the opposite direction. Cutting the spinnaker
halyard and sheets may save valuable time. Lay a trail of
any objects that float to help you find your way back.

In a shallow-draft vessel do not come alongside
to windward if there is a risk of drifting on top of the
person in the water. Make sure that the propeller is not
turning as you come alongside. It may be better to tie
something like a fender to the end of a rope and tow it in
an arc around the person so that he/she can catch hold of it
and can be hauled up to the boat with the engine stopped.

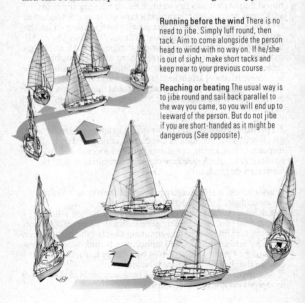

Running before the wind There is no
need to jibe. Simply luff round, then
tack. Aim to come alongside the person
head to wind with no way on. If he/she
is out of sight, make short tacks and
keep near to your previous course.

Reaching or beating The usual way is
to jibe round and sail back parallel to
the way you came, so you will end up to
leeward of the person. But do not jibe
if you are short-handed as it might be
dangerous (See opposite).

Getting the person back on board The first priority is to get a rope to him/her, preferably with a bight in it that can be securely placed under the arms.

It is very difficult to lift a person in wet clothes, who is very probably exhausted, into a high-sided boat without some form of mechanical assistance. Use the boarding ladder if you have one or make a 'step' out of rope. If the person can put his/her foot into a bight of rope and you have a winch, you can winch him/her up. In a sailing boat it may also help to lower a sail into the water [*see* below].

If you cannot get the person back on board launch the life raft or inflatable dinghy, if possible with someone else in it. If it is necessary for a second person to go into the water to assist, he/she should be wearing a life jacket. It is a good idea for everyone on a boat to be wearing a life jacket from the outset.

If no one saw the person go overboard sail back on the opposite compass course. Note the time when you turned back and calculate the time when you will reach the point where the person was last seen on board, so you can concentrate the search between those two points.

If you fall overboard do not try swimming after the boat if you cannot overtake it. Conserve your energy and concentrate on staying afloat.

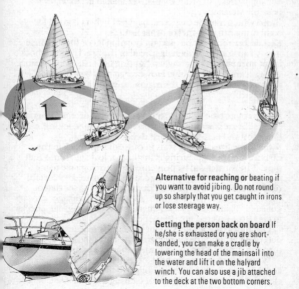

Alternative for reaching or beating if you want to avoid jibing. Do not round up so sharply that you get caught in irons or lose steerage way.

Getting the person back on board If he/she is exhausted or you are short-handed, you can make a cradle by lowering the head of the mainsail into the water and lift it on the halyard winch. You can also use a jib attached to the deck at the two bottom corners.

Firefighting

FIGHTING FIRE ON BOARD

1 Get everyone on deck and to a place of comparative safety from the flames. Everyone should put on a life jacket at the first available opportunity.

2 Tackle the fire as quickly as possible with extinguishers or by other means suitable to the type of fire. Speed is essential. Aim extinguishers at the base of the flames.

3 Launch the life raft or dinghy unless the fire can be brought under control immediately and certainly before there is any danger of the flames reaching it. It should be towed at a safe distance from the boat and anyone not involved in fighting the fire should get aboard.

4 Send a distress call if there is time and you have a radio. It is better to have to cancel a distress call than to leave it too late to send one.

Firefighting equipment Attention is drawn to the recommendations on page 123.

Fire extinguishers Dry powder types are the best general-purpose extinguishers for a yacht. Carbon dioxide [CO_2] or foam types are acceptable alternatives. BCF [bromo-chloro-difluoro-methane] or BTM [Bromo-trifluoro-methane] extinguishers may also be used but the fumes can be dangerous in confined places. CTC [carbon-tetrachloride] types, sold for use in automobiles, produce lethal phosgene gas and must *not* be used on yachts.

Fire blankets Asbestos fire blankets are useful for putting out small fires. An ordinary blanket soaked in sea water is a possible alternative.

Sand which may be carried in bags or buckets is good for combating burning fuel or other liquids.

Sea water must *not* be used for burning fat or fuel because it may cause an explosion or spread of the fire. Electric shock is not normally a danger when fighting fire on a yacht because voltages are generally low. However, it may be a danger if the boat is connected to the mains supply in a marina or yacht harbor.

Fire prevention The two most common sources of fire risk on a yacht are gasoline and bottled gas used for cooking, etc. Diesel oil and kerosene are less dangerous.

Gasoline fires usually start because of a spitback in the carburetor, spillage during refueling, or leakage from a fuel pipe. The former can be prevented by fitting gauze flame traps over air intakes. Spillage can be minimized by careful refueling procedure and checking afterward to see that no fuel has found its way into the bilges. Leakage can be guarded against by proper installation and regular checks to see that a leak has not developed.

Gas pipes can be checked for leakage by smearing detergent around the suspected part. You should always turn the supply off at the cylinder when not in use.

When returning to the boat after an absence always check for gas or fumes in the bilges before switching on any electrics, starting the engine, or causing a flame.

Refloating
AFTER RUNNING AGROUND

There are two basic methods of refloating a boat that has run aground—by reducing her draft or by using force. If she is well aground a combination of the two is often required.

Refloating methods You can reduce the draft of a boat by lightening her. In its simplest form this may mean having as many crew members as can be spared over the side, assuming that the water is shallow enough and provided that they can be got back on board afterward. This technique has the added advantage that they can also push. Alternatively, you can launch the dinghy and transfer people into that.

If more force is needed, besides using the engine, you can use the dinghy to lay out an anchor in the direction of deeper water. You may then be able to pull the boat off by hauling or winching in the anchor cable.

Sheeting in the sails makes the boat heel, thus reducing her draft. However, the sails should be lowered if they are tending to drive the boat farther aground. The boat can also be made to heel by concentrating crew weight on one side of the boat or having crew members sit on the boom while it is swung out over the side. In boats with long keels it may be more effective to alter the fore-and-aft trim by moving weight to the bow.

It is much easier to refloat a sailing boat if the bow is pointing toward the deeper water. Your first reaction, therefore, if you feel the keel touch bottom should be to try to spin the boat round before she becomes stuck fast.

Changing the fore-and-aft trim of a power craft is more likely to be effective than heeling her. However, if all the crew are gathered at the bow the propellers may be raised out of the water.

Motor boats have the advantage of more powerful engines than sailing craft, but they are also more susceptible to being holed, because they do not have deep keels.

Checking for leaks This should be done immediately on grounding if the impact was a hard one. Minor damage can often be stopped temporarily by covering it on the inside with a bunk cushion or similar, then wedging this in place with an oar, boat hook or anything that comes to hand.

State of the tide If the tide is rising there is not generally a problem, unless the boat is holed. If it is high or falling, however, speed is essential. If the boat is stranded by the retreating tide you should try to make sure that she settles against the uphill slope [if any] of a bank or shoal, by weight distribution or a line from the top of the mast. The most critical time is as the boat settles on her bilge, when damage may be caused by pounding. This phase can be eliminated by increasing the weight on that side at the critical time, either using crew weight or by bailing water *into* the boat.

Towing
AND BEING TOWED

Towing in anything but a calm sea places great strain on the tow rope and its point of attachment to both boats, unless the tow is a light one. Both the rope and the points of attachment must be strong enough for the job.

Passing the tow rope If it is too rough for the towing vessel to come alongside, the tow rope should be tied to a fender or life buoy and towed past the disabled craft so that her crew can catch hold of it. If the disabled boat is near a lee shore it is safer for the rescuer to anchor upwind of her and float the rope down.

Attaching the tow rope Most cleats on a yacht are not nearly strong enough to take the strains of towing. If you do not have a stout samson post you should tie the tow rope to the mast [if it is stepped through to the keel] or around the cabin top. The rope is then led through a fairlead at the stern of the towing vessel or the bow of the one being towed.

If you have to use cleats whose strength is suspect it is best to attach the rope to two cleats, one on either side. An alternative for the towed craft is to tie the tow rope to a stout piece of timber which is placed across the underside of the open forehatch. However, in rough seas waves or spray will come through the opening, and damage to the hatch coaming is also likely.

Pieces of cloth must be tied around the tow rope at all points where it may chafe.

Passing a tow rope [above] when disabled craft is on a lee shore.
Attaching a tow rope [right] Two cleats are stronger than one.
Towing in waves [opposite top] A drogue prevents towed vessel surging forward.
Towing alongside [opposite left] Slight toe-in improves maneuverability.
Reducing snatching [opposite right] using towed vessel's anchor.

To reduce snatching a heavy weight may be attached to the middle of the tow rope. This can often be achieved by attaching the tow rope to the towed vessel's anchor and towing her by her anchor cable. At the start of a tow the towing craft must move ahead very slowly until the strain comes on the tow rope. In waves the length of the tow rope should be equal to the distance between crests. The towed vessel may stream a drogue to stop her overtaking the towing craft.

Towing alongside is normally hazardous except in sheltered waters. However, since it makes for greater maneuverability it is better to bring the towed vessel alongside when entering the harbor. Towing alongside may also be the answer when the towing vessel is unable to steer or when the one towing is comparatively light. In the latter case both boats can be steered by the larger vessel's rudder.

Salvage claims Unless your boat is in danger no salvage claim can be made. If you accept a tow you should try to arrange payment, if there is to be any, before the tow begins. It is best if the rope used is your own and you steer your own boat. Do not take a member of the other vessel's crew on board unless necessary.

It is to be hoped that yachtsmen will not make claims of one another. If a claim is to be made it may prove useful to employ a Lloyd's salvage contract. The United States Coast Guard does not claim salvage or charge for its services.

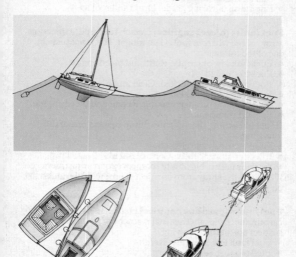

Engine faults
DIESEL AND GASOLINE ENGINES

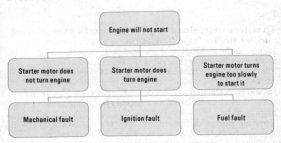

Starter motor does not start the engine
- Battery run down. Recharge or start engine by hand.
- Battery terminal loose or corroded. Tighten or clean.
- Battery lead faulty.
- Starter switch, solenoid or starter motor faulty.
- Starter motor brushes dirty. Clean or replace.
- Bendix gear jammed. Loosen starter motor to free.
- Starter motor not engaging. Starter motor turns but engine does not. Caused by fault or dirt in Bendix gear.

Starter motor turns engine too slowly to start it
- Battery run down.
- Battery lead or terminal faulty.
- Starter motor faulty.
- Engine oil of wrong grade. Drain and replace.

Fuel faults [diesel engines] Detach fuel pipe at injection pump to see whether fuel is reaching it. If it is *not* suspect one of the following.
- Fuel tank low or empty. Refill and bleed engine.
- Fuel tap turned off.
- Fuel pipe or filter blocked. Clear and bleed engine.
- Fuel tank vent blocked.
- Fuel pipe fractured or leaking. Repair and bleed engine.
- Fuel lift pump faulty.

If fuel *is* reaching the injection pump suspect one of the following.
- 'Stop' control not released.
- Injection pump faulty. Control rod may be sticking.
- Injector faulty. Normally requires expert adjustment.

Warning : the spray from an injector is powerful enough to penetrate the skin.

Fuel faults [gasoline engines] Detach fuel pipe at the carburetor to see whether fuel is reaching it. If it is *not* suspect one of the following.
- Fuel tank low or empty. Refill.
- Fuel tap turned off.
- Fuel pipe or filter blocked. Clear.
- Fuel tank vent blocked.
- Fuel pump faulty.

If fuel *is* reaching the carburetor suspect one of the following.
- Engine flooded. Remove spark plugs and turn engine several times.
- Fuel contaminated with water. Drain fuel tank and clean fuel pipes and carburetor.
- Choke defective. Check valve and cable.
- Jets blocked. Clear.
- Carburetor faulty.

Mechanical faults [diesel engines]
- Injection timing wrong.
- Compression poor. Normally the result of wear.
- Valve faulty.
- Air cleaner blocked.

Mechanical faults [gasoline engines]
- Intake manifold air leak. Check by squirting oil around intake connections. Tighten manifold.
- Cylinder head gasket leaking. Replace.
- Spark plug loose. Tighten.
- Compression poor. Normally the result of wear.
- Valves faulty.

Ignition faults [gasoline engines] Check for spark at plugs. If none suspect the following.
- Plugs fouled. Clean.
- Plug gaps incorrect. Reset or replace.
- Porcelain cracked. Replace plug.

Check for spark at plug leads. If none suspect the following.
- Plug lead loose or faulty. Tighten or replace.
- Distributor cap wet or dirty. Clean and dry.
- Distributor cap cracked. Replace.
- Condenser faulty. Replace.
- Rotor arm not making contact with carbon brush in distributor cap. Adjust.

Check for spark at HT lead. If none suspect the following.
- HT lead loose or faulty. Tighten or replace.
- Ignition coil faulty. Replace.
- Contact breaker points out of adjustment. Reset.

Engine stops [diesel engines] This may be caused by a fuel fault [*see* page 116]. In rough seas dirt or water may be stirred up from the bottom of the tank or air may be drawn into the fuel pipe if fuel is low. It may also be caused by a mechanical fault.
- Valve sticking.
- Governor idling setting incorrect.
- Injection timing too far advanced. Retard.

Engine stops [gasoline engines] This may be caused by a fuel fault [*see* page 116] or an ignition fault.
- LT lead loose. Tighten.
- Contact points dirty. Clean.
- Ignition switch faulty.

Engine loses power [diesel engine] This may be caused by a fuel fault [*see* page 116], a mechanical fault [*see* page 117] overheating [*see* below]. In addition, it may be caused by the following.
● Propeller fouled.
● Sterngear bearings picking up or seizing. Regrease.

Engine loses power [gasoline engines] This may be caused by a fuel fault [*see* page 116]. It may also be caused by one of the following.
● Fuel mixture too weak.
● Carburetor flooding.
● Valve faulty.
● Ignition timing incorrect. Advance or retard.
● HT lead shorting.
● Propeller fouled.
● Sterngear bearings picking up or seizing. Regrease.

Engine misfires [diesel engines] This may be caused by a fuel fault [*see* page 116] or overheating [*see* below].
Also suspect one of the following.
● Injector pipe fractured.
● Piston ring sticking.
● Valve sticking.

Engine misfires [gasoline engines] This may be caused by a fuel fault [*see* page 116], an ignition fault [*see* page 117] or overheating [*see* below]. In addition, it may be caused by the following.
● Plug leads crossed.

Engine overheating
● Header tank low or empty. Refill with fresh water.
● Drive belt slipping or broken.
● Sea water intake closed or blocked. Check that water is coming out of the system.
● Water pump faulty.
● Thermostat sticking.
● Engine oil low. Refill.
● Air in cooling system.
In diesel engines overheating may also be caused by the following.
● Injector faulty.
In gasoline engines overheating may also be caused by the following.
● Fuel mixture too weak.
● Ignition timing incorrect.

Bleeding the fuel system [diesel engines] Air may enter the fuel system of a diesel engine as a result of running out of fuel, leaks in pipes or connections, disconnection of pipes or changing filters. The following procedure is generally applicable to most diesel engines. However, the exact procedure varies from model to model.

1 Trace fuel pipe from lift pump to fuel filter. Open bleed screw on inlet side.
2 Operate priming lever until fuel free of air bubbles emerges around screw.
3 Open bleed screw on outlet side of filter and repeat procedure above.
4 Trace fuel pipe to injection pump. Open bleed screw and repeat procedure above.
If the engine runs for a few minutes and then stops, there is probably still air in the system so the whole procedure must be carried out again. If there is air in the system the engine may in fact run satisfactorily until stopped, then fail to start subsequently.

Outboard motors If the engine will not start suspect one of the following.
- Fuel tank empty or supply turned off.
- Fuel line blocked or kinked.
- Fuel system not primed. Squeeze priming bulb.
- Fuel tank vent closed.
- Engine flooded. Release choke, shut off fuel and turn engine over several times.
- Engine not choked.
- Spark plug fouled or faulty. Clean or replace.
If the engine lacks power suspect one of the following.
- Fuel line blocked or kinked.
- Carburetor out of adjustment.
- Spark plug faulty.
- Engine overheating.
If the engine will not idle suspect one of the following.
- Spark plugs dirty or faulty.
- Carburetor out of adjustment. Adjust idling speed.
- Fuel mixture incorrect.
If the engine overheats suspect one of the following.
- Water intake blocked.
- Water pump faulty.
- Prolonged low speed running

Outboards dropped in the water must be seen to quickly because corrosion sets in within about 3 hours. If you think that sand may have been drawn into the engine or there is any sign of binding when the flywheel is turned, do not turn the engine over.
1 Rinse motor with fresh water.
2 Remove plugs and dry them.
3 Clean carburetor, preferably with kerosene.
4 Turn engine over several times with plug hole facing downward.
5 Squirt oil into cylinders.
6 Refit plugs and carburetor.
7 Try to start engine.
If engine fails to start remove plugs and repeat procedure.
If all attempts fail and you cannot take the engine to a dealer immediately, resubmerge it in fresh water.

Navigating in fog
OR BAD VISIBILITY

In fog the great danger of any vessel is collision—with the shore or with another vessel. The following procedures are all designed to minimize one or both of these risks. It is also especially important in fog to know the Collision Regulations.

Slow down As well as giving you more time to take avoiding action, in a motor boat this will also make it easier to hear the sounds of other vessels.

Keep a good lookout This includes 'listening out' too. Every available person should be posted on deck, away from engine noise, etc., to look and listen. In particular, someone should be posted at the bow. Sounds can be deceptive in fog and the source of a sound may not lie in the direction from which it appears to be coming.

Make sound signals For the appropriate signals for a power-driven vessel, sailing vessel or vessel at anchor in restricted visibility *see* page 72.

Hoist a radar reflector The larger it is and the higher it is the better. At any event, it should be at least 18in [46cm] from corner to corner and not less than 12ft [4m] above sea level. It should be hoisted with one straight edge, *not* a corner, uppermost.

Keep clear of shipping lanes If you must cross one do so at right angles to the flow of traffic. The safest place for a small boat, other things being equal, is in water too shallow for a large vessel to enter.

If you find yourself becalmed or moving very slowly across a shipping lane you should start the auxiliary to get clear of it. Stop the engine at intervals, however, as you would in any other power-driven vessel.

In a motor boat the noise of the engine makes it difficult to hear sounds outside the boat, so you should stop it at regular intervals while you listen for the sounds of other vessels.

Navigation It is particularly important in fog to keep an accurate record of your course and distance run, and to plot your position regularly on the chart. This means steering as straight a course as possible, which is easy to forget when you are concentrating on keeping a lookout.

It is dangerous to close with the shore in thick fog, even if you know it well and it is free from outlying dangers. It is often better to anchor and wait for the fog to lift, provided you are clear of shipping lanes and other hazards. If you must approach the shore do so at right angles to the coast and go in slowly using the echo sounder. Echoes of your fog signals from the cliffs may also give you some warning of when land is just ahead.

General precautions All members of the crew should wear life jackets and the life raft should be ready for immediate launching. Keep some flares [preferably white] ready for instant use to draw attention to yourself if there is a danger of a collision with a larger vessel.

Gales at sea

HEAVY WEATHER TACTICS AND TECHNIQUES

The best action to take before and during a gale depends on many considerations, some of which are outlined below. Before you risk meeting foul weather you should study the wealth of published material on the subject and plan what you would do in different situations. It is best to gain experience of these conditions under an experienced skipper.

Making for shelter If a gale is forecast do not be obsessed with regaining your home port if another harbor is more accessible. If the refuge that you are trying to reach is, or will be, on a lee shore you must be certain that you will get there before wind and sea have risen, or your predicament will be much worse than it would be farther out to sea. Waves are much steeper near land and many harbors are extremely dangerous to enter under these conditions. In addition, deteriorating visibility is likely to make inshore navigation hazardous.

While a gale is in progress harbors likely to be safe to enter are those to windward. Even then, the approach must be either deep or sheltered since dangerous seas can be expected wherever large waves encounter shallowing water. Strong tidal streams also give rise to confused and breaking seas which are highly dangerous.

Making an offing If you cannot reach shelter it is essential to put as many miles as possible between yourself and any lee shore before the gale arrives. Bear in mind that the wind will almost certainly change direction during the course of a gale, and what is not now a lee shore may become one later.

Preparing for a gale Simple tasks, including sleeping, become extremely difficult in a rough sea and crew strength is likely to be reduced by seasickness. It is advisable, therefore, to do as many things as possible before the gale comes. These would include preparing food and getting ahead with the navigation, as well as checking safety equipment, making hatches secure, etc.

Riding out a gale at sea The procedure to adopt depends largely on the type of boat and the amount of searoom available to leeward. If you are close to a lee shore there is obviously no alternative but to work your way to windward.

⚠️ The mainsail should be reefed in good time. In a moderate gale you might be able to lie hove-to under a well reefed mainsail and storm jib. In a stronger wind it is often best to run before it under bare poles. If there is a risk of broaching you should trail a bight of stout rope at least 300ft [100m] long to slow the boat down and make waves break farther astern. In extreme conditions a well-found sailing yacht should be safe lying a-hull with battened-down hatches and helm lashed a-lee.

🛥️ In a motor boat the safest course may also be to run downwind trailing warps if you have enough searoom. Otherwise, the safest attitude is generally bow-on to the waves with a sea anchor streamed from the bow and perhaps a steadying sail at the stern.

Safety equipment

RECOMMENDATIONS

Personal safety equipment
● Safety harness—to USCG [United States Coast Guard] specification. One for each person on sailing yachts. One or more for each person on motor cruisers as may be needed when on deck.

Wear a safety harness on deck in bad weather or at night. Make sure it is properly adjusted. Experience has shown, however, that a harness can be dangerous if you happen to go overboard at speeds of eight knots or more.
● Life jackets—of USCG accepted type, except those wholly dependent upon oral inflation. One for each person on board.

Keep them in a safe place where you can get at them easily. Always wear a life jacket when there is any risk of being pitched overboard.

Rescue equipment for man overboard
● Life buoys—two at least. One life buoy should be kept within easy reach of the helmsman. For sailing at night, it should be fitted with a self-igniting light.
● Buoyant line—100ft [30m] minimum breaking strain of 250lb [115kg]. This too ought to be kept within easy reach of the helmsman.

Other floating equipment for longer journeys
● Inflatable life raft—to carry everyone on board. It should be carried on deck or in a locker opening directly to the deck and should be serviced annually; or
● Rigid dinghy—with permanent, not inflatable, buoyancy, and with oars and rowlocks secured. It should be carried on deck. It may be a collapsible type; or
● Inflatable dinghy—built with two compartments, one at least always kept fully inflated, or built with one compartment, always kept fully inflated, and having oars and rowlocks secured. It should be carried on deck.

If the vessel has enough permanent buoyancy to float when swamped, a dinghy with two compartments may be stowed. In sheltered waters a dinghy may be towed. Check that the tow is secure.

For short journeys
● Inflatable life raft or alternatives, as above. In sheltered waters the summer scale equipment, listed below, may usually be adequate.

For short summer journeys
● Life buoys—of USCG accepted type. One for every two people on board. Life buoys carried for 'man overboard' situations may be included. These support only one person.

General equipment
- Anchors—two, each with line or chain of appropriate size and length. Where line is used at least 18ft [5.5m] of chain should be used between anchor and line.
- Bilge pump.
- Efficient compass—and spare.
- Charts—covering intended area of operation.
- Distress flares—six with two of the rocket/parachute type.
- Daylight distress [smoke] signals.
- Tow rope—of adequate length.
- First-aid box—with anti-seasickness tablets.
- Radio receiver—for weather forecasts.
- Water-resistant torch.
- Fog horn.
- Radar reflector—of adequate performance. As large as can be conveniently carried. Preferably mounted at least 10ft [3m] above sea level.
- Life line—also useful in bad weather for inboard life line.
- Engine tool kit.
- Name, number or generally recognized sail number—should be painted prominently on the vessel or on dodgers in letters or figures at least 9in [22cm] high.

Fire-fighting equipment
- For vessels over 30ft [9m] in length and those with powerful engines, carrying quantities of fuel—two fire extinguishers should be carried, each of not less than 3lb [1.4kg] capacity, dry powder, or equivalent, and one or more additional extinguisher of not less than 5lb [2.3kg] capacity, dry powder, or equivalent. A fixed installation may be necessary.
- For vessels of up to 30ft [9m] in length, with cooking facilities and engines—two fire extinguishers should be carried, each of not less than 3lb [1.4kg] capacity, dry powder, or equivalent.
- For vessels up to 30ft [9m] in length, with cooking facilities only or with engine only—one fire extinguisher should be carried, of not less than 3lb [1.4kg] capacity, dry powder, or equivalent. Carbon dioxide [CO_2] or foam extinguishers of equal extinguishing capacity are alternatives to dry powder appliances. BCF [bromo-chloro-difluoro-methane] or BTM [bromo-trifluoro-methane] may be carried, but people on the boat should be warned that the fumes given off are toxic and are extremely dangerous in a confined space. A warning notice should be posted at each extinguisher point.

Additionally for all craft:
- Buckets—two, with lanyards.
- Bag of sand—useful in containing and extinguishing burning spillage of fuel or lubricant.
- Your craft should have been designed and built with the object of keeping fire risks to the minimum.

7

CRUISING & YACHT RACING
Cruising Abroad

Certain formalities are usually necessary on entering a port when a yacht has come from another country, and on leaving again. The requirements differ slightly from country to country. There may also be changes in the regulations from time to time. The following is intended as a guide only.

Flag etiquette Yachts entering a foreign port should wear their national ensign at the stern and a courtesy flag, consisting of a smaller version of the ensign of the country being visited, at the starboard crosstree.

Customs It is usually necessary to obtain customs clearance at your port of entry into a foreign country. In some countries certain ports have been designated for this purpose, and it is normally advisable to make your first call at a major port.

In most countries code flag 'Q' should be flown until customs clearance has been obtained.

Sometimes a yacht will be visited by a customs officer but more often one person must go ashore with the ship's papers and the crew's passports, to report to the customs.

Temporary importation Usually there are no restrictions on the temporary importation of a yacht into a foreign country if she does not stay for more than a year. However, it may be necessary to prove that she is foreign-owned.

Dutiable goods Yachtsmen are usually allowed to retain a certain amount of dutiable supplies for consumption on board during their stay, without having to pay import duty. Additional supplies may often be kept in a locker which is sealed by customs on arrival.

It is possible to obtain duty-free supplies in ports in some countries if you apply to the customs office.

Passports Passports should be carried by everyone on board. Although in some countries you may not be required to show your passport it is still advisable to have one.

Ship's papers Proof that a yacht is foreign-owned is often needed. In the case of a registered vessel this would be her registration certificate.

Health regulations Vaccination and other requirements vary from country to country and may change from time to time. If in doubt you should check well before leaving.

Certificates of competence are not generally required for yachtsmen navigating in coastal waters.

Canada Cruising craft must report to the first available Canadian port of entry. A permit will be issued authorizing you to cruise Canadian waters.

You should have identification for re-entry to the US. Naturalized citizens should carry naturalization papers. Dogs and cats must have proof of rabies vaccination.

Items for sale and gifts of value in excess of $15 are subject to excise or duty.

Holding tanks are required in Ontario waters; the system must be permanently installed and self-contained.

Mexico Mexico's east and west coast ports grow ever more popular as cruise destinations. You may apply to live in Mexico for two years at a time.

US citizens planning to visit Mexico's interior must have a tourist card whether they intend to stay only a few days or a full six months. There is a Single Entry card, which does not require a photo and a Multiple Entry card, requiring three 2″ × 2″ photos. Both cards are issued free of charge and are valid for a stay of 180 days [six months]. The tourist card must be obtained before entering Mexico. You can get a tourist card from officials at an entry point, from travel agents, or any Mexican consulate.

Clearance papers should be obtained ahead of time from a Mexican consul or a marine custom broker. They are required only at ports of entry and departure. There is no entry charge for boats under 5 tons. Sanitary inspection is made only at the port of entry. While visiting, the captain must tell naval authorities of his next destination.

If you plan to go ashore you should obtain the Multiple Entry tourist card. Personal baggage can be taken ashore. **Note:** The same crew and passengers must depart the country aboard the same boat on which they entered.

Bermuda Citizens of the US must show proof of their citizenship upon arrival; an expired passport, birth certificate, voter's certificate, or similar identification will suffice. This entitles you to stay in Bermuda for up to six months. No health documents are needed.

All yachts calling at Bermuda should contact the Harbor Radio Station prior to arrival. Visiting yachtsmen are required to clear customs and immigration in St. George's before proceeding elsewhere in Bermuda. This also applies to clearance on departure. Yachts should be flying the yellow quarantine 'Q' until clearance is obtained.

Bahamas US citizens do not need a passport or visa to enter the Bahamas provided their visit does not exceed 8 months. Proof of citizenship is required.

The health requirements in the Bahamas are minimal: smallpox vaccination and cholera inoculation certificates may be required only if a person is arriving directly from an area that is reported to have incidence of these diseases.

Departure tax is $3.00.

USYRU Rules

DEFINITIONS AND RIGHT-OF-WAY RULES

The following extracts are Parts I and IV of the
International Yacht Racing Rules as adopted by the United
States Yacht Racing Union. These rules govern yacht racing
throughout the world.

The rules of Part IV apply only between yachts that either
are intending to race or are racing in the same or different
races and, except when rule 3.2bii – Race continues after
sunset – applies, they replace the International Regulations
for Preventing Collisions at Sea or Government Right-of-
Way Rules applicable to the area concerned, from the time
a yacht intending to race begins to sail about in the vicinity
of the starting line until she has either finished or retired and
has left the course.

Part I - definitions

Racing A yacht is racing from her preparatory signal until
she has *either* finished and cleared the finishing line and
finishing marks *or* retired, *or* until the race has been
postponed, abandoned or canceled, *except* that in match or
team races, the sailing instructions may prescribe that a
yacht is racing from any specified time before the
preparatory signal.

Starting A yacht starts when, after fulfilling her penalty
obligations, if any, under rule 51.1c [Sailing the course],
and after her starting signal, any part of her hull, crew or
equipment first crosses the starting line in the direction of
the course to the first mark.

Finishing A yacht finishes when any part of her hull, or of
her crew or equipment in normal position, crosses the
finishing line from the direction of the course from the last
mark, after fulfilling her penalty obligations, if any, under
rule 52.2 [Touching a mark].

Luffing Altering course toward the wind until head to wind.

Tacking A yacht is tacking from the moment she is beyond
head to wind until she has borne away, when beating to
windward, to a close-hauled course; if not beating to
windward, to the course on which her mainsail has filled.

Bearing away Altering course away from the wind until a
yacht begins to jibe.

Jibing A yacht begins to jibe at the moment when, with the
wind aft, the foot of her mainsail crosses her centerline, and
completes the jibe when the mainsail has filled on the other
tack.

On a tack A yacht is on a tack except when she is tacking or
jibing. A yacht is on the tack [starboard or port]
corresponding to her windward side.

Close-hauled A yacht is close-hauled when sailing by the wind as close as she can lie with advantage in working to windward.

Clear astern and clear ahead; overlap A yacht is clear astern of another when her hull and equipment in normal position are abaft an imaginary line projected abeam from the aftermost point of the other's hull and equipment in normal position. The other yacht is clear ahead. The yachts overlap when neither is clear astern; *or* if, although one is clear astern, an intervening yacht overlaps both of them. The terms clear astern, clear ahead and overlap apply to yachts on opposite tacks only when they are subject to rule 42 [Rounding or passing marks and obstructions].

Leeward and windward The leeward side of a yacht is that on which she is, or, if luffing head to wind, was, carrying her mainsail. The opposite side is the windward side. When neither of two yachts on the same tack is clear astern, the one on the leeward side of the other is the leeward yacht. The other is the windward yacht.

Proper course A proper course is any course which a yacht might sail after the starting signal, in the absence of the other yacht or yachts affected, to finish as quickly as possible. The course sailed before luffing or bearing away is presumably, but not necessarily, that yacht's proper course. There is no proper course before starting.

Mark A mark is any object specified in the sailing instructions which a yacht must round or pass on a required side. Every ordinary part of a mark ranks as part of it, including a flag, flagpole, boom or hoisted boat, but excluding ground tackle and any object either accidentally or temporarily attached to the mark.

Obstruction An obstruction is any object, including a vessel under way, large enough to require a yacht, when not less than one overall length away from it, to make a substantial alteration of course to pass on one side or the other, *or* any object which can be passed on one side only, including a buoy when the yacht in question cannot safely pass between it and the shoal or object which it marks.

Postponement A postponed race is one which is not started at its scheduled time and which can be sailed at any time the race committee may decide.

Abandonment An abandoned race is one which the race committee declares void at any time after the starting signal, and which can be re-sailed at its discretion.

Cancellation A canceled race is one which the race committee decides will not be sailed thereafter.

Part IV—Right-of-Way Rules The rules of this part are suspended at night, when the normal collision regulations take over. For conditions under which the rules of Part IV apply *see* page 126.

SECTION A—Obligations and penalties

31 Disqualification
31.1 A yacht may be disqualified or otherwise penalized for infringing a rule of Part IV only when the infringement occurs while racing, whether or not a collision results.
31.2 A yacht may be disqualified before or after she is racing for seriously hindering a yacht which is racing, or for infringing the sailing instructions.

32 Avoiding collisions
A right-of-way yacht which fails to make a reasonable attempt to avoid a collision resulting in serious damage may be disqualified as well as the other yacht.

33 Rule infringement
33.1 ACCEPTING PENALTY A yacht which realizes she has infringed a racing rule or a sailing instruction is under an obligation either to retire promptly or to exonerate herself by accepting an alternative penalty when so prescribed in the sailing instructions, but when she does not retire or exonerate herself and persists in racing, other yachts shall continue to accord her such rights as she may have under the rules of Part IV.
33.2 CONTACT BETWEEN YACHTS RACING When there is contact between the hulls, equipment or crew of two yachts, both shall be disqualified or otherwise penalized unless *either*
a one of the yachts retires in acknowledgement of the infringement, or exonerates herself by accepting an alternative penalty when so prescribed in the sailing instructions, *or*
b one or both of these yachts acts in accordance with rule 68.3 [Protests].
33.3 When an incident is the subject of action by the race committee under rule 33.2 but under no other rule of Part IV, it may waive the requirements of rule 33.2 when satisfied that contact was minor and unavoidable.

34 Hailing
34.1 Except when luffing under rule 38.1, a right-of-way yacht which does not hail before or when making an alteration of course which may not be foreseen by the other yachts may be disqualified as well as the yacht required to keep clear when a collision resulting in serious damage occurs.
34.2 A yacht which hails when claiming the establishment or termination of an overlap or insufficiency of room at a mark or obstruction thereby helps to support her claim for the purposes of rule 42.

SECTION B—Principal right-of-way rules and their limitations These rules apply except when over-ridden by a rule in Section C.

35   Limitations on altering course
When one yacht is required to keep clear of another, the right-of-way yacht shall not so alter course as to prevent the other yacht from keeping clear; or so as to obstruct her while she is keeping clear, *except*
a to the extent permitted by rule 38.1, *and*
b when assuming a proper course: *either*
i to start, unless subject to rule 40, or to the second part of rule 44.1b, *or* **ii** when rounding a mark.

36   Opposite tacks—basic rule
A port-tack yacht shall keep clear of a starboard-tack yacht.

37   Same tack—basic rules
37.1 WHEN OVERLAPPED A windward yacht shall keep clear of a leeward yacht.

37.2 WHEN NOT OVERLAPPED A yacht clear astern shall keep clear of a yacht clear ahead.

37.3 TRANSITIONAL A yacht which establishes an overlap to leeward from clear astern shall allow the windward yacht ample room and opportunity to keep clear.

38   Same tack—luffing and sailing above a proper course after starting
38.1 LUFFING RIGHTS After she has started and cleared the starting line, a yacht clear ahead or a leeward yacht may luff as she pleases, subject to the proper course limitations of this rule.

38.2 PROPER COURSE LIMITATIONS A leeward yacht shall not sail above her proper course while an overlap exists, if when the overlap began or, at any time during its existence, the helmsman of the windward yacht [when sighting abeam from his normal station and sailing no higher than the leeward yacht] has been abreast or forward of the mainmast of the leeward yacht.

38.3 OVERLAP LIMITATIONS For the purpose of this rule: An overlap does not exist unless the yachts are clearly within two overall lengths of the longer yacht, and an overlap which exists between two yachts when the leading yacht starts, or when one or both of them completes a tack or jibe, shall be regarded as a new overlap beginning at that time.

38.4 HAILING TO STOP OR PREVENT A LUFF When there is doubt, the leeward yacht may assume that she has the right to luff unless the helmsman of the windward yacht has hailed 'Mast Abeam', or words to that effect. The leeward yacht shall be governed by such hail, and, when she deems it improper, her only remedy is to protest.

38.5 CURTAILING A LUFF The windward yacht shall not cause a luff to be curtailed because of her proximity to

the leeward yacht unless an obstruction, a third yacht
or other object restricts her ability to respond.

38.6 LUFFING TWO OR MORE YACHTS A yacht shall not luff
unless she has the right to luff all yachts which would
be affected by her luff, in which case they shall all
respond even when an intervening yacht or yachts
would not otherwise have the right to luff.

**39 Same tack—sailing below a proper course after
starting**

A yacht which is on a free leg of the course shall not sail
below her proper course when she is clearly within
three of her overall lengths of either a leeward yacht or
a yacht clear astern which is steering a course to pass to
leeward.

40 Same tack—luffing before starting

Before a right-of-way yacht has started and cleared the
starting line, any luff on her part which causes another
yacht to have to alter course to avoid a collision shall be
carried out slowly and in such a way as to give a
windward yacht room and opportunity to keep clear,
but the leeward yacht shall not so luff above a
close-hauled course, unless the helmsman of the
windward yacht (sighting abeam from his normal
station) is abaft the mainmast of the leeward yacht.
Rules 38.4; 38.5; and 38.6 also apply.

41 Changing tacks—tacking and jibing

41.1 BASIC RULE A yacht which is either tacking or jibing
shall keep clear of a yacht on a tack.

41.2 TRANSITIONAL A yacht shall neither tack nor jibe
into a position which will give her right of way unless
she does so far enough from a yacht on a tack to enable
this yacht to keep clear without having to begin to alter
her course until after the tack or jibe has been
completed.

41.3 ONUS A yacht which tacks or jibes has the onus of
satisfying the race committee that she completed her
tack or jibe in accordance with rule 41.2.

41.4 WHEN SIMULTANEOUS When two yachts are both
tacking or both jibing at the same time, the one on the
other's port side shall keep clear.

**SECTION C—Rules which apply at marks and
obstructions and other exceptions to the rules of
Section B** When a rule of this section applies, to the extent
to which it explicitly provides rights and obligations, it
overrides any conflicting rule of Section B, except rule 35.

42 Rounding or passing marks and obstructions

42.1 ROOM AT MARKS AND OBSTRUCTIONS WHEN
OVERLAPPED When yachts are about to round or pass a
mark, other than a starting mark surrounded by
navigable water, on the same required side or an
obstruction on the same side:

a An outside yacht shall give each yacht overlapping her on the inside room to round or pass the mark or obstruction, except as provided in rules 42.1c; 42.1d and 42.4. Room includes room for an overlapping yacht to tack or jibe when either is an integral part of the rounding or passing maneuver.
b When an inside yacht of two or more overlapped yachts either on opposite tacks, or on the same tack without luffing rights, will have to jibe in order most directly to assume a proper course to the next mark, she shall jibe at the first reasonable opportunity.
c When two yachts on opposite tacks are on a beat or when one of them will have to tack either to round the mark or to avoid the obstruction, as between each other rule 42.1 shall not apply and they are subject to rules 36 and 41.
d An outside leeward yacht with luffing rights may take an inside yacht to windward of a mark provided that she sails to that effect and begins to luff before she is within two of her overall lengths of the mark and provided that she also passes to windward of it.

42.2 CLEAR ASTERN AND CLEAR AHEAD IN THE VICINITY OF MARKS AND OBSTRUCTIONS When yachts are about to round or pass a mark, other than a starting mark surrounded by navigable water, on the same required side or an obstruction on the same side:
a A yacht clear astern shall keep clear in anticipation of and during the rounding or passing maneuver when the yacht clear ahead remains on the same tack or jibes.
b A yacht clear ahead which tacks to round a mark is subject to rule 41, but a yacht clear astern shall not luff above close-hauled so as to prevent the yacht clear ahead from tacking.

42.3 LIMITATIONS ON ESTABLISHING AND MAINTAINING AN OVERLAP IN THE VICINITY OF MARKS AND OBSTRUCTIONS
a A yacht clear astern may establish an inside overlap and be entitled to room under rule 42.1a only when the yacht clear ahead
i is able to give the required room *and*
ii is outside two of her overall lengths of the mark or obstruction, except when either yacht has completed a tack within two overall lengths of the mark or obstruction, or when the obstruction is a continuing one as provided in rule 42.3f.
b A yacht clear ahead shall be under no obligation to give room to a yacht clear astern before an overlap is established.
c When an outside yacht is overlapped at the time she comes within two of her overall lengths of a mark or an obstruction, she shall continue to be bound by rule 42.1a, to give room as required even though the overlap may thereafter be broken.
d A yacht which claims an inside overlap has the onus

of satisfying the race committee that the overlap was established in proper time.

e An outside yacht which claims to have broken an overlap has the onus of satisfying the race committee that she became clear ahead when she was more than two of her overall lengths from the mark or obstruction.

f A yacht clear astern may establish an overlap between the yacht clear ahead and a continuing obstruction such as a shoal or the shore or another vessel, only when at that time there is room for her to pass between them in safety.

42.4 AT A STARTING MARK SURROUNDED BY NAVIGABLE WATER When approaching the starting line to start, a leeward yacht shall be under no obligation to give any windward yacht room to pass to leeward of a starting mark surrounded by navigable water; but after the starting signal, a leeward yacht shall not deprive a windward yacht of room at such a mark by sailing either above the course to the first mark or above close-hauled.

43 Close-hauled, hailing for room to tack at obstructions

43.1 HAILING When two close-hauled yachts are on the same tack and safe pilotage requires the yacht clear ahead or the leeward yacht to make a substantial alteration of course to clear an obstruction, and when she intends to tack, but cannot tack without colliding with the other yacht, she shall hail the other yacht for room to tack and clear the other yacht, but she shall not hail and tack simultaneously.

43.2 RESPONDING The hailed yacht at the earliest possible moment after the hail shall *either*
a Tack, in which case the hailing yacht shall begin to tack *either*
i before the hailed yacht has completed her tack *or*
ii when she cannot then tack without colliding with the hailed yacht, immediately she is able to tack and clear her, *or*
b Reply 'You tack', or words to that effect, when in her opinion she can keep clear without tacking or after postponing her tack. In this case,
i the hailing yacht shall immediately tack *and*
ii the hailed yacht shall keep clear.
iii The onus of satisfying the race committee that she kept clear shall lie on the hailed yacht which replied 'You tack'.

43.3 LIMITATION ON RIGHT TO ROOM WHEN THE OBSTRUCTION IS A MARK
a When the hailed yacht can fetch an obstruction which is also a mark, the hailing yacht shall not be entitled to room to tack and clear the hailed yacht and the hailed yacht shall immediately so inform the hailing yacht.

b If, therefore, the hailing yacht again hails for room to tack and clear the hailed yacht she shall, after receiving room, retire immediately or exonerate herself by accepting an alternative penalty when so prescribed in the sailing instructions.

c When, after having refused to respond to a hail under rule 43.3a, the hailed yacht fails to fetch, she shall retire immediately, or exonerate herself by accepting an alternative penalty when so prescribed in the sailing instructions.

44 Returning to start

44.1 **a** After the starting signal is made, a premature starter returning to start, or a yacht working into position from the course side of the starting line or its extensions, shall keep clear of all yachts which are starting or have started correctly, until she is wholly on the pre-start side of the starting line or its extensions.
b Thereafter, she shall be accorded the rights under the rules of Part IV of a yacht which is starting correctly; but when she thereby acquires right of way over another yacht which is starting correctly, she shall allow that yacht ample room and opportunity to keep clear.

44.2 A premature starter while continuing to sail the course and until it is obvious that she is returning to start, shall be accorded the rights under the rules of Part IV of a yacht which has started.

45 Re-rounding after touching a mark

45.1 A yacht which has touched a mark, and is about to exonerate herself in accordance with rule 52.2 [Touching a mark], shall keep clear of all other yachts which are about to round or pass it or have rounded or passed it correctly, until she has rounded it completely and has cleared it and is on a proper course to the next mark.

45.2 A yacht which has touched a mark while continuing to sail the course and until it is obvious that she is returning to round it completely in accordance with rule 52.2 [Touching a mark], shall be accorded rights under the rules of Part IV.

46 Anchored, aground or capsized

46.1 A yacht under way shall keep clear of another yacht racing which is anchored, aground or capsized. Of two anchored yachts, the one which anchored later shall keep clear, except that a yacht which is dragging shall keep clear of one which is not.

46.2 A yacht anchored or aground shall indicate the fact to any yacht which may be in danger of fouling her. Unless the size of the yachts or the weather conditions make some other signal necessary, a hail is sufficient.

46.3 A yacht shall not be penalized for fouling a yacht in distress which she is attempting to assist or a yacht which goes aground or capsizes immediately ahead.

Performance Handicap Racing Fleet

Performance Handicap Racing Fleet [PHRF] is a fleet organization whose sole purpose is to equitably handicap sailing yachts so that differing designs and sizes can compete fairly in the same race.

The PHRF system is based on performance. Race results, accumulated from the many yacht clubs in an area which extends from Santa Barbara to San Diego – along 200 miles of race-sailing Southern California coastline – provide data on every yacht of every design that has ever raced in these waters using the PHRF handicapping system. This information enables the handicappers to determine the speed potential of one class or design in relation to that of others in the same race. If in consecutive race results the speed potential relationship remains the same, the board of handicappers can determine the degree to which one yacht design is faster or slower than another.

In making their calculations, the PHRF handicappers assume that every yacht is in absolute top racing condition. They assume that the bottom of each yacht is clean and smooth; any propeller is a folding type; the quality of sail is adequate for any race the yacht may enter. Furthermore, it is assumed that every skipper and crew is capable of racing the yacht to its speed potential as calculated from the past performances of yachts of the same design.

Headsail maximum sizes are established from information obtained from the manufacturers. Yachts with larger genoas or oversized spinnakers, or poles, or both are penalized in order to effect equitable racing between yachts of the same basic design as well as the other designs of the fleet.

How the system works Each member of the PHRF fleet has a PHRF rating assigned to his yacht in a one mile race, and this is deducted from the actual time it required to complete the one mile distance. The rating assigned to a yacht is not mathematically formulated for the yacht by itself, but is a time allowance for the yacht in relation to other yachts in the race. For example:

Yacht 'A' rating: 180 seconds per mile.
Yacht 'B' rating: 174 seconds per mile.
Time allowance differential = 6 seconds per mile.

Yacht 'B' has been rated by the handicappers as being 6 seconds per mile faster than Yacht 'A' and is, therefore, allowed 6 seconds less than Yacht 'A' to complete the mile.

Where the system is used. With the rapid changes in yacht design, the performance-based handicap system has emerged as the best assurance of continued opportunity for yachts of all designs to compete fairly. Since the PHRF system was established in California in 1959, it has spread to the Pacific Northwest, the Great Lakes, and the Gulf and Atlantic Coasts. In 1976, PHRF was sanctioned by CBYRA and is now recognized by USYRU as a subcommittee under its Offshore Racing Committee.

WEIGHTS AND MEASURES
Conversion factors

AMERICAN, METRIC AND IMPERIAL

Length and distance
1 inch = 25.4mm
1 inch = 2.54cm
1 foot = 0.3048m
1 yard = 0.9144m
1 mile = 1.609344km
1 millimeter = 0.0393701 in
1 centimeter = 0.393701 in
1 meter = 3.28084ft
1 meter = 1.09361yd
1 kilometer = 0.621371 miles

Area
1 square foot = 0.092903m²
1 acre = 0.404686ha
1 square meter = 10.7639ft²
1 hectare = 2.47105ac

Liquids
1 fluid ounce = 28.4131 milliliters
1 pint = 0.47318 liters
1 quart = 0.94635 liters
1 gallon = 3.78541 liters
1 milliliter = 0.351951fl oz
1 liter = 2.11337 pints
1 liter = 1.05669 quarts
1 liter = 0.26417 gallons

Avoirdupois weight
1 dram = 1.771844g
1 ounce = 28.3495g
1 pound = 0.453592kg
1 hundredweight = 0.0508023 tonnes
1 ton = 1.01605 tonnes
1 gram = 0.56438dr
1 gram = 0.035274oz
1 kilogram = 2.20462lb
1 tonne = 19.6841cwt
1 tonne = 0.984207 tons

Cubic capacity
1 cubic inch = 16.387064cm³
1 cubic foot = 0.0283168m³
1 cubic centimeter = 0.0610237in³
1 cubic meter = 35.314725ft³

American system
1 foot = 12 inches
1 yard = 3 feet
1 mile = 5280 feet
1 mile = 1760 yards

1 quart = 2 pints
1 gallon = 8 pints
1 gallon = 4 quarts

1 acre = 4840 square yards
1 square mile = 640 acres

1 ounce = 16 drams
1 pound = 16 ounces
1 stone = 14 pounds
1 hundredweight = 112 pounds
1 hundredweight = 8 stone
1 long ton = 2240 pounds
1 short ton = 2000 pounds

Metric system The following prefixes are used to form smaller or larger units from a basic unit.
Mega   × 1,000,000
Kilo   × 1,000
Hecto × 100
Deca   × 10
Deci   ÷ 10
Centi   ÷ 100
Milli   ÷ 1,000
Micro ÷ 1,000,000

1 milliliter = 1 cubic centimeter
1 liter = 1 cubic decimeter

Imperial measure
1 pint = 1.20095 US pints
1 gallon = 1.20095 US gallons

1 US pint = 0.832674 pints
1 US gallon = 0.832674 gallons

1 ton = 1.12 short tons
1 short ton = 0.892857 tons

Mariner's measure The old nautical mile 6080ft is now being replaced by the international nautical mile. The difference, however, is too small to be of any consequence for the yachtsman.
1 fathom = 6ft
1 fathom = 1.8288m
1 cable = 100 fathoms approximately
1 nautical mile = 10 cables
1 nautical mile = 6076.12ft [1852m]
1 nautical mile = 1.15 miles
1 nautical mile = 1.852km
1 knot = 1 nautical mile per hour

1 meter = 0.546807 fathoms

1 mile = 0.868976 nautical miles
1 kilometer = 0.539957 nautical miles

Electricity

Watts = Volts × Amperes

$$\text{Amperes} = \frac{\text{Volts}}{\text{Ohms}}$$

Maximum hull speed The following formulas give the approximate maximum displacement speed of a boat of a given length.

Speed in knots = $\sqrt{\text{length in feet}} \times 1.35$

Speed in knots = $\sqrt{\text{length in meters}} \times 2.45$

Estimating speed A rough idea of a boat's speed can be gained by noting the time it takes to travel its own length by reference to an object in the water.

Speed in knots = $\dfrac{\text{length in feet}}{\text{time in seconds}} \times 0.59$

Speed in knots = $\dfrac{\text{length in meters}}{\text{time in seconds}} \times 1.94$

Frequency/wavelength Frequencies and wavelengths are reciprocal. In other words, 300kHz = 1000m and 1000kHz = 300m. The formulas for converting them are as follows.

$$\text{Meters} = \frac{300000}{\text{kHz}}$$

$$\text{KiloHertz} = \frac{300000}{\text{m}}$$

1MHz = 1000kHz

Barometric pressure The following conversion factors are calculated at 0°C and standard gravity of 980.665cm/sec².
1 millibar = 0.02953in   1 inch = 33.86387mb

Temperature The formulas for converting degrees Celsius to degrees Fahrenheit and *vice versa* are as follows.

$$\text{Celsius} = \frac{5(°F - 32)}{9}$$

$$\text{Fahrenheit} = \frac{°C \times 9}{5} + 32$$

Conversion table [Fahrenheit to Celsius]

°F	°C	°F	°C	°F	°C	°F	°C	°F	°C	°F	°C
00	−18	24	−4	48	9	72	22	96	36	121	49
01	−17	25	−4	49	9	73	23	97	36	122	50
02	−17	26	−3	50	10	74	23	98	37	123	51
03	−16	27	−3	51	11	75	24	100	38	124	51
04	−16	28	−2	52	11	76	24	101	38	125	52
05	−15	29	−2	53	12	77	25	102	39	126	52
06	−14	30	−1	54	12	78	26	103	39	127	53
07	−14	31	−1	55	13	79	26	104	40	128	53
08	−13	32	0	56	13	80	27	105	41	129	54
09	−13	33	1	57	14	81	27	106	41	130	54
10	−12	34	1	58	14	82	28	107	42	131	55
11	−12	35	2	59	15	83	28	108	42	132	56
12	−11	36	2	60	16	84	29	109	43	133	56
13	−11	37	3	61	16	85	29	110	43	134	57
14	−10	38	3	62	17	86	30	111	44	135	57
15	−10	39	4	63	17	87	31	112	44	136	58
16	−9	40	4	64	18	88	31	113	45	137	58
17	−8	41	5	65	18	89	32	114	46	138	59
18	−8	42	6	66	19	90	32	115	46	139	59
19	−7	43	6	67	19	91	33	116	47	140	60
20	−7	44	7	68	20	92	33	117	47	141	61
21	−6	45	7	69	21	93	34	118	48	142	61
22	−6	46	8	70	21	94	34	119	48	143	62
23	−5	47	8	71	22	95	35	120	49	144	62

Conversion tables

METRIC AND AMERICAN

Inches to mm

in	mm
1/64	0.397
1/32	0.794
3/64	1.191
1/16	1.587
5/64	1.984
3/32	2.381
7/64	2.778
1/8	3.175
9/64	3.572
5/32	3.969
11/64	4.366
3/16	4.763
13/64	5.159
7/32	5.556
15/64	5.953
1/4	6.350
17/64	6.747
9/32	7.144
19/64	7.541
5/16	7.938
21/64	8.334
11/32	8.731
23/64	9.128
3/8	9.525
25/64	9.922
13/32	10.319
27/64	10.716
7/16	11.113
29/64	11.509
15/32	11.906
31/64	12.303
1/2	12.700
33/64	13.097
17/32	13.494
35/64	13.891
9/16	14.288
37/64	14.684
19/32	15.081
39/64	15.478
5/8.	15.875
41/64	16.272
21/32	16.669
43/64	17.066
11/16	17.463
45/64	17.859
23/32	18.256
47/64	18.653
3/4	19.050
49/64	19.447
25/32	19.844
51/64	20.241
13/16	20.638
53/64	21.034
27/32	21.431
55/64	21.828
7/8	22.225
57/64	22.622
29/32	23.019
59/64	23.416
15/16	23.813
61/64	24.209
31/32	24.606
63/64	25.003
1	25.400

Feet [fathoms] to meters

	ft	m		ft	m
	1	0.305		31	9.449
	2	0.610		32	9.754
	3	0.914		33	10.058
	4	1.219		34	10.363
	5	1.524		35	10.668
1	6	1.829	**6**	36	10.973
	7	2.134		37	11.277
	8	2.438		38	11.582
	9	2.743		39	11.897
	10	3.048		40	12.192
	11	3.353		41	12.497
2	12	3.658	**7**	42	12.802
	13	3.962		43	13.106
	14	4.267		44	13.411
	15	4.572		45	13.716
	16	4.877		46	14.021
	17	5.182		47	14.326
3	18	5.486	**8**	48	14.630
	19	5.791		49	14.935
	20	6.096		50	15.240
	21	6.401		51	15.545
	22	6.706		52	15.850
	23	7.010		53	16.154
4	24	7.315	**9**	54	16.459
	25	7.620		55	16.764
	26	7.925		56	17.069
	27	8.230		57	17.374
	28	8.534		58	17.678
	29	8.839		59	17.983
5	30	9.144	**10**	60	18.288

Meters to feet

m	ft	m	ft
1	3.281	31	101.706
2	6.562	32	104.987
3	9.843	33	108.267
4	13.123	34	111.549
5	16.404	35	114.829
6	19.685	36	118.110
7	22.966	37	121.391
8	26.247	38	124.672
9	29.528	39	127.953
10	32.808	40	131.234
11	36.089	41	134.514
12	39.370	42	137.795
13	42.651	43	141.076
14	45.932	44	144.357
15	49.213	45	147.638
16	52.493	46	150.919
17	55.774	47	154.199
18	59.055	48	157.480
19	62.336	49	160.761
20	65.617	50	164.042
21	68.898	51	167.323
22	72.179	52	170.604
23	75.459	53	173.885
24	78.740	54	177.165
25	82 021	55	180.446
26	85.302	56	183.727
27	88.583	57	187.008
28	91.864	58	190.289
29	95.144	59	193.570
30	98.425	60	196.850

Gallons to liters

gals	liters	gals	liters
1	3.785	31	117.348
2	7.571	32	121.133
3	11.356	33	124.919
4	15.142	34	128.704
5	18.927	35	132.489
6	22.713	36	136.275
7	26.498	37	140.060
8	30.283	38	143.846
9	34.069	39	147.631
10	37.854	40	151.416
11	41.460	41	155.202
12	45.425	42	158.987
13	49.210	43	162.773
14	52.996	44	166.558
15	56.781	45	170.343
16	60.566	46	174.129
17	64.352	47	177.914
18	68.137	48	181.700
19	71.923	49	185.485
20	75.708	50	189.270
21	79.494	51	193.056
22	83.279	52	196.841
23	87.064	53	200.627
24	90.850	54	204.412
25	94.635	55	208.198
26	98.421	56	211.983
27	102.206	57	215.768
28	105.991	58	219.554
29	109.777	59	223.339
30	113.562	60	227.125

Liters to gallons

liters	gals	liters	gals
1	0.264	31	8.189
2	0.528	32	8.453
3	0.793	33	8.718
4	1.057	34	8.982
5	1.321	35	9.246
6	1.585	36	9.510
7	1.849	37	9.774
8	2.113	38	10.038
9	2.378	39	10.303
10	2.642	40	10.567
11	2.906	41	10.831
12	3.170	42	11.095
13	3.434	43	11.359
14	3.698	44	11.624
15	3.963	45	11.888
16	4.227	46	12.152
17	4.491	47	12.416
18	4.755	48	12.680
19	5.019	49	12.944
20	5.283	50	13.209
21	5.548	51	13.473
22	5.812	52	13.737
23	6.076	53	14.001
24	6.340	54	14.265
25	6.604	55	14.529
26	6.868	56	14.794
27	7.133	57	15.058
28	7.397	58	15.322
29	7.661	59	15.586
30	7.925	60	15.850

NAUTICAL TERMS
Six language dictionary
ENGLISH, FRENCH, GERMAN, DUTCH, DANISH, SPANISH

English	French	German
Types of vessel		
catamaran	catamaran	Floß
dinghy	youyou	Beiboot
motor boat	bateau à moteur	Motorjacht
sailing boat	bateau à voiles	Segelboot
Parts of a vessel		
backstay	étai arrière	Achterstag
boom	gui	Baum
bow	avant	Bug
cabin	cabine	Kajüte
deck	pont	Deck
draft	tirant d'eau	Tiefgang
forestay	étai avant	Vorstag
halyard	drisse	Fall
hull	coque	Rumpf
jib	foc	Fock
keel	quille	Kiel
mainsail	grand'voile	Großsegel
mast	mât	Mast
oar	rame	Riemen
propeller	hélice	Schraube
rudder	gouvernail	Ruder
sail	voile	Segel
seacock	vanne	Seeventil
sheet	écoute	Schot
shroud	hauban	Want
spinnaker	spinnaker	Spinnaker
stern	poupe	Heck
tiller	barre	Ruderpinne
winch	winch	Winsch
Parts of an engine		
diesel engine	moteur diesel	Dieselmotor
two-stroke	à deux temps	zweitakt
four-stroke	à quatre temps	viertakt
outboard motor	moteur hors-bord	Außenbordmotor
battery	batterie	Batterie
belt	courroie	Riemen
carburetor	carburateur	Vergaser
coil	bobine	Spule
cylinder	cylindre	Zylinder
exhaust pipe	tuyau d'échappement	Auspuffrohr
fuel filter	filtre à combustible	Brennstoff-filter
fuel pump	pompe à combustible	Brennstoffpumpe
gasoline engine	moteur à essence	Benzinmotor
gearbox	boîte de vitesses	Getriebegehäuse

Dutch	Danish	Spanish
vlot	katamaran	catamaran
bijboot	jolle	bote
motorboot	motorbåd	motora
zeilschuit	sejlbåd	barco de vela
achterstag	bagstag	burda
boom	bom	botavara
boeg	bov	proa
kajuit	kahyt	camarote
dek	dæk	cubierta
diepgang	dybgående	calado
voorstag	fokkestag	estay del trinquete
val	fald	driza
romp	skrog	casco
fok	fok	foque
kiel	køl	quilla
grootzeil	storsejl	vela mayor
mast	mast	palo
riem	åre	remo
schroef	propeller	hélice
roer	ror	timón
zeil	sejl	vela
buitenboordskraan	søhane	grifo de fondo
schoot	skøde	escota
want	vant	obenque
spinnaker	spiler	espinaquer
achtersteven	agter	popa
helmstok	rorpind	caña
lier	spil	winche
dieselmotor	dieselmotor	motor diesel
tweetakt	totakt	dos tiempos
viertakt	firetakt	cuatro tiempos
buitenboordmotor	påhængsmotor	motor fuera de borda
batterij	batteri	bateria
riem	rem	correa
carburateur	karburator	carburador
spoel	spole	bobina
cylinder	cylinder	cilindro
uitlaatpijp	udblæsningsrør	tubo de escape
brandstoffilter	brændstof-filter	filtro de combustible
brandstofpomp	brændstofs pumpon	bomba de combustible
benzinemotor	benzinmotor	motor de gasolina
versnellingsbak	gearkasse	caja de cambio

English	French	German
generator	dynamo	Dynamo
handle	manivelle	Griff
injector	injecteur	Injektor
piston	piston	Kolben
propeller shaft	arbre d'hélice	Schraubenuelle
sparking plug	bougie	Zündkerze
starter motor	démarreur	Anlasser
tappet	poussoir	Stößel
valve	soupape	Ventil

Places on the shore

English	French	German
bakery	boulangerie	Bäckerei
bank	banque	Bank
butcher	boucherie	Schlachterei
dentist	dentiste	Zahnarzt
fishmonger	poissonnerie	Fischhändler
grocer	épicerie	Krämer
hospital	hôpital	Krankenhaus
pharmacy	pharmacie	Apotheke
physician	médecin	Arzt
police station	poste de police	Polizeiwache
post office	bureau de poste	Postamt
sailmaker	voilier	Segelmacher
street	rue	Straße
town	ville	Stadt
village	village	Dorf
yacht chandler	fournisseur de marine	Jachtausrüster

Stores

English	French	German
anti-seasickness pills	pillules contre le mal de mer	Antiseekrankheits-mittel
antiseptic cream	onguent antiseptique	antiseptische Salbe
bacon	lard fumé	Speck
bandage	bandage	Binde
band-aid	pansement adhésif	Heftplaster
beer	bière	Bier
biscuits	biscuits	Kekse
bread	pain	Brot
bulb	ampoule	Birne
butter	beurre	Butter
cheese	fromage	Käse
coffee	café	Kaffee
cooking oil	huile	Öl
corkscrew	tire-bouchon	Korkenzieher
detergent	détergent	Reinigungsmittel
drinking water	eau potable	Trinkwasser
dry battery	pile sèche	Trockenbatterie
eggs	œufs	Eier
fish	poisson	Fisch

Dutch	Danish	Spanish
dynamo	dynamo	dinamo
hengsel	håndtag	mango
inspuiter	injektor	inyector
zuiger	stempel	émbolo
schroefas	skrue-aksel	árbol de la hélice
bougie	tændrør	bujía
startmotor	startmotør	motor de arranque
klepstoter	medbringer-knast	taqué
klep	ventil	válvula
bakkerij	bageri	panadero
bank	bank	banco
slagerij	slagteri	carnicería
tandarts	tandlæge	dentista
vishandel	fiskehandler	pescadería
kruideniers	købmand	tienda de comestibles
zeikenhuis	hospital	hospital
apotheek	apotek	farmacía
dokter	læge	médico
politiebureau	politistation	comisaría
postkantoor	postkontor	officina de correos
zeilmaker	sejlmager	velero
straat	gade	calle
stad	by	ciudad
dorp	landsby	pueblo
scheepsleverancier	skibshandler	almacénista de efectos navales
pillen tegen zeeziekte	søsyge-tabletter	pildoras contra el mareo
antiseptische zalf	antiseptisk cream	pomada de sulfamidas
spek	bacon	tocino
verband	bandage	venda
kleefpleister	hæfteplaster	esparadrapo
bier	øl	cerveza
beschuits	kiks	galletas
brood	brød	pan
lampje	pære	lampara
boter	smør	mantequilla
kaas	ost	queso
koffie	kaffe	café
olie	spise-olie	aceite
kurketrekker	proptrækker	sacacorchos
wasmiddel	rensemiddel	detergente
drinkwater	drikkevand	agua potable
batterij	tørbatteri	pila seca
eieren	æg	huevos
vis	fisk	pescado

English	French	German
fruit	fruit	Obst
funnel	entonnoir	Trichter
gas	gaz	Gas
insulating tape	ruban isolant	Isolierband
matches	allumettes	Streichholzer
meat	viande	Fleisch
milk	lait	Milch
needle and thread	aiguille et fil à voile	Nadel und Garn
newspapers	journaux	Zeitungen
pepper	poivre	Pfeffer
safety pin	épingle de sûreté	Sicherheitsnadel
salt	sel	Salz
soap	savon	Seife
sugar	sucre	Zucker
tea	thé	Tee
thermometer	thermomètre	Thermometer
tin opener	ouvre-boîtes	Dosenöffner
toilet paper	papier hygiénique	Toilettepapier
vegetables	légumes	Gemüse
washing-up liquid	détergent liquide	Abwaschmittel
wine	vin	Wein

In harbor

bridge	pont	Brücke
cast off	dégager	loswerfen
customs	douane	Zoll
dock	bassin	Dock
fend off	écarter	absetzen
harbor master	capitaine de port	Hafenkapitän
insurance certificate	certificat d'assurance	Versicherungs- zeugnis
jetty	jetée	Anlegesteg
mooring buoy	coffre d'amarrage	Festmachetonne
passport	passeport	Reisepaß
pile	pieu	Pfaht
quay	quai	Kai
slipway	cale de halage	Helling
yacht club	yacht club	Jacht-Klub
yacht harbor	bassin pour yachts	Jachthafen
Where can I moor?	Où puis-je amarrer?	Wo soll ich anlegen?

Chandlery

adhesive	colle	Leim
anchor	ancre	Anker
batten	latte	Latte
block	poulie	Block
bolt	boulon	Bolzen
bottle screw	ridoir	Wantenspanner
bucket	seau	Pütze
charts	cartes marines	Seekarten
cleat	taquet	Klampe

Dutch	Danish	Spanish
fruit	frugt	frutas
trechter	tragt	embudo
gas	gas	gas
isolatieband	isoleringsbånd	cinta aislante
lucifers	tændstikker	fósforos
vlees	kød	carne
melk	mælk	leche
naald en garen	nål og tråd	aguja e hilo de velas
kranten	aviser	periódicos
peper	peber	pimienta
veiligheidsspeld	sikkerhedsnål	imperdible
zout	salt	sal
zeep	sæbe	jabón
suiker	sukker	azúcar
thee	te	té
thermometer	termometer	termómetro
blikopener	dåseåbner	abrelatas
toilet papier	toiletpapir	papel higiénico
groenten	grønsager	legumbres
afwasmiddel	opvaskemiddel	detergente
wijn	vin	vino

Dutch	Danish	Spanish
brug	bro	puente
losgooien	smide los	largar amarras
douane	told	aduana
dok	dok	dique
afduwen	fendre af	abrir
havenmeester	havnefoged	capitán de puerto
verzekeringsbewijs	assurance certifikat	certificado de seguro
pier	mole	muelle
meerboei	fortøjningstønde	boya de amarre
paspoort	pas	pasaporte
paal	pæl	estaca
kaai	kaj	muelle
sleephelling	ophalingsbedding	varadero
jacht-club	yacht klub	club náutico
jachthaven	yachthaven	dársena de yates
Waar kan ik vastmaken?	Hvor skal jeg fortøje?	¿Dondé puedo amarrar?

Dutch	Danish	Spanish
lijm	klæbestof	adhesivo
anker	anker	ancla
lat	sejlpinde	enjaretado
blok	blok	motón
bout	bolt	perno
wantspanner	vantskrue	tensor
emmer	pøs	balde
zeekarten	søkort	cartas náuticas
klamp	klampe	cornamusa

English	French	German
compass	compas	Kompaß
distress flares	feux de détresse	Notsignalfeuer
echo sounder	échosondeur	Echolot
ensign	pavillon	Nationalflagge
fender	défense	Fender
fire extinguisher	extincteur d'incendie	Feuerlöscher
foghorn	corne de brume	Nebelhorn
hank	mousequeton	Stagreiter
jubilee clip	collier de serrage	Schlangenklemme
life buoy	bouée de sauvetage	Rettungsboje
life jacket	gilet de sauvetage	Schwimmjacke
life raft	radeau de sauvetage	Rettungsfloß
log	loch	Log
nail	clou	Nagel
nut	écrou	Schraubernmutter
oilskins	cirés	Ölzeug
paint	peinture	Anstrich
paint brush	pinceau	Pinsel
pencil	crayon	Bleistift
pilot	instructions nautique	Seehandbuch
pipe	tuyau	Rohr
radiotelephone	radio-téléphone	Sprechfunk-Gerät
rivet	rivet	Niete
rope	corde	Seil
sandpaper	papier de verre	Sandpapier
screw	vis	Schraube
shackle	manille	Schäkel
sheave	réa	Scheibe
snap shackle	manille rapide	Schnappschäkel
split pin	goupille fendue	Splint
thimble	cosse	Kausch
tide tables	annuaire de marées	Gezeitentafeln
varnish	vernis	Firnis
washer	rondelle	Unterlegsscheibe
whipping twine	fil à surlier	Takelgarn
wing nut	vis papillon	Flügelmutter
wire rope	cable d'acier	Drahtseil

Materials		
alloy	alliage	Legierung
aluminum	aluminium	Aluminium
brass	laiton	Messing
copper	cuivre	Kupfer
cotton	coton	Baumwolle
fibreglass	fibre de verre	Glasharz
galvanised iron	fer galvanisé	galvanisiertes Eisen
iron	fer	Eisen
laminated plastic, Tufnol	plastique stratifié, Céloron	laminiertes Plastik

Dutch	Danish	Spanish
kompas	kompas	compás
noodseinen	nødlys	bengala
echolood	ekkolod	sonda acústica
natie vlag	nationalflag	pabellón
stootkussen	fender	defensa
brandblusser	ildslukker	extintor
misthoorn	tågehorn	bocina de niebla
knipleuver	fokkehage	garrucho
slangklem	slangebinder	abrazadera
reddingsboei	redningskrans	guindola
zwemvest	redningsvest	chaleco salvavidas
reddingsvlot	redningsflåde	balsa salvavidas
log	log	corredera
nagel	søm	clavo
moer	møtrik	tuerca
oliegoed	olietøj	chubasquero
verf	maling	pintura
kwast	malerpensel	brocha
potlood	blyant	lápiz
zeemansgids	kursangiver	derrotero
buis	rør	tubo
radio telefoon	radiotelefon	radio teléfono
klinknagel	nagle	remache
touw	tov	soga
schuurpapier	sandpapir	papel de lija
schroef	skrue	tornillo
sluiting	sjækkel	grillete
schijf	skive	roldana
snapsluiting	sjækkel	grillete de enganche
splitpen	split	pasador abierto
kous	kovs	guardacabo
getijtafels	tidevandstabeller	tabla de mareas
vernis	fernis	barniz
ring	spændeskive	arandela
garen	taklegarn	piolilla
vleugelmoer	fløjmøtrik	tuerca de orejas
staaldraadtouw	ståltov	cable
legering	legering	aleación
aluminium	aluminium	aluminio
messing	messing	latón
koper	kobber	cobre
katoen	bomuld	algodón
fiberglas	fiberglas	fibra de vidrio
ijzer galvaniseerd	galvaniseret jern	hierro galvanizado
ijzer	jern	hierro
gelamineerd plastic	lamineret plastic	plástico laminado

English	French	German
metal	métal	Metall
nylon	nylon	Nylon
plastic	plastique	Plastik
stainless steel	acier inoxydable	rostfreier Stahl
steel	acier	Stahl
Terylene, Dacron	Tergal	Diolen
timber	bois	Holz

Tools

drill bits	forets	Bohrer
hacksaw	scie à metaux	Metallsäge
hammer	marteau	Hammer
hand drill	chignolle à main	Drillbohrer
pliers	pinces	Drahtzange
screwdriver	tournevis	Schraubenzieher
wrench	clef à écrous	Schrauben-schlüssel

Fuels

diesel oil	gas-oil	Diesel-Kraftstoff
distilled water	eau distillée	destilliertes Wasser
engine oil	huile	Schmieröl
gasoline	essence	Benzin
grease	graisse	Schmiere
hydraulic fluid	liquide hydraulique	hydraulisches Öl
kerosene (paraffin)	pétrole	Petroleum
T.V.O.	pétrole carburant	Traktoren-Kraftstoff

Maintenance and Repairs

adjust	régler	einstellen
bleed	purger d'air	entlüften
broken	cassé	gebrochen
corrosion	corrosion	Korrosion
haul ashore	tirer à terre	an Land holen
launch	mettre à l'eau	zu Wasser lassen
leak	voie d'eau	Leck
marine engineer	ingénieur du génie maritime	Schiffbauingenieur
overhaul	revision	besichtigen
repair	réparer	reparieren
replace	remplacer	ersetzen
rot	pourriture	Fäulnis
scrub the bottom	nettoyer la carène à la brosse	das Unterwasser-schrubben
tow	remorquer	schleppen
weld	souder	schweißen

General

left	gauche	links
right	droite	rechts
in front	devant	davor
behind	derrière	hinten
please	s'il vous plaît	bitte

Dutch	Danish	Spanish
metaal	metal	metal
nylon	nylon	nilon
plastic	plastic	plástico
roestvrij staal	rustfri stål	acero inoxidable
staal	stål	acero
Dacron	Terylene, Dacron	terilene, dacron
hout	tømmer	madera
boren	drilbor	broca
metaalzaag	nedstryger	serrucho
hamer	hammer	martillo
handboor	håndbor	taladro de mano
buigtang	tang	alicates
schroevedraaier	skruetrækker	destornillador
moersleutel	skruenøgle	llave de tuerca
dieselolie	dieselolie	gasoil
gedistilleerd water	destilleret vand	acqua destilada
olie	maskinolie	aceite de motor
benzine	benzin	gasolina
smeer	smørelse	grasa
hydraulische olie	hydraulisk vædske	aceite hidráulico
petroleum	petroleum	petróleo
tractor-petroleum	T.V.O.	T.V.O. petróleo
verstellen	justere	ajustar
ontluchten	lufte ud	purgar
gebroken	knækket	roto
corrosie	rust-tæring	corrosión
op de wal halen	hale på land	varar
te water laten	søsætte	botar
lek	læk	via de agua
machinist	maskinofficer	ingeniero de la marina
grondig nazien	at efterse	examinar
repareren	reparere	reparar
vervangen	at erstatte	reemplazar
rot	råd	putrición
het onderwater schoonmaken	skrubbe bunden	limpiar fondo
slepen	slæbe	remolcar
lassen	svejse	soldar
links	venstre	izquierda
rechts	højre	derecha
voorop	forpå	delante
achter	bag efter	detrás
alstublieft	vær [så] venlig	por favor

English	French	German
thank you	merci	bitte [affirm] danke [neg]
How much does it cost?	Combien?	Was kostet es?
Please direct me to . . .	S'il vous plaît, voulez-vous m'indiquer la route pour . . . ?	Bitte ziegen Sie mir den Weg nach . . .
Where can I get . . . ?	Où puis-je obtenir . . . ?	Wo kann ich . . . bekommen?

Navigation

English	French	German
anchorage	mouillage	Ankerplatz
awash	à fleur d'eau	überspült
bay	baie	Bucht
beacon	balise	Bake
bearing	relèvement	Peilung
breakers	brisants	Brandung
buoy	bouée	Tonne
calm	calme	glatt
channel	canal	Fahrwasser
course	cap	Kurs
current	courant	Strom
ebb	marée descendante	Ebbe
estuary	estuaire	Flußmündung
flood	marée montante	Flut
gale	coup de vent	Stürmischer Wind
headland	cap	Vorgebirge
high water	pleine mer	Hochwasser
hill	colline	Hügel
island	île	Insel
leading line	alignement	Leitlinie
lighthouse	phare	Leuchtturm
lightship	bateau-phare	Feuerschiff
low water	basse mer	Niedrigwasser
magnetic	magnétique	magnetisch
mountain	montagne	Berg
mud	vase	Schlamm
overfalls	remous et clapotis	Stromkabbelung
rain	pluie	Regen
reef	récif	Riff
rock	roche	Felsen
rough sea	grosse mer	grobe See
sand	sable	Sand
shoal	haut fond	Untiefe
thunder	tonnerre	Donner
true	vrai	rechtweisend
wave	vague	Welle
weather forecast	previsions météorologique	Wettervorhersage
wind	vent	Wind
wreck	épave	Wrack

Dutch	Danish	Spanish
dank u	tak	gracias
Hoeveel kost het?	Hvad koster det?	¿Cuanto cuesta?
Alstublieft, kunt U mij de weg wijzen naar ...	Vil De være venlig at vise mig vegen til ... ?	¿Tendria la bondad de decirme dondé está ...?
Waar kan ik ... verkrijgen?	Hvor kan jeg få ...?	¿Dónde puedo conseguir ...?
ankerplaats	ankerplads	fondeadero
overspoeld	overskyllet	flor de agua
baai	bugt	bahia
baken	sømærke	baliza
peiling	pejling	marcación
branding	brænding	rompientes
ton	tønde	boya
vlak	stille	calma
vaarwater	kanal	canal
koers	kurs	rumbo
stroom	strøm	corriente
eb	ebbe	vaciante
mond	flodmunding	estuario
vloed	flod	entrante
storm	hård blæst	duro
voorgebergte	kap	promontorio
hoogwater	højvande	pleamar
heuvel	høj	colina
eiland	ø	isla
geleidelijn	ledelinie	enfilación
vuurtoren	fyrtårn	faro
lichtschip	fyrskib	buque faro
laagwater	lavvande	bajamar
magnetisch	magnetisk	magnético
berg	bjerg	monte
modder	mudder	fango
stroomrafeling	strømsø	escarceos
regen	regn	lluvia
rif	rev	arrecife
rots	skær	piedra
ruwe zee	grov sø	picada
zand	sand	arena
droogte	grund	bajo
donder	torden	trueno
rechtwijzende	sand	verdadero
golf	bølge	ola
weersvoorspelling	vejrudsigt	previsión metereólogica
wind	vind	viento
wrak	vrag	naufragio

Index

Further reading
The following publications are available from the US Department of
Commerce, National Oceanic and Atmospheric Administration, National
Ocean Survey, Rockville, Maryland:
Tidal Current Tables
The Nautical Almanac
Tide Tables
Nautical Charts

The following are available from the Defense Mapping Agency Hydrographic/
Topographic Center:
Radio Navigational Aids
International Code of Signals
American Practical Navigator
Light Lists [published by the United States Coast Guard]

Also:
Waterway Guide, the authoritative reference for cruising boatmen, is published
in three editions: *Northern*, which covers Atlantic coastal cruising from New
York to Maine and inland waters in New York and Canada including Lakes
Ontario and Erie; *Mid-Atlantic* covering Atlantic coastal cruising from New
York to Florida; and *Southern* which covers Florida East Coast, Bahamas, and
Gulf Coast cruising.
Special features include mile-by-mile navigational advice, descriptions of
harbors, anchorages, marine facilities listings, boatmen's restaurant guide, and
visitor discounts to shoreside attractions.

Illustrations: Marilyn Bruce, John Dower Associates, Chris Forsey,
 Colin Salmon and Alan Suttie
Photographs on pages 98–99: Royal Meteorological Society (Cave Collection),
 R.K. Pilsbury